KT-501-163

MA Year 2

2002 — 2003

WHAT TEACHERS DO: CHANGING POLICY AND PRACTICE IN PRIMARY EDUCATION

see grouping

WS 2305880 3

Also available:

Sandra Acker: *The Realities of Teachers' Work*
Patricia Broadfoot *et al.*: *Promoting Quality in Learning*
Paul Croll (ed.): *Teachers, Pupils and Primary Schooling*
Ann Filer and Andrew Pollard: *The Social World of Pupil Assessment*
Michael Fullan: *The New Meaning of Educational Change*
Andy Hargreaves: *Changing Teachers, Changing Times*
Gary McCulloch *et al.*: *The Politics of Professionalism*
Andrew Pollard with Ann Filer: *The Social World of Children's Learning*
Andrew Pollard and Ann Filer: *The Social World of Pupil Career*
Andrew Pollard *et al.*: *Changing English Primary Schools?*
Andrew Pollard *et al.*: *What Pupils Say: Changing Policy and Practice in Primary Education*

WHAT TEACHERS DO:

Changing Policy and Practice in Primary Education

Marilyn Osborn, Elizabeth McNess and Patricia Broadfoot
with Andrew Pollard and Pat Triggs

CONTINUUM
London and New York

Continuum

The Tower Building	370 Lexington Avenue
11 York Road	New York
London SE1 7NX	NY 10017–6503

© 2000 Marilyn Osborn, Elizabeth McNess, Patricia Broadfoot, Andrew Pollard and Pat Triggs

All rights reserved. No part of this publication may be reproduced or transmitted in any form or by any means, electronic or mechanical, including photocopying, recording or any information storage or retrieval system, without prior permission in writing from the publishers.

First published 2000

British Library Cataloguing-in-Publication Data
A catalogue record for this book is available from the British Library.

ISBN 0–8264–5072–5 (hardback)
    0–8264–5073–3 (paperback)

Typeset by YHT Ltd, London
Printed and bound in Great Britain by TJ International, Padstow, Cornwall

Contents

List of Figures and Tables

Figures

Tables

Preface
Jennifer Nias

This and its companion volume (Pollard *et al.*, 2000) are important books. Grounded in data collected in the last decade of the twentieth century, they point forward to the twenty-first. *What Teachers Do* describes and analyses the response of English primary school teachers and headteachers, of all lengths of experience, to the changes in policy which followed from, and after, the Education Reform Act, 1988. *What Pupils Say* documents the parallel impact on the lived experience of pupils aged between 5 and 11. The focus of the books is the introduction of the National Curriculum and its associated assessment procedures, but because the Primary Assessment, Curriculum and Experience (PACE) Project was longitudinal in its approach, they also take note of the changes in inspection procedures, school governance and funding which took place in the years 1989 to 1997. What emerges from the mass of quantitative and qualitative data which the Project team accumulated is a vivid and disturbing picture of teachers' and pupils' evolving experience of the new requirements for curriculum, pedagogy and assessment, and of the cumulative effects of this experience upon their sense of autonomy, their motivation and their attitudes to, on the one hand, teaching and, on the other, learning.

The books are vivid because they draw extensively upon painstaking classroom observations and on sensitively conducted interviews with participants, as well as on appropriate statistical evidence. They are disturbing because they point up some of the unintended consequences of, and tensions within, the policies of three different governments, each intent on raising educational standards by the use of centralization and control together with an appeal to the power of competition and parental choice. The PACE evidence suggests that an apparent rise during the 1990s of measured standards in English, Mathematics and Science has been achieved by sacrificing, at least in part, some of the characteristics of teaching and learning in

English primary schools which have attracted the attention of visitors and researchers from over the world. Among these are a warm affective climate and encouragement of pupils' autonomy, creativity, activity and reflexivity. The curriculum has narrowed, despite the initial promise of the National Curriculum, sometimes bringing boredom in its wake. More fundamental, the cumulative pressures of additional curricular content, of assessment, recording and reporting have eroded time for affective contact between teachers and pupils. Partly as a result of this, many teachers have begun to replace their sense of moral responsibility for their work – deriving from their relationship with individuals – with one of contractual accountability for the achievement of externally set targets.

Indeed, a theme running through all the Project findings is the growth among teachers and pupils of an instrumental and pragmatic view of education. As pupils grew older, they increasingly came to equate 'success' with producing what teachers wanted in the narrow curricular areas of reading, writing, mathematics and, to a lesser degree, science. In addition, they showed limited understanding of the learning purposes which their work was intended to fulfil. For their part, teachers too, though in most cases reluctantly, began to define their own success in terms of their ability to meet performance targets over which they had little or no control. For both sets of participants, schooling during this decade often became a question of task accomplishment, a process in which quality was constantly overtaken by quantity, teacher facilitation of pupils' self-defined learning goals by instruction, pupil activity by sitting, listening and writing, and spontaneity, creativity and inquiry by satisfactory performance on school and national tests.

This pervasive instrumentalism has had the further effect of creating a new type of differentiation between pupils and among teachers. One of the stated aims of all governments since 1988 has been to reduce the impact of economic and social class differences on access to, and the ability to profit from, education. The National Curriculum was conceived as 'curriculum entitlement' and the rhetoric of this aspiration has persisted. Similarly, the drive to raise standards in 'the basics' derives in part from a desire that all children should achieve equality of educational opportunity. Whatever the outcome in terms of test results of this emphasis by central government, the PACE project makes it clear that a new form of differentiation has replaced, or perhaps been added to, the familiar distinctions which are associated with social and economic status. Pupils who did well in primary schools during the 1990s and whose SAT results, especially at Key Stage 2, were satisfactory or better, were those who showed obvious signs of self-confidence and self-esteem as learners. Similarly, the teachers who rose above the pressures of constant modifications to curriculum and assessment, an intensified workload, the need for new curricular knowledge, OFSTED inspections and media attacks were those whose self-confidence as teachers was not eroded or was, in some cases, enhanced by these policy changes. By contrast, pupils and teachers who experienced anxiety and loss of confidence when faced with what they perceived as their failure to meet externally imposed, and often apparently arbitrary, goals did not thrive under the new conditions. When such pupils could, they devised strategies to get by or to avoid overt censure, thus achieving some sense of control over their environment, if not over their learning. The toll among teachers who were anxious or who lost professional self-esteem was more obvious. Illness and early retirement rose to unprecedented levels during this period, especially among the more experienced.

Of course, the confidence that one can succeed in meeting the standards set by others, or successfully afford to ignore them, derives from many sources. Evidence from this Project indicates the importance of support by other people. Teachers benefited from working in collaborative environments; pupils tended to receive support from teachers, but also, and crucially, from parents, peers and siblings. This further complicates the problem of how to achieve equality of opportunity. Differentiation based upon degrees of self-confidence, self-esteem (as teachers or learners) and support is not likely to be susceptible of easy solutions, especially in a social and political climate which favours competition and individualism.

As an instrumental view of schooling has gained ground in the minds of pupils, parents and teachers, a further tension in government policy has emerged. The present system of curricular instruction, external target-setting, regular assessment and measured outcomes encourages a performance view of the learner and the teacher. This is in line with the official doctrine that Britain's economic future depends upon the existence of a skilled, competitive and reliable work force. *Mutatis mutandis*, this argument is little different from that used in the late nineteenth century to justify the curriculum, pedagogy and assessment of the elementary schools. But the social, economic and technological background from which school entrants come and into which leavers must fit has radically changed. Business leaders, politicians, educationalists and many parents are all aware that now and in the foreseeable future, society and, more narrowly, economic enterprise needs citizens who are flexible, resourceful and capable of 'life-long learning'. The evidence presented in these two volumes suggests that the structured pursuit of higher standards in English and mathematics may be reducing the ability of many children to see themselves as self-motivating, independent problem-solvers taking an intrinsic pleasure in learning and capable of reflecting on how and why they learn. It also highlights the fact that primary schools can strongly affect pupils' willingness as learners to take risks and to engage emotionally with their learning. Too great or inflexible an emphasis upon pupils as products may inhibit the emergence of a society whose members are also capable of acting as agents, wanting to learn, confident of their capacity to do so, responding to economic and technological challenges in active yet reflexive ways. There is little indication that politicians are yet aware of this tension in the goals which they espouse. Similarly, the fact that their teachers have tacitly been defined as technicians whose skills can be judged against externally set criteria has reduced the sense of moral commitment which most feel to their work. It has been replaced by a narrower, more bureaucratic sense of accountability which, in its turn, may prove too limited and inflexible to meet the future needs of a 'learning society'. At the same time, those teachers who have retained a sense of moral responsibility for pupils often experience dysfunctional levels of stress, because they feel required to act in ways which they believe to be contrary to the latter's best interests.

Paradoxically, the answer to these apparent conflicts may also lie within the Project data. Pupils have only one education and although their attitudes to it are influenced by parents and older siblings, they are less likely to question innovations than are teachers. The latter are older, their beliefs and values are more firmly established. Even if they have been teaching for only a short time, it may cost them a great deal in personal terms to alter or surrender these. *What Teachers Do* shows the ways in which a fluctuating number of 'creative mediators' have taken active, but selective, control of the changes imposed upon them, with the result that they have sometimes become makers rather than simply implementers of educational policy. These teachers and headteachers have retained their educational beliefs, and a sense of their professional efficacy and autonomy. In their classrooms and schools, instrumentalism is often reconciled with creativity, and the fulfilment of external targets with affectivity and pupil-directed learning. It seems as if relatively small reductions in the pressures currently bearing upon teachers and pupils would free some learning time and space into which both could grow. If the imbalance between instrumentalism and individual development, between extrinsic and intrinsic motivation, were corrected, teachers might begin to regain their sense of professional autonomy and with it their feeling of moral, rather than contractual, accountability for their work. In their turn, pupils might become more concerned with their own learning and less with mere task-fulfilment.

The data presented in these volumes and the conclusions drawn from them are thought provoking and potentially far reaching in their consequences. These books are a fitting outcome from a decade of rigorous and insightful inquiry with which I have been glad to be associated. I hope that they will reach a wide and appropriate readership.

Jennifer Nias
University of Plymouth
July 2000

Books from the PACE Project

This book derives from the three phases of the Primary Assessment, Curriculum and Experience project (PACE), which ran from 1989 to 1997. The value of the book may be enhanced by reading it in conjunction with the other PACE books, and the structure of these is as indicated below:

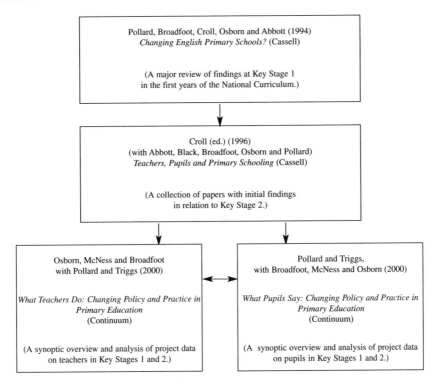

Pollard, Broadfoot, Croll, Osborn and Abbott (1994)
Changing English Primary Schools? (Cassell)

(A major review of findings at Key Stage 1
in the first years of the National Curriculum.)

Croll (ed.) (1996)
(with Abbott, Black, Broadfoot, Osborn and Pollard)
Teachers, Pupils and Primary Schooling (Cassell)

(A collection of papers with initial findings
in relation to Key Stage 2.)

Osborn, McNess and Broadfoot
with Pollard and Triggs (2000)

*What Teachers Do: Changing Policy and Practice in
Primary Education*
(Continuum)

(A synoptic overview and analysis of project data
on teachers in Key Stages 1 and 2.)

Pollard and Triggs,
with Broadfoot, McNess and Osborn (2000)

*What Pupils Say: Changing Policy and Practice in
Primary Education*
(Continuum)

(A synoptic overview and analysis of project data
on pupils in Key Stages 1 and 2.)

As would be expected, there are many design and theoretical elements that are shared between our two parallel synoptic books reporting six years of fieldwork findings on teacher and pupil experiences. Their origins, and the coherence of the project as a whole are reflected by some shared text, particularly in the introductions and chapters on research design.

A fifth book deriving from the PACE projects is being considered (Broadfoot and Pollard). Provisionally entitled *The Assessment Society*, this would address the emphasis on 'performance' within modern education, taking its influence on primary education as a case-study.

Members of the PACE teams have been engaged in other, closely related projects. For international comparisons, see Broadfoot, Osborn, Planel and Sharpe (2000). For studies at a further level of detail concerning pupil 'life-stories' through primary schooling, with particular foci on learning, career and assessment, see Pollard with Filer (1996), Pollard and Filer (1999) and Filer and Pollard (2000).

Details of other publications from the PACE projects are available on the ESRC database, Regard, at *http://regard.ac.uk* (search on authors or the ESRC project reference numbers: R000231931, R000233891, R000235687).

Acknowledgements

The three phases of the PACE projects between 1989 and 1997 were each funded by the UK's Economic and Social Research Council (ESRC). We gratefully acknowledge this support.

Pupils, teachers and headteachers, and LEA staff have faced many challenging years since 1989, and yet they have found both the time to talk with us and the generosity to welcome us into their schools. Although they must all remain anonymous, we thank them.

We would like to acknowledge the support of many academic colleagues, in particular those of our Consultative Group, in discussing ideas, problems, strategies and the many other issues which arise during a longitudinal study of this sort. Jennifer Nias and Basil Bernstein have been particularly influential in the evolution of our thinking. We are also grateful to the two universities from which the project derived (the University of the West of England and the University of Bristol), and to staff of the ESRC, who have helped us in many ways throughout the programme.

We are enormously grateful to our colleagues who have been members of the PACE team at various stages: Dorothy Abbott, Paul Croll, Edie Black, Mike Taysum and Jenny Noble. Their work has contributed to the analysis which is reported in this book, and its companion volume. Jenny Noble's work formed the basis of Chapter 10 of this volume. We have also had superb assistance from support staff during the project, including Jacquie Harrison, Viki Davies, Sheila Taylor, Sarah Butler, Stephanie Burke, Elspeth Gray and Jenny Wills.

This book is dedicated to all primary teachers, particularly those in the PACE study, whose commitment to children and to the quality of education remains undiminished.

Part 1

The Primary Assessment, Curriculum and Experience Project

Chapter 1

Introduction: The Context and Research Questions

1.1 CHANGING TIMES

Primary education in England and Wales will never be the same again. The 1988 Education Reform Act was the most radical education legislation in half a century, and a decade of unremitting change followed it. As the tidal wave of new policy initiatives began to ebb, it revealed a shoreline in which many of the principal features had been rearranged: the role of the headteacher and the way schools were managed; teachers' priorities and ways of working together; curriculum content, teaching methods and forms of assessment. Perhaps to the casual observer, classroom practices and the activities of teachers and pupils may appear little altered. The constants of classrooms everywhere – talk, activity, display, busyness; a single teacher occupied with a large group of children – these remain the defining characteristics of formal education across the globe. For the present, notwithstanding the new learning technologies of the information society, schools and teachers, pupils and lessons, are constants which we both recognize and understand. They are a familiar feature of our contemporary culture.

All the more difficult, then, to appreciate the subtle yet profound redefining of the educational project that the introduction of the National Curriculum and associated initiatives has produced in English primary schools; the changes in relationships between headteacher and staff; between the teachers themselves and between teachers and their pupils; and the product of these changes: different attitudes, different goals, different concerns; different skills. The result in the 1990s was an education system in which teachers' priorities in practice reflected a hard-won, and often uneasy, compromise between new obligations and an enduring vision that had its roots in a different era. For pupils, the new requirements introduced into their schooling a more specified curriculum, tighter framing of classroom life and a new level of assessment activity. On the other hand, it was 'still school', whether they answered to the idiosyncrasies of their allotted class teacher, or to a common, national statutory requirement.

The Primary Assessment, Curriculum and Experience (PACE) project was established in 1989 to monitor the impact of the momentous changes then occurring following the passing of the 1988 Education Reform Act. Funded in three stages, 1989–92, 1992–4 and 1994–7, the PACE project was uniquely placed to document the unfolding story of change in primary schools and, in particular, the impact of the new National Curriculum and assessment requirements on headteachers, teachers and pupils. As Chapter 2 describes in detail, we chose a national sample of primary schools which afforded us access throughout the years of the project to collect information about the changes teachers and pupils felt they were experiencing; to document the evolving school experience of a particular group of pupils throughout the course of their primary schooling; and to observe these experiences for ourselves by sitting in classrooms and staffrooms. The project amassed an enormous quantity of material which provides a unique resource for both current and future analyses of English primary education in the final years of the second millennium. As with all data, its value is realized by exposing it to the filter of particular questions and to the subsequent interpretation of theoretical analyses.

In this book we present one such account. Its focus is on teachers. We report their changing experiences and perceptions during the period of the study and how these in turn have led to changes in their professional practice. Our account is matched by that in the companion volume on pupils (Pollard *et al.*, 2000). But whilst we seek to describe, our primary goal is to go beyond mere description in order to analyse and explain; to understand and to assess the significance of the responses to policy that our data document. Our fundamental aspiration is to generate insights that can help to provide the basis for more generalized explanations of the relationship between educational policy and teachers' practice. In presenting the particular case-study which this period of educational history represents, we hope to illuminate in a more enduring way the educational issues which must be confronted in any era.

The central questions that informed the PACE study of teachers were as follows:

- What are the principal changes that have taken place in English primary teachers' attitudes and practice as a result of recent policy initiatives?
- How can the nature of these changes best be explained?
- What is their significance for the teachers themselves, their pupils, their schools and for the education system and society as a whole?

The rest of this chapter sets out the context both for the policy initiatives themselves and for the PACE research project. The first part of what follows presents a brief overview of some of the key elements of the recent reforms and the particular combinations of historical situation and political circumstances which gave rise to them. Then, arising from this analysis, we introduce in more detail the three key questions which are listed above. The chapter concludes with a review of the contents of the book as a whole.

1.2 THE CONTEXT FOR CHANGE

Educationists in other countries are frequently amazed that there was no tradition of a national curriculum in England and Wales until the 1988 Education Reform Act was implemented. Previously, the only formal control of the content of education concerned the requirement to teach religious education, which had been established in the 1944 Education Act. Historically, then, England has been almost unique in not having a national curriculum. Instead it has traditionally relied on various kinds of assessment, particularly public examinations, to control the system. As in other countries, the existence of so-called 'high-stakes' public examinations at 11 +, 16 + and 18 + provided a powerful focus for schools which were otherwise free to make their own decisions about content. At primary school level, relatively far from the constraints of the exam system, teachers had considerable autonomy to develop their interests, commitments and particular areas of expertise. Further, 'topic work' and other integrated forms of curriculum planning flourished in the years following the Plowden Report (CACE, 1967). Overall, however, there were significant problems in providing coherence, continuity and progression within the curriculum, with the result that children were sometimes exposed to the same content or activities on several occasions – whilst other curricular entitlements could unwittingly be neglected (HMI, 1978). Thus one of the main stimuli for the introduction of a national curriculum was the desire to provide a broad, balanced and coherent curriculum for the years between age 5 and age 16, Years 1–10.

Other straws in the wind were also significant in prompting legislation. The 1980s had seen a growth in international economic competition. This, together with growing financial pressures and an increased demand for state institutions to be accountable, underpinned a desire to curb the professional autonomy of teachers and to replace it with a much greater measure of central control. A key ingredient in providing for such control was seen as the generation of comprehensive information about standards, about finance and about many different aspects of educational provision; hence the simultaneous and significant development of a variety of forms of monitoring of performance.

From the 1960s onwards, a series of international surveys began to reveal how standards in England compared to those in other countries (see, for example, Husen, 1967; Keys and Foxman, 1989). The Third International Mathematics Survey (Keys *et al.*, 1997) provided a recent illustration of this kind of concern, showing as it did that English pupils apparently compare well with their peers in other countries on science achievement, but are well down when it comes to mathematics. How far it is appropriate to trust such statistics is perhaps less important than recognizing the effect of such high-profile studies on policy-makers, who are keen to be seen to be responding to public concern about standards.

In addition to these general concerns, there were also a number of more specific developments. One of these was the 'fallout' from the virtual abandonment of eleven-plus testing with the advent of comprehensive schools during the 1970s. This development left primary schools free of almost any kind of formal curriculum or assessment control. It also meant that there was very little information about the standards being achieved in primary schools and in the lower years of secondary schools. Although the Assessment of Performance Unit had been set up in the 1970s to monitor national performance in particular subject areas, this was a spasmodic exercise and was not sufficient to calm public disquiet.

Concern about education, and primary education in particular, grew throughout the 1970s. The publication of the first 'Black Paper' (Cox and Dyson, 1969) was an early manifestation, but debate was fanned by the furore over the management and teaching at Tyndale Junior School (Dale, 1981). Other key events of 1976 were the publication of Neville Bennett's book *Teaching Styles and Pupil Progress*, and Prime Minister Jim Callaghan's Ruskin College speech. Callaghan, with an eye on the public critique of 'progressivism', argued that the educational aims of the time were unbalanced. As he put it:

> The goals of our education are clear enough. They are to equip children to the best of their ability for a lively, constructive place in society and also to fit them to do a job of work. Not one or the other, but both.

Concern about the relevance and control of education continued following the 1979 election of Mrs Thatcher's Conservative government. New thinking by her education ministers, such as Sir Keith Joseph, and by various New Right pressure groups led to the publication of a White Paper, *Better Schools* (1985), and subsequently the 1988 Education Reform Act, which was to prove a watershed in English educational provision.

1.3 THE 1988 EDUCATION REFORM ACT

The expressed aim of the 1988 Education Reform Act – a policy initiative almost unprecedented in its ambition and scope – was, quite simply, to raise standards. This was to be achieved by raising expectations about pupil achievement and, through the imposition of a broad and balanced national curriculum for all pupils, to provide continuity and coherence in their learning experience. The introduction of the National Curriculum was complemented by provision for a standard and comprehensive assessment system. This national system was designed not only to measure the performance of pupils at the end of four Key Stages (Years 1–2, 3–6, 7–10 and 11–12), but also to make it possible for market forces to operate by providing a currency of information which would fuel competition between schools.

The original aim of the national assessment system was that it should provide formative and diagnostic information to guide teachers in the classroom as well as summative information for students, teachers and parents about the level of attainment of a given child at a given stage. Thus the government's Task Group on Assessment and Testing (TGAT) envisaged an elaborate, criterion-referenced structure of attainment targets. Pupils' achievement was to be recorded and reported at the end of Key Stages 1, 2 and 3 by means of a combination of teacher assessment and results from externally provided standard assessment tasks. At the end of Key Stage 4, external assessment was to be in the form of the newly introduced GCSE examination. Significantly, such a comprehensive national assessment system could, and subsequently did, provide attainment data with which to compare not only individual students, but also the results of their schools, of local education authorities (LEAs) and indeed of the nation as a whole in comparative league tables. Slowly the formative purpose of assessment waned in significance, and its significance as a summative measure of performance became dominant.

Innovation on the scale described was likely to cause turbulence in any education system, and the English reforms were no exception. Earlier books based on the PACE study (Pollard *et al.* 1994a; Croll 1996) documented the anger and despair of teachers in the early 1990s as they struggled to implement both the National Curriculum and new assessment procedures. Both proved to be too demanding in terms of teachers' time and were perceived as being over-prescriptive. The National Curriculum was therefore reviewed by Sir Ron Dearing, and a second version was introduced in September 1995. This 'slimmed down' the curriculum content and changed the elaborate structure of criterion-referenced attainment into a simpler system of 'level descriptions' for 'best-fit' assessment judgements and reporting. National tests were statutory only in the core subjects of English, maths and science, and, for Key Stages 2 and 3, external markers were to be provided to lighten the load on classroom teachers.

The first PACE book, *Changing English Primary Schools?* (Pollard *et al.*, 1994a), reported the project's findings concerning teachers' experiences with, and attitudes to, both the National Curriculum and the assessment system during the early 1990s. It made clear that teachers found the workload of implementing the new requirements both an unacceptable burden in terms of the time required and equally unacceptable in terms of the prominence given to subject knowledge and the explicit labelling and categorizing of pupils in terms of their levels of achievement. The 'child-centred' commitment of primary teachers was still very strong at the time, with considerable support for 'topic work' and for the significance of developing close teacher–pupil relationships. Subject knowledge, however, was weak in a number of areas. Assessment practices were undeveloped, since primary schools in most parts of the country had had little or no tradition of formal assessment since the demise of the eleven-plus selection examination. Further, many teachers were ideologically opposed to conducting tests which they felt were neither meaningful nor helpful. However, as with subject knowledge, many teachers also lacked professional experience in conducting such formal assessments and thus were faced with the need to develop new skills in this respect.

In 1993 many teachers, suffering low morale from the sustained public critique combined with the work pressure of the overloaded curriculum, refused to do the national tests on a formal basis. This revolt was initiated by English teachers at Key

Stage 3 who were objecting to the content of the tests and their inevitable washback effect on curriculum priorities. However, the fact that the boycott rapidly spread into primary schools provides a good illustration of the extent of the antipathy towards national assessment and government policy that existed among primary teachers at that time. As *Changing English Primary Schools?* makes clear, the causes of this antipathy were at a number of levels. Amongst the most obvious were issues of workload and time. Teachers objected strongly to a procedure that would take many days of effort for themselves and their pupils but would not, in their view, contribute to the facilitation of pupil learning.

Beneath this, though, were more fundamental concerns about the anticipated effect of such tests on the priorities and practices of English primary schooling. For instance, it was already clear to many teachers that the well-established English tradition of controlling schools by means of external assessment requirements was being redeployed in a new and powerful way to impose a particular set of curriculum priorities on schools. Further, the steadily growing emphasis year by year on the use of national assessment results as an external indicator of school standards meant that the reliability of the information became increasingly important. In the context of the publication of 'league tables' of test results at school and LEA level in the national media, assessment procedures had to be rigorously controlled in order to ensure fairness in comparisons between schools. The consequence was a steady trend towards the use of formal, externally controlled paper-and-pencil tests at all levels, and with this came a wash-back on to the curriculum so that teaching and curriculum planning became increasingly designed to maximize test performance.

Another major development under the Conservative administrations of the 1990s was the introduction of the school inspection system. Established through the 1992 Education Act, this was designed to monitor and make public the quality of management, teaching and pupil attainment at each school. Once again, there was a rationale in terms of providing public information based on independent judgement, but the system, led by the Chief Inspector of Schools, Chris Woodhead, was seen by many as a vehicle for 'teacher-bashing'.

Overall, the period of PACE data-gathering during the early and mid-1990s was a time of considerable tension between the government and the teaching profession, a tension that was only partially ameliorated by Sir Ron Dearing's 1995 review. At the end of the period, teachers eagerly anticipated a new start from a more sympathetic government.

1.4 DEVELOPMENTS UNDER NEW LABOUR

When the Labour government came to power in May 1997, the White Paper *Excellence in Schools* (DfEE, 1997) was published rapidly, and it was evident that the pace of new education policy-making was to continue. However, there was a reappraisal of focus and priorities, and this resulted in a new concern for social inclusion and an ever-increasing emphasis on the basics of literacy and numeracy. Indeed, in January 1998 the Secretary of State for Education, David Blunkett, announced that some of the requirements of the primary National Curriculum were being suspended for the following two years to enable more time to be spent on these 'basics' prior to a comprehensive revision of the National Curriculum. Thus although primary schools were 'expected' to continue teaching history, geography, design and technology, art, music and physical education, only English, mathematics, science, information technology and religious education remained as required subjects. In the other subjects the content and the amount of coverage were left to the discretion of schools. The goal of this initiative to suspend and focus the National Curriculum was expressed in terms of the government's desire to ensure that all children would leave primary school equipped with the necessary competence in the basics of literacy and numeracy. Others criticized the focus on 'the basics' of literacy and numeracy for undermining the previous commitment to a broad and balanced curriculum.

In 1999 plans for a revised National Curriculum were published. This *Curriculum 2000* (DfEE, 1999b) was the result of much more extensive consultation with classroom teachers than previous versions. Nevertheless, the radically slimmed-down curriculum that had earlier been anticipated, which would give more scope for teachers' professional judgement, did not materialize.

New Labour also increased pedagogic prescription through the competency requirements of the Teacher Training Agency, the frameworks of the literacy and numeracy hours, the naming and shaming of 'failing' schools, and the specification of school inspection. The effects of these developments have been further reinforced by the gradual development of sophisticated target-setting systems for schools and local education authorities, and the linking of teachers' classroom performance to salary enhancement. Taken as a whole, these various policy initiatives have ensured that primary school teaching has become increasingly framed by requirements and pressures that are external to the school itself.

The policy developments that have followed the period covered by the PACE study represent a continuation of the major themes which we have identified. Although there are differences between the earlier Conservative administrations and that of New Labour, post-1997, remarkable continuities also remain in terms of the underlying assumptions driving the search for higher educational standards. Thus as we demonstrate in what follows, the lessons to be learned from the PACE project in terms both of policy and of practice have a continuing significance both for England and for the many other education systems around the world where similarly informed policy initiatives aimed at raising standards are also being pursued.

1.5 THE PACE PROJECT

The overall goals of the PACE project were broad: to describe the impact of the English National Curriculum and to evaluate its significance for pupils, teachers and the process of education as a whole. Its focus was on the process of change in primary schools – its origins and progress; its management and effects.

Expressed in terms of specific objectives the PACE project sought:

1. to monitor changes in teachers' practices and pupil experiences in terms of curriculum, pedagogy and assessment;
2. to investigate the consequences of national policies and mediating effects which are associated with teacher perspectives, cultures and behaviour, and, in particular, their perceptions of professional responsibility; and
3. to investigate the consequences of national policies and mediating effects which are associated with pupil perspectives, cultures and classroom behaviours.

Whilst our first priority was to describe and analyse the impact of the Education Reform Act on primary schools, we also aimed to consider the changes in primary schooling as an illustration of wider social developments. In particular, we came to see the changing focus of education policy as a reflection of the tensions between modern and 'post-modern' society, with new priorities and new forms of contestation, regulation and discourse. Our study has a strongly empirical flavour, and we feel a responsibility to report fully the patterns of opinion, behaviour and practice which we have recorded. However, we have also attempted to theorize these findings and set them in the wider context of social change.

After eight years of data collection, from 1989 to 1997, the PACE project represents what is arguably a uniquely comprehensive picture of the changes which took place for pupils, teachers and headteachers during this time. In this book we focus particularly on teachers' experience during these turbulent years – on their evolving professionalism and on changes in their classroom practice. This book, and its partner volume on pupils' perceptions and classroom experiences, aspire both to *describe* the developments in primary education that have taken place and to *understand* them as part of wider social developments at the end of the twentieth century. Our further proposed synoptic PACE volume 'The Assessment Society' (Broadfoot and Pollard) will have as its central focus an analysis of the impact of recent policy changes in assessment. It will explore the nature of contemporary educational discourse as a case-study of underlying trends in society and, in particular, of the significance of the gradual establishment of the new hegemony of 'performance' which the PACE project has documented.

Given that, from its inception, the PACE project has aspired not only to describe but, crucially, to *explain* the nature of the changes taking place, it has also been concerned with evaluating the significance of these changes, both for the business of education specifically and, more generally, for the nature and conduct of social life. In 1994a we described the PACE project as 'one of the many stepping stones in the quest to understand the nature of the educational enterprise and hence, how to provide for it most effectively in a changing context' (p. 4). Thus our research was designed to help understand the origin and significance both of the policy initiatives imposed by government and of those which were the product of the attempts by teachers and headteachers to reconcile these requirements with their professional values and understandings. Why were these policy initiatives set in motion in the England of the late 1980s and what, ultimately, is likely to be their significance for the nature and quality of pupils' learning? If it is important to find the answer to this question in order to inform subsequent policy-making in England, this is also an important project more globally since many of the recent English policy initiatives which are the subject of this volume have also been enthusiastically imitated in other parts of the world.

From the outset, the work of Basil Bernstein has proved particularly apposite as a foundation for our theoretical interpretations. The capacity of Bernstein's conceptualization to embrace curriculum, pedagogy and assessment, and its concern with power, knowledge and consciousness as key variables, enabled us to integrate the diverse perspectives of the PACE project into three core themes which we identified as 'values', 'understanding' and 'power'. We also used Bernstein's well-established concepts of classification and framing to develop various cubic representations, facets of which portray the different, but interrelated, trends which have taken place in primary schools over the period. Thus, for instance, our early data suggested that classroom life reflected the move to a more classified, subject-based curriculum, increasingly controlled and framed forms of pedagogy, and more explicit and categoric forms of assessment (see Figure 1.1).

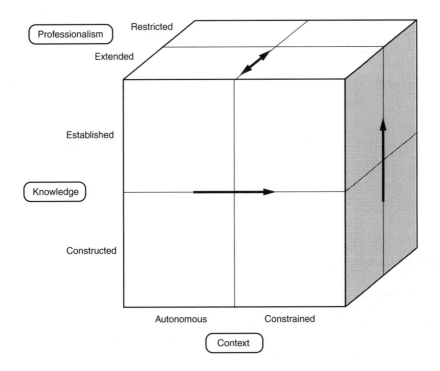

Figure 1.1 Changing dimensions of teacher professionalism

Similarly, the demands on teachers and the nature of teaching also changed. Professional autonomy became more constrained and the pressure for accountability grew. Teachers' views of their own professional responsibilities began to become more pragmatic. Over time, there was a gradual acceptance of the National Curriculum and assessment, particularly as older teachers retired, new teachers were inducted into a new set of professional expectations, and the worst excesses of prescription were moderated. Teachers also began to recognize the value of subject knowledge, and to see it as complementing the previous emphasis on children constructing their own understandings. We conceptualized these developments as shown in Figure 1.2.

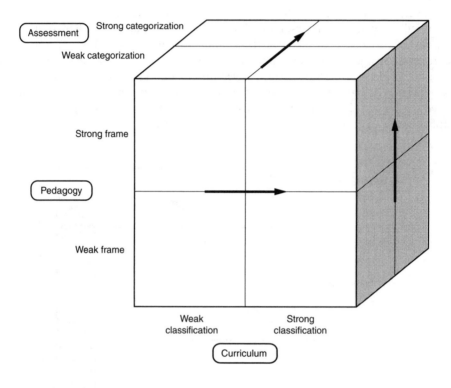

Figure 1.2 Changing dimensions of curriculum, pedagogy and assessment

In a subsequent PACE book, edited by Croll (1996), we explored at greater length the ways in which these changing characteristics of the organization and delivery of primary education in England were being experienced and managed by those affected. The findings reported in the book reinforced the salience of values, understanding and power as key themes in the explanation of both the rationale for the changes that were being imposed and teachers' responses to them.

We argued that schools, as well as teachers and pupils, are 'embedded in a dynamic network of personal identity, values and understandings that are constantly developing in the light of internal and external interaction, pressure and constraint' (Croll, 1996, p. 156). Because of this, policy directives are translated into classroom practice through a series of 'mediations'. Such 'mediations', we argued, should not be conceptualized in engineering terms as a series of articulated levers that relay a load through the structure. Rather, they are the creative reinterpretation by the actors involved at each successive stage of the process of delivering education. Once again, Bernstein's analysis of the pedagogic code and its power to define, and hence control, provided a powerful theoretical model with which to examine the significance of the changes documented in the PACE data. We will explore this further in Chapter 11.

Now, at the end of the empirical phase of the longitudinal study as a whole, we have tried to produce both a comprehensive descriptive picture of how things have changed in primary schools since 1989 and an analytic framework for summarizing these developments.

1.6 A STUDY OF TEACHERS AND TEACHING

As has already been made clear, this book is about how life has changed for English primary school teachers in recent years. It describes their response to imposed policy initiatives in the context of a more general analysis of the traditions of primary teaching in England, the professional ideologies and ways of working, the patterns of perceived obligations, and the strategies that have evolved to reconcile the diverse and evolving pressures which they experience.

How did teachers perceive and experience the introduction of the National Curriculum and assessment?

We believe that this is an important question since it touches on fundamental issues of professional responsibility and motivation. In the context of an education system characterized by a long tradition of professional autonomy, it is important to consider what the effects on teachers' attitudes and practice of a more dirigiste education system have been. Did the steadily tightening framework of expectations and requirements that English teachers experienced in the years since 1988 lead to a reinvigorated professionalism characterized by a clearer pedagogic focus and higher aspirations for pupil learning?

In the context of the long-running debates between the traditions of elementary and developmental education in English primary education, what part did teachers' own professional values play in influencing what educational priorities were in practice? 'Child-centred education' or 'progressivism' became a powerful professional ideology for English primary teachers following the Plowden Report of 1967. The developmental tradition was very much a part of the beliefs and values of the majority of the teachers at the beginning of the PACE study. Yet as we have seen, the context in which the National Curriculum and assessment were introduced was characterized by a strong discourse linking education to international competitiveness and asserting its 'accountability'. Such concerns articulate closely with the elementary tradition and were reflected in the content and structure of the curriculum. Thus the Education Reform Act of 1988 and, more recently, the National Literacy and Numeracy Strategies evoke the very different priorities of the elementary tradition of the Victorian era, which prioritized the inculcation of basic skills through 'cheap and efficient' mass instruction. Teachers, then, were faced with a profound tension between the priorities being imposed upon them and the continued desire of many to prioritize their 'caring' role and to derive much personal pleasure from children's individual development and achievement.

As we argued in the first PACE book (Pollard *et al.*, 1994a, ch. 2), the developmental education tradition was underpinned by the way in which 'childhood' has been idealized and sentimentalized in English culture. Today the debate concerning different educational values and practices which has characterized English primary education in recent years raises the most profound questions about the role of education at the dawn of the third millennium. Indeed, our companion volume (Pollard *et al.*, 2000) concludes by asking: what priorities should inform the preparation of children who will live their lives in the very different world of the twenty-first century?

The central theme of this book, however, concerns teachers' perceptions of their role as professionals and how they feel they have responded to change. It teases out the deep-seated, often taken-for-granted value systems that inform well-established assumptions about both the goals and the techniques of teaching. As we set out in Chapters 3 to 5, teachers have struggled to defend their traditionally 'extended' conception of their role against pressures to accept a more narrow, 'technicist' conception. Despite their escalating workload, they have been unwilling to give up their deep-rooted sense of caring about their pupils. However, our evidence suggests that they seem to have become more instrumental, moving from a 'covenant'- to a 'contract'-based work ethic, whilst at the same time preserving a good measure of their traditional personal and moral accountability. In these chapters we explore how and why the more traditional professional discourse is being eroded as new teachers enter the profession, and whether, as Nias (1999b) suggests, to the extent that this is so, it may actually lead to both greater professional satisfaction for teachers and a clearer focus on learning *per se*.

Campbell (1996) identifies three contemporary pressures on English teachers' work. He defines these as shifts along continua from specificity towards diffuseness; from the generalist towards the specialist; and from restricted to extended professionalism. Ironically, perhaps, this first dimension relates to the ever-widening range of educational goals for which teachers in English primary schools are deemed to be responsible, including, for example, moral and civic education, religious awareness and social and health education. Yet at the same time, teachers are increasingly being expected to become subject specialists, a trend which, paradoxically, prioritizes the academic achievement of pupils. The issue of the new subject knowledge demands that have been placed on teachers by the advent of the National Curriculum appears as an important strand in our study, which records how teachers generally have developed new curriculum expertise whilst at the same time, in many cases, losing confidence in their capacity to deliver.

The combined impact of new requirements which appear to pull teachers in different directions is necessarily complex to unravel. Many contemporary studies have stressed the need to understand teachers' responses as a series of mediations. Troman (1996), for example, in the light of his detailed study of change in one primary school, is clear that he had found neither a wholesale clinging to the past, nor a comprehensive embrace of new constructions of the work of teaching in the new 'managerialist' culture. Rather, the reactions he observed were typically 'ambivalent, complex and contradictory', with some changes being accepted and others resisted.

This capacity of teachers creatively to mediate change, how and why they do it, and the implications of this process, are arguably the central themes of this book. In the first stage of the project, PACE 1, we described the multiple strategic responses of the teachers in our study, which ranged from compliance, through incorporation, creative mediation, resistance and retreatism. This capacity of teachers to adapt policy prescriptions in the light of their own beliefs, skills and circumstances has grown in prominence during the course of the project. In 1996, reporting on the second phase of the project, PACE 2, we described how teachers were becoming 'policy-makers in practice' (Croll, 1996). We suggested that their capacity to be so depended on their ability to reconcile new ways of working with their fundamental professional values on the one hand and their own knowledge, skills and abilities on the other. Those teachers who believed that they had managed the new requirements in this way were feeling both positive and empowered, in contrast to those who continued to feel overwhelmed by their new responsibilities and/or fundamentally out of sympathy with the rationale of the reforms.

What is the significance of recent education policy in terms of teachers' professional skills and engagement?

Part 2 of this book describes in detail teachers' evolving attitudes and practices, and how their varied responses translated into different ways of working with colleagues, with the headteacher and with pupils in the classroom. We report, too, changes in headteachers' beliefs and practices, their varied responses to the pressure of new responsibilities and how these in turn impacted on their schools. In line with our overall goal, however, we seek to understand not only the interactive processes that underpin *individual teachers'* ways of coping with change, but also the part placed by the school as an institution, its leadership and culture in facilitating or inhibiting this process. More fundamentally still, our analysis teases out the way in which, as different groups within the education system seek to accommodate the new requirements on them through a variety of mediations, they have gradually changed the discourse through which the ideology and practice of primary education are expressed. As Woods and Wenham (1995) argue, it is not just at the level of the individual teacher that policy initiatives become reinterpreted. This is also true at every other level of the system where different interest groups 'interpret them, using different discourses to imbue sense to, rather than take sense from them' (p. 119).

The Bernsteinian focus of the PACE analysis teases out these various stages of the 're-creation' of the original policy message in order to explore possible explanations for the changing perceptions of the role of primary education in England. It underpins the attempt to discover the particular reasons which have led in England to the scapegoating of teachers as part of the public debate over standards in contrast to other, in many ways comparable, countries such as France or Germany –

or even Scotland, where policy initiatives have taken a very different shape, despite being part of the same broad governmental jurisdiction (Broadfoot *et al.*, 1996).

This is a book about the impact of policy-making on practice. It traces the way in which teachers' practice has changed in terms of the balance of emphasis given to different subjects, modes of classroom organization and grouping, the balance of different pedagogic approaches and the choice of assessment practices. The extent of the changes documented here represent the heart of the educational change project initially launched in 1988. They represent the extent to which external forces have been successful in redefining teachers' understanding of means and ends, and hence, how far teachers have acquired new professional values about the priority to be accorded to particular activities – forms of instruction and evaluation. The significance of these developments however, must ultimately be judged in terms of their impact on pupils – their achievements, their attitudes and, perhaps most important of all, their learning dispositions.

Nevertheless, maximizing the effectiveness of education will continue to depend in large part on the quality and commitment of teachers. How best to provide for this is currently a central concern of government policy. *A Fast Track for Teachers* (DfEE, 1999) sets out a vision of a teaching profession in which individual performance management and an explicit structure of incentives constitute the central policy planks towards achieving higher professional standards. It is a policy that reflects the same set of assumptions about how to improve performance as those currently informing the approach to pupil attainment and school quality. It assumes that an explicit framework of expectations coupled with a system of sanctions and rewards will result in enhanced performance. It is this 'performativity' ethos that lies at the heart of the policy changes studied by the PACE project. Its contemporary pervasiveness in all aspects of education policy underlines the importance of exploring how far the assumptions on which it is based are borne out by the lived experience of teachers and pupils. How successful have been the attempts over the past decade or so to shift the world of primary education on its axis? What have been the effects of these changes on teachers' teaching and pupils' learning? In what way are these effects likely to be significant?

These are the questions that we explore in the chapters that follow.

1.7 THE STRUCTURE OF THE BOOK

Chapter 2 describes in some detail the complex range of data-collection methods that the PACE project adopted in order to explore as comprehensively and representatively as possible the different perspectives and experiences of teachers and pupils over a considerable period of time. It describes some of the particular challenges that such a broad and lengthy research project inevitably faced and how these were addressed, in an attempt to draw out some of the unique methodological lessons that can be learned from this experience.

Part 2 (Chapters 3, 4 and 5) of the book explores teachers' own perspectives. Chapter 3 documents their sense of professionalism and accountability, and the impact of policy changes on their fundamental values. In examining teachers' perceptions of what motivates them and gives them professional satisfaction, it highlights some of the profound tensions that teachers have had to negotiate in recent years and the ways in which this has been achieved. Chapter 4 explores some of the reasons for teachers' different responses to the pressures they experienced and the implications of these differences in terms of their subsequent capacity to experience such changes as a source of professional renewal. Chapter 5 complements the essentially personal tone of the two earlier chapters in this section in highlighting the very significant part played by a web of professional relationships in helping teachers to cope with the new demands being experienced. For many teachers, one of the most positive effects of recent policy initiatives has been a significantly increased level of collaboration with colleagues. This has been a source of both professional development and emotional support for many teachers, and in Chapter 5 we explore the factors underpinning its development as well as the more general significance of different professional relationships as an influence on teachers' work.

Part 3 of the book documents the changes that have taken place in teachers' classroom practice. Chapter 6 uses the Bernsteinian concept of classification to explore the way in which the boundaries between subjects within the curriculum have become increasingly sharply drawn and, in the process, have provided for an increasingly explicit and externalized definition of what counts as knowledge. Chapter 7 applies the parallel concept of 'framing' to explore the changes that have taken place in relation to pedagogy. The balance of power between pupils, teachers and external agencies in determining the nature of the educational interaction taking place is taken as a central theme to explore the implications of recent shifts in emphasis in favour of whole-class teaching, ability grouping and the level of engagement of different pupils. Finally, in this part of the book, Chapter 8 addresses the central issue of assessment, once an implicit and almost exclusively covert activity in the primary classroom. Chapter 8 documents how assessment increasingly constitutes an explicit message system that categorizes both the quality of pupils' work according to overt criteria and the individual as a whole. How teachers have responded to the pressures to engage in such activity, their efforts to protect pupils from what they considered to be its worst effects and the growing inevitability of 'teaching the test' are central themes in the PACE analysis.

Part 4 of the book (Chapters 9 and 10) shifts the focus to a more individual level. In presenting in rather more detail accounts of individual teachers' responses to the changes they experienced, Chapter 9 highlights the way in which common and individual factors combined for each individual to mediate their response to the pressures being experienced. It highlights the importance of 'context' – interpersonal, institutional and managerial – and examines the different pressures and responses that were evoked by the impact of common requirements on individuals, schools and pupils very differently equipped to cope with them. Some of these themes are pursued in more detail in Chapter 10, which examines the particular part played by headteachers in managing the process of change and in protecting teachers as far as possible from the worst pressures. Again this chapter illustrates the considerable variation that characterized different heads' capacity both to cope themselves with the range of new pressures and to provide an effective managerial climate to facilitate coping by their teachers.

1.8 CONCLUSION

The PACE project is not just about policy change. Nor is it just about primary teachers' lived experience and what makes them 'tick' as professionals. It is rather about the concatenation of the two: about the way in which systems and institutions, directives and materials are made a reality by the subjectivities of individuals. As such it is a study of policy-making in practice with lessons to offer of both a specific and a more general kind concerning how efforts to change practice may most effectively be managed. But beyond this specific focus, the PACE study also addresses more general issues of structure and agency and the way in which social activity is regulated and constituted through interaction both between individuals and with texts. Last but not least, it is a study of power, of the various stages in the creation and dissemination of a discourse that has the power both to define what is normal and to impose this through the three message-systems of education: curriculum, pedagogy and assessment. Ultimately, the issues at stake here are those concerning values and understanding – values concerning the ultimate goals of education and understanding about how these may best be achieved. The picture of English primary teachers that we present in this book is one that may be unique in the world in its description of a profession committed to the academic, social, moral, physical and emotional development of every child – a commitment that may be unique in terms of the professional hours and effort expended by individual teachers; a commitment that may be unique in terms of the capacity to collaborate and to generate a level of institutional synergy. The story of English primary education that we have briefly rehearsed in this chapter is one of both change and chagrin in recent years. It invites the question that forms the implicit heart of this book of whether, if and when the dust eventually settles, it will all have been worth it.

Chapter 2

Research Design and Data-Gathering Methods

2.1 INTRODUCTION

This chapter outlines the research design of the PACE project and its implementation over the eight years of the project's duration from 1989 to 1997. It considers some of the methodological challenges that emerged, together with the ways in which the team attempted to resolve them. In the concluding part of the chapter we discuss some of the issues that arose as part of the collaborative work of a team of five researchers over such a considerable period of time.

As we saw in Chapter 1, PACE aimed to monitor the impact of the curricular and assessment structures introduced by the 1988 Education Reform Act (ERA) for primary schools, teachers and pupils. There was a particular focus on teacher and pupil perspectives and on classroom practices and experiences, though we also gathered data on school policies and management. In developing our research design, we were considerably helped by Bernstein's conceptualization of three educational 'message systems': curriculum, pedagogy and assessment. He argues that these message systems convey the 'education codes' of their particular society (Bernstein, 1975, 1990, 1996) and thus signify values, priorities and understandings.

Table 2.1 represents our design, embracing national policy, school contexts and classroom contexts, with our particular focus on teachers and pupils, and on curriculum, pedagogy and assessment.

Table 2.1 Research design: data to be gathered

	Teachers	**Pupils**
Curriculum		
Pedagogy		
Assessment		

The national policy context

↓

The local government context

↓

Change in the school context

↓

Change in the classroom context

Note: This framework was applied to (a) the natural policy context; (b) change and experience in the school context; and (c) change and experience in the classroom context

As we discussed in the first chapter, the project was wide-ranging from the start and it became even more complex as the phenomenon of almost continuous educational change evolved in the 1990s. A considerable variety of data collection procedures were used in the research in an attempt to capture the processes involved in multiple innovation (Wallace, 1991). Over the eight years of the study personal interviews with headteachers, teachers and children were one of the most important sources of data. These included both open-ended and structured questions. The early interviews with children included special techniques of 'embedded interviews' involving visual stimuli and discussion of activities that the researcher had observed earlier (Pollard *et al.*, 1994a). Self-completion questionnaires were used with teachers in order to collect demographic and career data, and also for attitude scales and similar data. Other procedures included observation in classrooms using both systematic, quantitative procedures and qualitative approaches with open-ended or partially structured field notes. Sociometric data on children's friendship patterns and tape-recordings of teachers' interactions with children were also collected. These methods are described in more detail in later sections of this chapter.

Throughout the three phases of the study the major priority was to map the educational experiences of a pupil cohort as those pupils developed within the new structures. The core of the PACE study was thus a longitudinal study of 54 children from nine schools drawn from across England as they moved through their schools. However, if children moved away or left the school they had to be replaced by others. In total, 87 children – 43 boys and 44 girls – participated in the study as target pupils for observation and interview over the six-year period. These children, their classrooms and teachers were studied in some detail over the years. However, to meet the objectives of the PACE study we needed to balance the need for a highly detailed study of children's and teachers' experience of the National Curriculum and assessment with the desirability of also having representative data from a broader sample. The nine classroom study schools were therefore embedded in a larger sample of schools drawn from across the country in which a larger number of teachers and headteachers were interviewed.

Since the longitudinal element was designed with the aim of following, as far as was possible, the same children throughout their primary school experience, the focus on their teachers was on a largely different population over the course of the study. In each round of interviews we talked to teachers of the year groups in which our target children were currently placed. This design enabled us to chart teacher perspectives throughout the primary school during this period of rapid multiple change. However, we needed a cross-sectional element in the study in order to examine change in teacher perspectives. Therefore, during PACE 2 we returned to the same schools to interview a sample of Key Stage 1 teachers two years on, so that comparisons could be made between teacher perspectives in 1992 and 1994. We were also fortunate in that a number of teachers in the sample stayed with their pupils for several years as they moved through the primary school. This made possible several qualitative case-studies of individual teachers which analysed changes in perspectives as the reforms moved into successive phases (Osborn, 1996a, c).

Regarding the tracking of change over a longer period, we designed many of our research instruments so that our new, post-ERA data on classroom practice in primary schools would be broadly comparable with earlier studies such as the ORACLE research (Galton *et al.*, 1980), the Junior Schools Project (Mortimore *et al.*, 1988) and the Bristaix project (Broadfoot *et al.*, 1993). The latter project was based on comparisons between teachers in France and England regarding their views of professional responsibilities in the mid-1980s. During the 1990s further international comparisons were made possible by a directly comparable project which used the PACE teacher data together with questionnaires and interviews with teachers in France, following recent policy reforms (Broadfoot *et al.*, 1996).

The PACE project was thus designed to track pupil experiences and monitor change on a very wide front, though not least amongst the project aims was the concern to analyse and theorize the new developments. Although we take the view that all social science is, inevitably, somewhat inexact, our task has nevertheless been to gather data as carefully as we can and to analyse those data to provide a meaningful interpretation of developments since the 1988 Education Reform Act. This will, we hope, have as much policy relevance for government as it does for teachers.

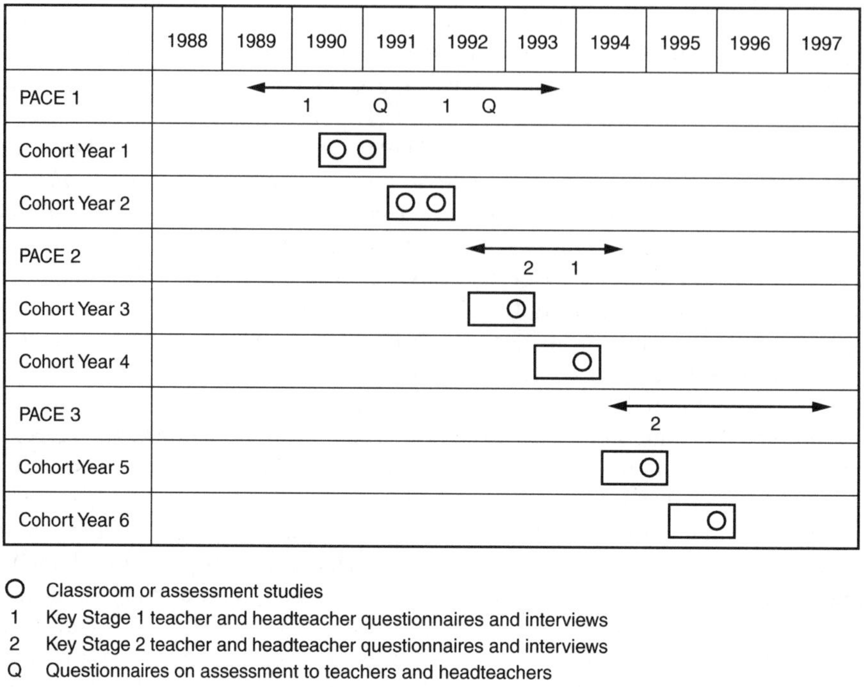

	1988	1989	1990	1991	1992	1993	1994	1995	1996	1997
PACE 1		←	1	Q	1	Q →				
Cohort Year 1			O O							
Cohort Year 2				O O						
PACE 2					← 2	1 →				
Cohort Year 3					O					
Cohort Year 4						O				
PACE 3							← 2		→	
Cohort Year 5							O			
Cohort Year 6								O		

O   Classroom or assessment studies
1   Key Stage 1 teacher and headteacher questionnaires and interviews
2   Key Stage 2 teacher and headteacher questionnaires and interviews
Q   Questionnaires on assessment to teachers and headteachers

Figure 2.1 Major phases of data-gathering in the PACE project

In each phase of the project there were two rounds of both interviews and questionnaires administered to a large sample of teachers, and two rounds of both classroom and assessment studies, using multiple data-gathering methods. In the sections of this chapter that follow, we provide more details on data-gathering methods, beginning with an outline of the data-gathering schedule and an explanation of how our national sample of schools was drawn.

2.2 THE DATA-GATHERING SCHEDULE

The study was organized in three phases: PACE 1, from October 1989 to December 1992; PACE 2, from January 1993 to December 1994; and PACE 3, from January 1995 to August 1997. This made it possible to request funding within the relatively limited budget of the Economic and Social Research Council (ESRC) research grants scheme. Some of the problems which arose for the team because of the need to obtain funding in this way are discussed in the concluding section of this chapter.

The major phases of data collection are shown in Figure 2.1, which provides an overview and illustrates both the longitudinal and the cross-sectional features of the research design.

In PACE 1 and 2 there were also several meetings of a 'federated network' of related research projects. This aimed to link into a significant group of studies on the impact of the National Curriculum being conducted by other researchers, some of whom were working alone in smaller-scale studies. The PACE study aimed to provide a broader contextualization for some of these other studies through ongoing debate and exchange of papers, together with a linkage at the level of findings.

2.3 THE NATIONAL SAMPLE OF SCHOOLS, CLASSROOMS, TEACHERS AND PUPILS

Through careful sampling design, the study aimed to provide data which were broadly representative of schools, teachers and pupils across the whole of England. At its most general level our analysis was derived from 150 teachers and headteachers in 48 schools in eight English local education authorities. At its more specific level, it was based on the perspectives and practices of nine teachers for each year of the study (54 classrooms and teachers being reported over the whole study) and six children in each school moving through their primary school careers in those classrooms (a total of 54 pupils). Given the enormous national significance of the innovation being studied and, not least, its cost, it would have been desirable to have a larger sample. However, given this impossibility and the scarcity of funding for educational research, we took steps to attempt to ensure that our sample represented a full range of primary school practices and circumstances.

The main LEA and school sample

An initial strategy, following ESRC advice, was to sample in local education authorities (LEAs) that were regarded as having 'positive support structures' for the implementation of the National Curriculum. A comparison of different types of support at LEA level was not one of the project's aims, and it was felt that this strategy could reduce some extraneous variables from our data-gathering. After consultation with Her Majesty's Inspectorate (HMI) and others, we identified eight such LEAs, aiming for a balance in terms of socio-economic factors, urban/rural areas and a geographical spread in the north, Midlands, south-east and south-west of England, as well as making some allowances for ease of access. The chief education officer in each LEA was approached in the first instance for permission to carry out the research in his or her authority and, with permission obtained, local primary inspectors were designated as liaison officers.

To identify schools within each LEA a random sample of twenty infant schools or departments was drawn from a sector of the LEA that had been nominated by local advisers as being broadly representative of the LEA as a whole. From each of these lists, six schools were then selected to reflect different socio-economic locations and distinctive features such as religious denomination or styles of internal organization. Overall, in producing the final selection of 48 schools, the aim was to obtain a sample that encompassed the considerable variety of educational approaches that currently exist within primary schools. Both schools with separate infant departments and schools where infant and junior sections were integrated were chosen in order to explore any differences that these organizational variations might have produced. Infant schools that were not attached to any one junior school were excluded in order to ensure the capacity for longitudinal study.

The sample schools were classified broadly in terms of location and social class, as shown in Table 2.2. The spread of the sample in terms of school size was as shown in Table 2.3.

Table 2.2 Sample schools by location and predominant social class of local communities

	Number	Percentage
Rural, mixed social class	9	19
Urban, settled working/lower middle class	13	27
Inner city, deprived working class	15	31
Urban/suburban middle class	7	15
Urban, mixed social class	4	8
Total	48	100

Table 2.3 Sample schools by size

Number on roll	Number	Percentage
Under 150	12	25
151–350	29	60
351–650	7	15
Total	48	100

When, at the end of PACE 2, the target pupils left infant schools to move into separate junior schools, an additional sample of twenty schools was generated. These were in the same broad socio-economic catchment areas as their linked infant schools.

The school sub-sample

In the light of analysis of data collected from the advance questionnaire and first round of interviews, a sub-sample of nine schools was selected for more detailed and observational study in our 'classroom studies' and 'assessment studies'.

Two of these schools were in a relatively accessible area for the research team and one was in each of the other LEAs. We attempted to achieve a school sub-sample reflecting the range of socio-economic circumstances, school size and responses to change which we had found, but it cannot be claimed to be strictly representative.

Negotiations regarding access moderated our initial selection to avoid problems such as major building works and staff illness. The result was that our final sub-sample was not quite as well balanced as had been hoped. For example, both small rural schools and Roman Catholic schools were over-represented in terms of their occurrence nationally. Nevertheless, the sub-sample schools did, we feel, reflect most of the common characteristics and circumstances of English primary schools.

Brief details of the sub-sample schools are as follows:

St Bede's was a Roman Catholic primary school of 230 pupils in an established suburb of a medium-sized city in the south of England. It opened in the early seventies and was built to a single-storey open-plan design around a central courtyard which recently had been developed, with the help of the PTA, into an environmental area with plants and a pond. Inside the building, dividing walls had been gradually added to mask classes from noise from cloakrooms and corridors which were also used as teaching spaces. Outside there was a large playground with climbing apparatus, grass and trees. As a denominational school it had a wide catchment area and children were bussed to and fro each day. The school had close links with the local parish, and the parish priest was a frequent visitor. It was popular with parents. The approach was fairly traditional: pupils were organized in year groups, routines and values were clearly established and the ethos was cohesive. Most children wore school uniform. The school was led by a strong, experienced (female) headteacher and the atmosphere in the staffroom was noisy and good-humoured.

Kenwood Infant School was situated in very similar surroundings in the same city as St Bede's. It was built early in the twentieth century and was set in a concrete playground relieved by a new nature area. It had a well-stocked library and resource rooms. There was an emphasis on good behaviour and on making progress, and considerable effort was made to involve children in planning their own work. Children transferred to the nearby Kenwood Junior School at age 7. Like the infant school, this was a large and somewhat rambling urban school situated on an estate which was mainly council houses but with some private housing. The school also served families from surrounding areas of private terraced housing. The 331 children, organized in year groups, were mostly from white working-class families. There were very firm school structures in place with strong central control emanating from the (male) headteacher and a tightly defined timetable. Staff turnover was very rapid, reflecting the conflict which existed between the staff and the headteacher. A new (male) head was appointed in Year 6 of the project.

Meadway First School was an open-plan single-storey primary school built in the 1970s. It was set in a metropolitan inner-city housing estate and was surrounded by high-rise blocks of flats. The area suffered from high unemployment, significant crime rates and considerable vandalism. The school was light, airy and attractively decorated with children's work and other displays, and its pupils and staff reflected the multi-ethnic character of the local community. Amongst the teachers there was a high degree of joint planning, but their efforts often had to be directed towards the behavioural needs of the children. Ancillary support staff were provided to help.

During the course of the project, the LEA reorganized its schools from first/middle/secondary to primary/secondary. As a consequence, the pupils in our sample moved in Year 3 to Meadway Junior (previously a middle school), where the staff, led by a very long-standing and experienced (female) head, was also ethnically mixed. This school, located only a few yards from the infants', occupied two large Victorian red-brick buildings beside the road and shared an adjacent games field. Pupils in Years 3 and 4 (the Lower School) were taught in one building and Years 5 and 6 (the Upper School) were taught in the other. At the time of the study there were 235 pupils on roll, which was below capacity and allowed spare rooms to be used for a variety of purposes. There was a strong emphasis on behaviour, effort and achievement, and a very public reward system. The pedagogy tended to be teacher centred, though behaviour was often challenging. Fifty per cent of the pupils had special needs statements. There were support staff for both special educational needs (SEN) and English as a Second Language. The school made considerable efforts to involve parents in its work.

Greenmantle Primary School was located in a market town in central southern England, where traditional agricultural occupations coexisted with modern light industry. Its buildings were a mixture of Victorian and newer architecture with a scatter of temporary classrooms. The playground, though small, had plenty to interest the children. Most of the 270 children lived in the town or close by. The school was popular locally, and a high proportion of the pupils had prosperous, professional family backgrounds. It acquired grant-maintained status during the project. Pupils were organized in mixed-age classes throughout; teaching methods were fairly traditional and used a good deal of positive reinforcement. In Years 5 and 6 the model was semi-secondary: pupils from three classes were set for maths, English and physical education (PE); for some other subjects they were taught by 'specialists' from the three teachers. The school was led by a strong (male) headteacher and a supportive deputy (also male).

St Anne's was a Roman Catholic primary school in one of the country's least affluent LEAs in the north of England. The school population of 270 pupils (plus a nursery class) was drawn from a large council estate of very disadvantaged families. There was a high take-up of free school meals. Many parents were unemployed and some children were on the 'at risk' register or closely supported by social services. Some were living with extended family members: grandparents, relatives or friends, rather than with their own families. The school had a caring, close-knit family ethos, deriving in part from its Roman Catholic philosophy. This provided a stabilizing influence, which, in the early years of the study, was reinforced by daily visits by the local priest and by the assemblies led by the (male) headteacher, who had grown up in the city.

Although the school was in a highly disadvantaged area, its surroundings were not unpleasant. The main building was between 40 and 50 years old and had a new wing which was attached to the Catholic church next door. It was surrounded by a concrete playground, but behind this were large green playing-fields and trees that belonged to the Catholic comprehensive which many of the children would eventually attend. Unusually, pupils in the study were taught by male teachers for five of the six years. Classes in Key Stage 2 were mixed-age, with high achievers taught with older pupils. Teaching at Key Stage 1 was normally fairly structured around particular 'topics', while allowing for pupil choice of activities for part of each day. At Key Stage 2, lessons were structured by the subject timetable with strong teacher direction and little choice of activity for pupils.

Orchard was a small rural primary school of 116 pupils located in a pleasant village in central England. The school was an attractive purpose-built modern building surrounded by trees and fields. During the course of the study an extension, housing a new library and other facilities, was added. The school was very popular amongst local parents, who were mainly employed in the professions, business and farming. Because of its reputation, built up by the (female) head who led the school when the study started, children were drawn from a wider area of neighbouring villages and were either bussed in or driven to and from school by parents. Parental expectations were high and pupils were well motivated. Because of the school's small size, all the children were in mixed-age classes, some of these spanning three year groups. The three class teachers, all female, had considerable classroom autonomy, and teaching methods were varied. Both the staff and the headteacher knew the children's families well, and the relationship between home and school was relatively close. During the course of the study there was a change of headship and a new (male) headteacher, who had been a deputy in a neighbouring school, took over. The school continued to enjoy a high reputation in the local community.

Lawnside Primary School was set in a village near a large Midlands conurbation. The population consisted of a mixture of commuters and local families with agricultural connections. The school was opened in the thirties, and conditions were cramped, with a small original building, a brick structure and temporary classrooms. During the course of the project a new school was built on the site, which pupils and teachers moved into at the beginning of school year 1995. In Year 6, at the move, the school population was 186, with a planned expansion to 500, including a nursery. Pupils came from the immediate locality but were also brought by car from the surrounding area. Children eligible for free school meals or with special educational needs were numbered in single figures. All children had English as a first language. The school was welcoming and provided for a number of travellers' children from a nearby site. Pupils were taught in mixed-age classes spanning two years; all those in the study were taught by female teachers. The long-standing (male) head had led the school's expansion. The ethos was caring and structured. School uniform was almost universally worn and parents were supportive.

Valley was another rural school, set in a traditional village in the south-west of England. The core of the school was stone-built Victorian but there were modern extensions and two portable classrooms and good facilities. The school had a small playground, imaginatively equipped, a netball pitch and a large playing-field. It had a strong Christian ethos and close relationship with the village church and rector. The local population was a socio-economic mixture including local farming families and professional people who worked in nearby small towns. The school attracted its 111 pupils from largely middle-class and professional backgrounds from the village and the surrounding area. The level of support was high, and parents and other local residents acted as adult helpers. Uniform was limited to a sweatshirt. The school was led by an experienced (female) teaching head who shared a class of pupils in Years 4–6 with a part-time teacher. The small, all-female staff worked closely together and teaching methods were eclectic.

Audley Infant School was built between the wars. It was somewhat overcrowded but busy and well resourced. The location was an industrial village in the north-west where there was little unemployment compared with the surrounding area. Nevertheless, few local people were particularly affluent. There was a fairly high degree of teacher control, but children were allowed a degree of freedom within tasks. Children transferred to the neighbouring Audley Junior School at age 7. Audley Juniors amalgamated with the infants' school in Year 5 of the project to form a new voluntarily assisted primary school. The amalgamation was associated with a period of disruption and uncertainty over staffing. In Year 6, as well as the head (male) and deputy, the school had nine teachers, eight of them female. The school was housed in an old Victorian building with a Tarmac yard at the front and back and a small playing-field. It had a mixed social intake of 207 pupils plus a nursery, drawing the children mainly from lower middle-class and working-class families. The curriculum was taught mostly as separate subjects.

All the schools and LEAs were provided with outlines of the project's aims, design and ethical guidelines. As the project progressed they received project newsletters and occasional papers and eventually copies of the books. They were also aware that ongoing findings were being disseminated to policy-makers and that the research might have an influence on the review of the National Curriculum which took place in the latter phases of the research. At a time when they had so many other demands and pressures on their time it is particularly remarkable that none of the schools wanted to withdraw from the project. We have been grateful for the very high degree of support and cooperation which they have offered. Pseudonyms are, of course, used in this book for all LEAs, schools, teachers and pupils.

The pupil sample

In each year of the study we focused our observation and interviews on six children from one class in each of the nine schools – 54 pupils per year. These children were initially selected by relating a list of random numbers to each class list. However, there was some turnover of sample pupils from year to year, because of either family mobility or pupil absence from school during the particular annual period of our data-gathering, and this effect was particularly marked in Years 1 and 2. In such circumstances, the targeted pupil was replaced by a child of the same sex, and as similar as possible in terms of socio-economic background and attainment. In phases 2 and 3 of the project, where possible, gaps were filled by pupils previously in the sample to maintain the longitudinal data set. Overall, of the original 54 children, 21 remained in the project throughout. For another 16 children five years' worth of data were collected, and we have data on four or more years for 48 (57 per cent) of the total sample.

In total, 87 children, 43 boys and 44 girls, participated in the study as target pupils for observation and interview over the six-year period. Of these children, 54% of the total sample were drawn from families in which the wage-earner was in a skilled or non-skilled manual occupation, with 46% being non-manual. Ninety-three per cent were white. Six UK-born black children participated in the study over the period, five of whom were from Meadway. Overall teacher ratings classified 7% of the sample as being of 'low' attainment, 16% 'below average', 32% 'average', 29% 'above average' and 15% 'high', and this distribution was broadly confirmed by SAT scores in both Year 2 and Year 6.

Many other children were interviewed in relation to SATs. For instance, in Years 2 and 6 over 100 interviews were conducted. In Year 6, in each school, the six target pupils were interviewed plus six other pupils identified as higher and lower achievers. In addition, in Year 6 almost 270 'SAT Story' comic strips were completed by pupils from the classes being studied. (For further details, see p. 39.)

In the following sections we discuss sampling methods in more detail with regard to each method of data-gathering.

2.4 THE ADVANCE QUESTIONNAIRE TO TEACHERS

During the course of the three phases of the study there were four rounds of questionnaire surveys of the teachers and headteachers in our main sample of 48 schools.

In 1990 an initial 'advance questionnaire' was distributed by post to the main sample of 48 schools. This was designed to gather evidence of headteacher and class teacher perceptions on topics such as accountability, professional responsibility and educational aims, as well as providing background information on age, gender, length of teaching experience etc. In the first instance, questionnaires were completed by headteachers and by teachers of Reception and Year 1 classes, since the children who would later form the cohort to be studied were at that time in reception classes. For cross-sectional comparative purposes, identical questionnaires were again distributed and completed two years later, in the Summer Term of 1992, when heads and teachers of Year 1 and Year 2 classes took part.

Questionnaires were distributed again at the beginning of PACE 2 to teachers of Years 3 and 4 and their headteachers, and finally at the beginning of PACE 3 to teachers of Years 4, 5 and 6 and their headteachers. The inclusion of Year 4 teachers once again was designed to provide a cross-sectional comparison.

The response rate from schools was 100% in the first round when the researchers collected the questionnaires personally, but slightly less good in the second round (85%). In subsequent rounds the response rate declined still further (75% and 71% respectively), when we relied upon schools to return questionnaires by post, prompted by follow-up letters and telephone reminders. Apart from one open-ended question, the questionnaires used pre-coded scaling techniques in order to ensure rapid completion. Questions about gender and age group, for example, were answered by the ticking of boxes, while the importance teachers attributed to various educational objectives was indicated on a five-point scale. Teachers' views of their relative accountability to such categories as colleagues, parents, pupils, the government and society in general were similarly graded on a five-point scale. However, the final question was open-ended: respondents were asked: 'What does professional responsibility mean to you?' These questions and procedures were modelled on the Bristol–Aix study (Broadfoot *et al.*, 1993) and enabled comparisons to be made with a sample of English teachers questioned before the introduction of the National Curriculum, and with teachers in France.

The pre-coded questions were processed for statistical analysis using the SPSS statistical package. Cross-tabulations and factor analyses were carried out together with appropriate tests of statistical significance. Responses to the open-ended question on professional responsibility were analysed for themes and categories, and subsequently coded along four dimensions reflecting different dimensions of responsibility.

The resulting analysis was tabulated, where appropriate, and circulated among team members using data analysis record sheets. These recorded data codes, sources, descriptions, dates and modes of analysis, summaries of findings and introductory comments on significance. This system of sharing and disseminating analysis was used for all strands of the research.

2.5 STRUCTURED INTERVIEWS WITH TEACHERS

Overall, five rounds of interviews took place with the teachers and headteachers in our 48 schools. First, in the same 48 primary schools, a round of interviews was conducted in the Summer Term of 1990. In each school the headteacher, the teacher of the Reception class and a Year 1 infant teacher took part. The interviews, which took approximately one hour, were based on a structured schedule, but many questions were open-ended and exploratory. They aimed to explore staff perceptions of the impact of National Curriculum requirements on their own work and on the life of the school as a whole.

The main areas of discussion were:

- headteachers' perceptions of the changes needed and their strategies for providing for these. In addition to the more obvious obligations enshrined in the curriculum and assessment arrangements, issues here also included perceived changes in the school ethos, in the head's role, in staff relationships, and in relations between staff, parents and other outside bodies;
- teachers' perceptions of the impact of National Curriculum and assessment arrangements on the curriculum and pedagogy of the school as a whole and of their own individual classrooms. Topics here included changes in curriculum content or in time allocation to different subjects, in teaching style, in assessment and record-keeping, in the quantity and quality of extra-curricular activities and in relations with parents.
- perceived changes in pupils' responses to schooling both in their attitudes and in their learning;
- teachers' responses to the preparation they had been given to help them meet the novel requirements being placed upon them. During the initial stages of the project such discussion focused on the in-service training itself, whereas later on it was possible to gather some data on teachers' actual experiences with implementing new procedures, especially the standard assessment tasks (SATs).

Interviewers made detailed notes of the interviews, marking particularly illuminating responses for later transcription from tape-recordings, which were used for subsequent extension or cross-referencing as necessary.

Similar interviews and questionnaires were again completed two years later, in the Summer Term of 1992, when headteachers and teachers of Year 1 and Year 2 classes took part. The core of the interviews remained unchanged to make it possible to trace changes taking place in teachers' perceptions during the study period. However, in view of the multiple changes in government policy during the intervening period, schedules were adjusted to take account of such innovations as 'league tables' of schools' assessment performance and the strengthened role of governors. Similar adjustments were made in the later rounds of interviewing, which took place in the summer of 1993 with teachers of Years 3 and 4 and their headteachers, in 1994 when we revisited the Key Stage 1 teachers in order to provide for direct cross-sectional comparison, and in the autumn of 1995 and in early 1996 when we interviewed Year 4, 5 and 6 teachers (the inclusion of Year 4 again was designed to provide cross-sectional comparison).

A coding schedule and coding sheets were constructed after pilot analysis of a few interviews, with the schedule being developed to allow for diversity as well as for typicality. Most coding categories allowed for 'other' responses, which were included in the subsequent analysis when they occurred in significant numbers.

Statistical analysis of the coded data was carried out using SPSS and evaluated by all members of the research team. Methods of analysis included comparisons of frequency distributions of variables for each successive sweep. Tests of statistical significance (chi-square) were used to assess the significance of the changes. Cross-tabulations and factor analysis were also used for investigative analysis.

2.6 CLASSROOM STUDIES

Detailed case-studies of individual classrooms from the nine case-study schools provided the next element of data collection. These began in the Year 1 classrooms in 1990 and continued every year through Years 2, 3, 4 and 5, ending after we had studied the Year 6 classrooms in 1996.

All the sub-sample classrooms selected for closer study were visited for a full week during each successive year. This phase of the research included gathering of documentary, evidence, qualitative observation, systematic observation and interviews with pupils and teachers. The research focused primarily on curriculum and pedagogy, whilst assessment processes, although observed and recorded, were the prime focus for a separate element of the study. This is discussed in Section 2.7.

When the sample school and class had been identified according to the criteria discussed earlier and cooperation had been agreed, the headteacher and class teacher were sent an overview of the week's data collection plan (see Figure 2.3). The classroom study data collection plan set up a schedule for each day, which provided blocks of time for particular types of data-gathering and ensured efficient sequencing of the process.

Six children from each of the nine classrooms were sampled. (For further details,

In advance	*Ask for:*	Class list	
		Curriculum plan	
		Sociometry	
	Give:	Overview of research intentions for week	

During week	a.m.	p.m.	Other
Monday	Field notes	Teacher interview	In evening: analyse sociometric data, consider friendships in relation to pen sketches
		Field notes	
Tuesday	Teacher audio-recording	Two child interviews (A + B)	
	Systematic observation of two children and teacher (child A + B + teacher)	Systematic observation of two children and teacher (child C + D + teacher)	
Wednesday	Recording and observation as Tuesday (child C + D + teacher)	Interviews with child C + D	Over lunch, etc. on Tuesday, Wednesday and Thursday: hold general discussions with teacher
		Observation as Tuesday	
Thursday	Recording and observation as Tuesday (child E + F + teacher)	Interviews with child E + F	
		Observation as Tuesday (child A + B + teacher)	
Friday	Field notes	Teacher interview	
	Contingency time		

Figure 2.2 The classroom studies timetable

see p. 28.) Prior to the visit by a member of the research team, each teacher was asked to provide copies of key documents: the class list, a curriculum plan and sociometric data collected from all the children in the class. The latter, and each of the other major data-gathering methods used in the classroom studies, are described in more detail below.

Sociometry

Each child was asked to write the names of three friends within her or his own class on a sheet specially designed for this purpose. These sheets were later used to complete a sociometric grid showing children's friendship patterns and group membership.

Field notes

Field notes were relatively open-ended. The aims were to provide a rich and detailed account of the various routine procedures and phases of a school day and, at other times in the week, to record any particularly interesting or theoretically significant events, statements or activities.

Systematic observation

Systematic observation was carried out during the mornings and afternoons of the three central days of the week of classroom study, so that a wide spread of activities could be observed. Break times were not observed.

Each of the six 'target children' in each class was observed during both a morning and an afternoon, and a rotational system was used to focus successive periods of observation on target children and the teacher.

Observations were recorded on coding forms relating to a ten-minute period (see Figure 2.3). Six minutes of systematic observation, using a ten-second interval, were followed by four minutes of contextualizing notes.

When focusing on the teacher, the observer coded 'Interaction' and 'Teacher Activity' simultaneously at ten-second intervals.

When a pupil was being observed, the observer coded 'Child Activity' and 'Interaction' at all ten-second intervals. 'Teacher Activity' was recorded only when the target child was directly interacting with the teacher or with another adult.

The sheet also carried a list of 'Curriculum Context' categories – English, maths, etc. – and another of 'Pedagogic Context', including class teaching and individual and group work. These were recorded, at the end of each six-minute observation period, in terms of the 'main' or 'part' aspects of the curriculum and pedagogic context. Where more than one curriculum context or pedagogic context had been observed, then both 'main' and 'part' were used. More qualitative contextualizing notes were also completed immediately after the timed recording and these were structured by the headings of curriculum, pedagogy, interactions/relationships, assessment, other/general.

PACE CHILD OBSERVATION

Observer	Teacher	Pupil year	LEA
....	....	....	....
Target child	Pupil code	Time	Date
....	....	....	...../...../.....

Child activity

Child interaction

Teacher activity

Child activity

Child interaction

Teacher activity

CHILD ACTIVITY		**CHILD INTERACTION**		**TEACHER ACTIVITY**	
TE	Task engagement (apparent)	O	Alone	I	Instruction (curriculum)
TM	Task management	TC	With teacher in whole class	C	Control (behaviour)
D	Distracted	TO	With teacher in one-to-one	D	Direction (task management)
B	Both distracted and TM	TG	With teacher in group	A	Assessment (explicit)
A	Assessment (explicit)	AO	With other adult one-to-one	E	Encouragement (support,
W	Waiting for teacher	G	With individual girl		facilitating)
X	Waiting (other)	B	With individual boy	N	Negative (discouragement,
O	Out of room/sight	X	With a group of boys		criticism)
R	Reading to teacher	Y	With a group of girls	R	Hearing children read
		M	With a mixed group	O	Other

PEDAGOGIC CONTEXT

	Main	Part
Class teaching		
Individual work		
Co-operative group work		
Group with teacher		
Other (specify)		

CURRICULUM CONTEXT

	Main	Part
RE		
English		
Maths		
Science		
History		
Geography		
Music		
Art		
Physical education		
Technology		
Personal and social		
Non-curriculum		

Figure 2.3 The child observation schedule
Note: The teacher observation sheets contained no 'child activity' categories and listed 'teacher interaction' rather than 'child interaction'

Observer	Teacher	Class	LEA	Date	Target Child	Time

NOTES:

Notes to yourself where necessary

Curriculum
Classification
(strength of subject boundaries)

Pedagogy
Framing
(control over pacing and organisation of tasks)

Interactions/Relationships

Assessment

Other/General

Child interviews

Each target child was interviewed, individually, following the period during which he or she had been a focus for classroom observation. The aim here was to complement observational data with material on pupil perspectives so that explanatory analyses could be attempted. More details of the content of the interviews and the way in which they were carried out are given in the PACE book on pupils (Pollard and Triggs *et al.*, 2000).

Teacher interviews

Structured interviews with the class teachers took place on the first and last afternoons of the observation week. Notes were made on a schedule during the interview, but the whole conversation was also tape-recorded for transcription.

The first day's interview was aimed at obtaining the following:

- pen sketches of target children;
- brief descriptions of attainment, behaviour and social relationships of each child in the class;
- curriculum plans;
- details of the procedure for the allocation of work to children; and
- normal routines of the teacher's morning.

The last day's interview covered:

- teacher assessment;
- the teacher's views of work and changing role;
- the teacher's views of pupil control of learning; and
- the teacher's views of relationships with children.

Unstructured discussions, throughout the week, supplemented these pre-specified interviews. Observers took whatever opportunities arose to seek clarification or ask questions suggested by observation or field notes, and teachers' views were written up in full as soon as possible afterwards.

Tape-recorded interaction

In some classes, teachers agreed to carry small cassette recorders fitted with throat microphones for some teaching sessions. Tapes were not transcribed in full, but extracts were used for analytical purposes in conjunction with field notes to provide a more detailed picture of pedagogy and of teacher–child interaction.

Analysis of classroom studies data

As with all other elements of data-gathering in the PACE study, responsibility for data analysis was shared and data analysis sheets were produced to record and summarize results for circulation among the team. Sociometric diagrams were completed for each class, revealing sociometric status and the membership of friendship groups. Systematic observation data were entered and analysed using SPSS. Questions from both child interviews and teacher interviews were distributed among team members for initial analysis and tabulation.

In each round of data-gathering, the analyses from the various empirical aspects of the classroom studies were compared, and integrated where possible. Sociometric data, attainment data, teacher interview data and systematic observation data were entered on the same Access database. This provided for a degree of methodological triangulation and a more multifaceted analysis. For instance, teachers' views of children's achievement levels could be compared with pupil perceptions on both their own and their classmates' attainments, related to other data from the pupil interviews, and then linked to patterns that had been produced from the systematic observation of teacher or pupil classroom behaviour. Fieldnotes and transcripts of tape-recorded teacher–pupil interaction were also used to augment emerging analysis. The possibilities of such analysis were considerable, but there were also significant technical difficulties in interpreting the scale and variety of data on a year-by-year basis. The data became most meaningful at the end of the study when the patterns and trends of six years of data were apparent.

2.7 ASSESSMENT STUDIES

Key Stage 1

During the early part of the Summer Term, 1991, Year 2 classes in the nine schools of our sub-sample were visited for two days each while Standard Assessment Tasks (SATs) were in progress. This meant that pupils who were one year older than our longitudinal pupil sample, and their teachers, were observed and interviewed while the first round of SATs took place. This was our first use of an anticipatory cross-sectional strategy (see Section 2.1) and was designed to enable us to make comparisons of change as our main pupil cohort experienced the SATs in the following year, and to monitor the piloting of SATs.

Observers watched whichever SATs teachers had chosen to carry out in the data-gathering period, and the unit of analysis was taken to be the SAT as a complete classroom episode. An attempt was thus made to observe each SAT in operation from beginning to end and to record, using field notes, as much detail of the interaction and classroom processes as possible. Following SAT observation, interviews were conducted, on an individual basis, with as many as possible of the pupils who had experienced the observed SAT.

During the 1992 assessment study the process was similar, but this time the cohort of pupils on which we focused *was* that of our continuing study. This was, in other words, our third major period of sustained observation and interviews with these children. This time data were gathered for three days in each classroom and qualitative observations were more focused. Again, as many pupils as possible were interviewed. Observers made sure that these included the six target pupils in each class.

Further details of the data-collection processes follow.

Classroom observation during the SATs

Observers used open-ended observation methods, making field notes and written records of teacher–child and child–child conversation and other interaction, whilst recording at intervals brief notes on such pre-selected categories as preparations for the SAT, arrangements for the rest of the class, extra help, if any, provided for the teacher and post-SAT events. Various SATs were observed in use. However, when the same SAT was observed in different classrooms it was possible to examine the effect of different styles of teacher presentation and of physical circumstances on the perceptions and performance of pupils.

In the 1992 assessment studies there were some adjustments to the data-gathering programme to increase standardization of data. Schools were also asked if observers could be present when one specific SAT, Maths 3, was carried out. It was thus possible to record, for an apparently 'standardized' test situation, the effects of different contexts and interaction.

Interviews with teachers about assessment

Teacher interviews were structured in both rounds and covered such areas as teachers' perceptions of the role assessment should have in infant classrooms, the relative degree of value they found in SATs and in teacher assessment, and the support they were given in carrying out the process. Further topics covered were their perceptions of their pupils' experience, including the question of whether National Curriculum assessment procedures reinforced a sense of academic hierarchy among the children and whether they took steps to address this issue. Interviews conducted one year later during the second SAT period differed only slightly from the first set, so that changes in perceptions could be tracked.

Interviews with pupils about assessment

Children were asked about whether they had enjoyed the tasks observed, how they rated their own performances and those of their classmates, whether they discussed the work at home and how they saw the purpose of the tasks carried out. These data were coded and entered on our database for analysis.

Assessment questionnaires

After the completion of the 1991 and 1992 SAT procedures, all 48 schools in the main PACE sample received questionnaires for all teachers involved in carrying out SATs. The response rate was 92 per cent of schools in 1991 and 81 per cent in 1992. Teachers were asked to note, using five-point scales, their views of the degree of difficulty in organizing the tasks, the degree of value they attached to the results, the support they received within their schools and the reactions of their pupils. Headteachers were asked an open-ended question about the experience of the process in their schools. Both quantitative and qualitative material was therefore available for analysis on this major innovation.

Key Stage 2

Since the arrangements for the Key Stage 2 SATs which our cohort of children took in 1996 were significantly different, a different research strategy was required. The Key Stage 2 SATs involved pencil-and-paper tests, centrally set and taken on a prescribed day. The 1996 SAT study was therefore designed to focus on a number of rather different key issues. These included issues of continuity and progression, investigating the extent to which teachers used assessment data to work towards continuity and individual matching in curriculum provision. In particular, we were concerned to investigate how far teachers perceived SAT data as likely to be useful in secondary school transfer. We were also interested in teachers' reactions to the SATs in terms of their perceived manageability, reliability, and impact on children, as well as their utility in comparison with teacher assessment.

The study was also designed to document teachers' changing assessment practices at Key Stage 2, especially in Year 6; how far SAT requirements were influencing teaching and learning, and classroom priorities; and the impact of SATs and the prevailing assessment climate on pupils and their sense of themselves as learners.

To gather data for the study, researchers spent time in each of the nine PACE classroom study schools during Key Stage 2 SAT week in May 1996. They observed tests across the subject range, making field notes on the preparation and application of the SAT, together with what they observed as the children resumed their normal timetable. The English writing SAT was observed in all nine schools concurrently and hence gave useful data on comparability. Researchers went back into the nine schools the following week to interview, in each case, the Year 6 teacher, the cohort of six target pupils, together with an additional six Year 6 children. The additional children were chosen to create a sample of equal numbers of high attainers, average attainers and low attainers. Each of these children, twelve in each school, then completed a cartoon story-based questionnaire eliciting their feelings at each stage of the SAT.

A postal questionnaire was also sent to all schools in the larger sample of 48 to be completed by teachers who had been involved in the Key Stage 2 testing.

2.8 DOING RESEARCH AS A COLLABORATIVE TEAM

The research design and data collection and analysis procedures outlined above were an excellent resource and provided a data-set of unusual range and richness. However, the scale and magnitude of the research together with the nature of the task we had to undertake raised a number of issues that had to be confronted whilst we were working as a collaborative team over the six years of the project. From the point of view of the research design, there were two related problems.

First, there was the issue of multiple innovation (Wallace, 1991). Whilst the phenomenon we set out to study, change in primary school classrooms following the introduction of the National Curriculum and assessment, itself had several dimensions, these were set in an even wider context of many other changes. These included local management of schools, the roles of local education authorities, school inspection requirements and the introduction of OFSTED, school account-ability structures, teacher appraisal systems and the introduction of the market philosophy to education through open enrolment, opting out and publication of league tables of assessment performance. The project team could not address the ramifications of all these issues, nor yet could we ignore them. Our solution to this dilemma was to attempt to liaise with other research teams and to maintain awareness of the wider social, political and historic context in which our study was set, whilst maintaining our prime focus at the classroom level. The study can thus contribute to a holistic understanding of the many facets of change in the 1990s, but its contribution, whilst necessary and perhaps unique, is not sufficient to embrace the full complexity of the system-wide innovation that has occurred.

The second major challenge to our research design concerned when, how and from whom to gather data which would be as nationally representative as possible and also provide valid indications of trends in perspectives, classroom practices and provision. Of course, research resources are always limited and judgements are always required to identify the most worthwhile data-gathering strategies and scheduling. However, in this case, these routine decisions were complicated further by the continuing process of change. The study had to aim for as much comparability as possible and yet at the same time respond to evolving policy change. We also needed to take into account the increasing age and sophistication of the children who were at the heart of the study, so that comparability of research instruments sometimes needed to take second place to the need to talk to children in an appropriate way. Therefore, with the child interviews we aimed for continuity of topics, rather than continuity in the way questions were framed.

Another set of issues were related to the nature of the project itself and the consequences for the researchers within it working as a collaborative team. Initially the study was located within two institutions, the University of Bristol and the University of the West of England, with two of the directors located at the University of the West of England and one at the University of Bristol. One full-time contract researcher was based in each institution. Later the project team moved entirely to the University of Bristol when one of the West of England directors left and the other became a professor at Bristol. The logistical challenge of working in two sites and then later moving all the data and resources plus half the project team to Bristol was considerable. In addition there were other issues to be resolved, deriving from the differences in culture of the two institutions together with dual financial arrangements, computer systems and indeed of different research paradigms held by some members of the research team. The latter provided both a creative and a constraining tension.

Other issues derived from the nature of the funding of social science research in the UK. This had implications for the way in which the project was designed, for the career structure of both the contract researchers and the directors, and for maintaining continuity in the team. The relatively limited funds available for social science research meant that the research had to be designed in three consecutive phases and as three separate projects which would both provide a basis for a subsequent stage and be self-contained and complete in themselves if no further funding were to become available. This created the necessity to leap-frog strategically from one project to another without knowing until near the end of one phase whether further research would be funded. As in all such funded projects, the conditions of the professional researchers' employment were uncertain so that there were times when members of the team were compelled to follow up other career opportunities in order to maintain continuity of career. The directors of the research were also undertaking a wider range of responsibilities, leaving a greater load of fieldwork and other responsibilities for the contract researchers. Some of these tensions will be familiar to the participants in any funded research project but others may have been relatively unusual and particular to a longer-term longitudinal project.

All these conditions, together with the natural progression of team members' careers and life cycles over a six-year period, meant that there were considerable changes in the research team during the life of the project. When the research drew to a close only two of the directors and one senior researcher remained from the original team. There had been three other part-time research associates plus a consultant working on the research in the interim. The complexity of the project sometimes posed problems for new team members joining later. They needed to get a grasp fairly quickly of what had gone before and to have time to acquire feelings of ownership in the research. However, there were a number of ways in which we attempted to resolve these issues which may be of interest to other research teams. First, the team meetings and the way in which responsibilities were allocated attempted to build on individuals' strengths and expertise, and to allocate themes and tasks in accordance with these. For example, different team members took prime responsibility for one or other of the major themes of the project: pupil and classroom experience, teachers' professional perspectives, whole-school change, and assessment. These were followed through, where possible, throughout the life of the project and also carried through into writing responsibilities.

There were particular methodological issues involved in teamwork of this nature. Because of the relatively large number of researchers involved, the research needed to have a very structured focus, which was discussed and agreed in team meetings. Research instruments had to be carefully designed to ensure comparability from one researcher's classroom to another, and after intensive rounds of data-collection there were brainstorming, mind-mapping sessions in which the whole team participated and in which emerging issues from the fieldwork fed into a number of themes and where the beginnings of a conceptual framework emerged. Earlier parts of this chapter have described the data analysis sheets which were used and circulated amongst the team so that everyone had a grasp of new issues emerging.

Different members of the team took responsibility for the fieldwork in particular classroom study schools and maintained their contact with the school, as far as possible, throughout the life of the project. This ongoing relationship played a considerable part in the trust and goodwill which were built up between the researchers and the schools, so that, as mentioned earlier, all the study schools remained with the project throughout, in spite of the many other pressures they were experiencing.

2.9 CONCLUSION

The procedures outlined above provided large quantities of varied data allowing for analysis on several levels. Some of the problems they posed for the research team working over the eight years of the project have been discussed.

Throughout the research there was a potential risk that the scale of empirical work would steer the project towards description of change, rather than providing the foundation for analysis and theorization. As we were engaged in one of very few independently funded social science projects on changes in primary schools following the Education Reform Act, we felt that we had a particular responsibility to stand back from simple evaluation of the innovation and to attempt to discern and articulate more fundamental developments and consequences.

In this we were able to build on some of our previous work. For instance, one of our major theoretical concerns was the influence of external constraints on teachers' professional perspectives, and here it was possible to develop work from the ESRC project Teachers' Conceptions of Their Professional Responsibilities in England and France (Bristaix) (Broadfoot *et al.*, 1993) and later from other related work. Another theoretical issue centred on teacher–pupil interaction and strategies in classrooms, on which we were able to develop the work of Pollard (1985) and others in tracing the changes in classroom practices adopted by teachers and children as they responded to new curricular and assessment arrangements. For complementary insights on learning and 'pupil career' through their primary schooling we drew on the longitudinal ethnography of the Identity and Learning Programme (ILP) of Pollard and Filer (1996, 1999, 2000).

At the end of the eight years of the PACE project we have therefore tried to describe primary schools that have changed substantially but have also tried to map a model which may have wider implications for understanding the process of educational change.

Part 2

Teachers' Work, Values and Culture

Chapter 3

Teachers' Work, Professional Identity and Change

3.1 INTRODUCTION

The introduction of a national curriculum and national assessment and the multiple changes which followed this were inevitably likely to have a profound impact on the way in which primary teachers' work and role were defined by government policy directives. The more recent changes introduced by New Labour – introducing a literacy and numeracy hour and proposing, in the Green Paper (DfEE, 1999), a change in career structure linked to performance for teachers – were likely to continue these pressures.

Ball (1990) has shown how a general public sense of unease about the state of teaching was created by a continuous battery of 'discourses of derision' which were used to justify subsequent government attempts to reconstruct teachers' work and notions of the 'good teacher'. The power of such discourses is that they begin to shape definitions of reality in a way that is not politically neutral but which makes it possible to redefine the nature of teaching and teachers' work (Gewirtz, 1997). These discourses were successful in justifying the policy changes which took place in terms of 'common-sense' understandings using terms such as 'curriculum delivery', 'target-setting', 'performance-setting' and 'accountability' (Helsby, 1999).

What was less certain was the longer-term influence of these discourses and policy changes on how the teachers themselves defined their professional role and identity as teachers. One of the assumptions underlying centrally directed policy change is certainly that teachers, where necessary, will be both willing and able to adapt their practice in appropriate directions. Yet the research evidence suggests that this is not so. Indeed, far from their being mere puppets pulled by the strings of policy-makers, it can be argued that teachers mediate the external pressures upon them through the filter of their own values and practice. The result is a blend of both personal ideologies and external constraints (Acker, 1999; Fullan, 1982; Osborn *et al.*, 1997b). The implementation of government policy in the classroom will thus reflect both the general beliefs that inform teachers' practice and the perspectives likely to be held by any particular group of teachers at a particular time and place.

Therefore the policy changes outlined above provide an ideal focus for exploring the mediating influence of teachers' professional perspectives on the impact of educational policy initiatives and, in effect, for examining the complex interplay of structure, agency and culture in influencing the outcomes of educational reforms (Acker, 1999; Helsby, 1999).

This is the subject of this and the next two chapters. In this chapter we begin to delineate from the teachers' own point of view some of the issues surrounding their sense of their work and their professional selves. In the chapter which follows we look in more depth at the strategies adopted by the PACE teachers in response to change, and consider the argument that some teachers in effect became policy-makers in practice in the classroom. Finally, Chapter 5 considers the impact of the changes on how teachers worked collaboratively as distinct from autonomously and the extent to which this altered what it meant to be a primary teacher.

In this chapter we begin by considering changes in the power context of teachers' work. We explore whether there has been a shift in teachers' perception of their work from relative autonomy to constraint, from a commitment to teaching which is largely expressive to one which is relatively instrumental, and from concerns which are strongly affective to those which are more technical. Has there been a move from a perception of teaching as a covenant which emphasizes moral responsibility to one of teaching as a contract which emphasizes external accountability? Do teachers feel that their work has been deskilled, or is there a sense of reskilling, even of re-professionalization?

In order to provide a baseline on teachers' professional perspectives prior to the 1988 Education Reform Act (ERA), we draw upon previous comparative research carried out by two of the authors: the 'Bristaix' project (Broadfoot *et al.*, 1993). This research studied teachers' conceptions of professional responsibility through the comparative focus of the two very different education systems of England and France before both these systems started to undergo major changes. It showed teachers' conceptions of their responsibility in the two countries to be characterized by two very different models of professionalism.

To summarize briefly, French teachers had a narrower, more 'restricted' (Hoyle, 1974) and more classroom-focused conception of their role, which centred on what they saw as their responsibility for children's academic progress. English teachers, in contrast, saw themselves as having a more wide-ranging, diffuse and 'extended'

(Hoyle, 1974) set of responsibilities relating to work outside as well as inside the classroom, including extra-curricular and sometimes even community activities, all aspects of school relationships, accountability to parents, colleagues and the head. At each extreme, a French teacher's perception of her role centred on 'meeting one's contractual responsibility', whilst a typical English teacher characterized her role as 'striving after perfection'. For some English teachers this meant a certain amount of conflict and confusion about their role and a sense that they were setting themselves, and being set, goals they could not hope to fulfil.

The Bristaix research suggests that before the ERA, although English teachers were becoming increasingly constrained on all sides, they nevertheless believed in their autonomy (in contrast with French teachers, who believed they had very little autonomy), and saw it as central to their 'extended' role that they be able to define and decide for themselves both what they would teach and how they would change it. Here we explore how far these beliefs have been influenced by the recent policy changes.

In the sections that follow, we focus particularly on how teachers in the PACE study saw the complex network of obligations which made up their accountability to others – to pupils, parents, colleagues, governors and indeed to themselves – and how this web of obligations was shifting over the years of the project. We draw on the voices of the Year 5 and 6 teachers to try to understand the meaning for them of being a primary teacher and we look at the statistical data to set these selected voices in a wider context. Did teachers still regard the emotional and affective components of teaching as important in a climate where teaching skill was increasingly being externally assessed in terms of technical skills and measurable outcomes, with an emphasis on 'performativity' rather than on creativity or spontaneity?

3.2 ACCOUNTABILITY: A NETWORK OF COMPETING OBLIGATIONS

Many of the imposed changes described above and in Chapter 1 might be expected to have transformed teachers' work and role from that of semi-autonomous professional to managed employee or even technician. Public discourses about accountability, together with discourses about 'failing teachers' whose professional judgement cannot be trusted, and who are in need of external regulation, might be assumed to have altered teachers' sense of accountability (Helsby, 1999; Poulson, 1996). Previous research suggests that teachers have long made a distinction between formal, contractual accountability to governors, heads and administrators, and increasingly parents, and moral accountability to those with whom they have a different kind of relationship, for example their pupils and colleagues (Elliott *et al.*, 1981). Whereas they have accepted both, it is their sense of moral accountability which has most influenced their beliefs and actions in the past. As Nias (1999b) argues, moral accountability implies that individuals need to be as free as possible from externally imposed constraints in order to be able to make decisions about how best to meet their pupils' interests.

Consequently, if teachers were internalizing the policy changes of the past few years and complying uncritically with them, one might expect to observe a shift in teachers' sense of obligation to various groups in the educational process. A change might be expected from a personal or moral focus to an external focus in response to increasing demands for external accountability. In a short questionnaire given to teachers in each data-gathering round between 1990 and 1995, we were able to assess the extent of teachers' feelings of accountability to various groups by means of a question asking 'As a teacher, to whom do you feel accountable and to what extent?' Replies were measured on a five-point scale ranging from 'not at all accountable' to 'very accountable'. Results are summarized in Table 3.1, which compares the PACE findings with those from English primary teachers in the earlier 'Bristaix' study, which focused on teachers of children aged 7 to 11 in 1985.

Table 3.1 Changes in teachers feeling 'very accountable' (percentages)

Source of accountability		KS1		KS1	
	1985/6	1990/1 R/Y1	1992/3 Y1/2	1993/4 Y3/4	1995/6 Y4/5/6
	Bristaix	PACE	PACE	PACE	PACE
Yourself	89.4	95.1	95.0	94.0	88.2
Pupils	81.8	86.3	78.5	81.0	79.8
Headteacher	32.9	56.4	56.3	28.0	49.6
Colleagues	24.3	47.5	42.8	42.0	36.1
Parents	43.1	65.4	63.0	63.0	51.3
Society	31.7	6.3	13.5	15.0	16.8
Governors	0.0	26.1	20.4	32.0	18.5
Inspectors/advisers	3.0	–	–	14.0	16.8
Employers	–	9.2	5.4	13.0	16.0
Government	–	3.4	1.1	4.0	3.4
	$n = 360$	$n = 88$	$n = 93$	$n = 92$	$n = 128$

Source: PACE 1, 2, 3 teacher questionnaires and Bristaix questionnaires
Sample: 94 Key Stage 1 teachers, 360 English Bristaix teachers
Date: 1985, 1990, 1992, 1993, 1995
Note: Totals do not equal 100 per cent since each item was rated on a five-point scale

These findings suggest that although external obligations still appeared to be less significant for primary teachers in England than internal ones, there had been a shift in accountability since the successive reforms which began with the 1988 ERA. Teachers' sense of 'personal and moral' accountability as indicated by responsibility to pupils and to themselves as professionals remained strong but there was a marked increase in accountability towards colleagues and parents. Accountability towards headteachers is more complex, with initially a striking rise at Key Stage 1 shortly after the ERA, but later a decrease at Key Stage 2, perhaps as accountability to governors became much more important. Overall comparisons over time seem to suggest that there has been a significant increase in teachers' feelings of external, contractual accountability yet no diminishing of the personal and moral account-ability they feel particularly towards their pupils and their own consciences. Therefore, teachers are now having to take into account a wider range of what might be seen as conflicting obligations.

This had begun with the Key Stage 1 teachers. When interviewed earlier in the study, a Key Stage 1 teacher had said:

> There is a continual feeling of harassment caused by contradictory signals from the 'powers that be'. It pre-dates the National Curriculum but it's got worse since ... At the same time, we have got parents to think about – they may be different again – and, most important of all, there are the needs of the children.

It is also illustrated by what some of the Year 5 and 6 teachers said to us about their sense of responsibility:

> It is a very important part of my life. My whole approach to my work and my attitude towards my class and colleagues is hinged on how I view my professional responsibility within the school. In my role as head of year, I need to support my colleagues and make decisions when necessary based on professional judgements. My whole approach in my teaching career has been founded on the belief that I have a total professional commitment to the school and society in general. (Year 5 teacher)

> [Professional responsibility means] to create a happy, caring environment for your pupils. To have clear aims and objectives. To provide them with the very best teaching you can, by planning well and good delivery of the National Curriculum. To ensure equal opportunities for all pupils. To maintain good order in class. To give pupils confidence and improve their self-esteem. To teach them the basic skills and how to use the skills. To work closely with other colleagues and to communicate the pupils' progress to parents. (Year 6 teacher)

For these teachers their responsibility to their pupils clearly came first, but they were also expressing a strong sense of accountability for delivering the National Curriculum and towards colleagues, parents, school and society in general, providing a sharp contrast with the conception of responsibility characteristic of French teachers and described earlier in the chapter.

Interestingly, in spite of the PACE teachers' moral commitment to a caring environment for their pupils, as they themselves felt more externally controlled they were also compelled to exert more control over pupil experience in the classroom, allowing pupils less choice of activity in the classroom and increasing the pressure towards measurable achievement (Chapter 7) (Pollard *et al.*, 2000).

Teachers' feeling of loss of autonomy has thus been paralleled by a tightening of control over pupil activity in the classroom and a loss of autonomy for pupils. As one Year 6 teacher said:

> Well, I don't know the children any more. Well, I know them but there's no time to chat really. You feel that you are under this obligation to get work done and as a consequence ... no, I don't know the children ... This notion that we've got a certain amount to get through is just pressurizing – for the teacher and for the children. It's difficult to include the education of the whole child because of it.

For these teachers there was clearly a sense of sometimes conflicting and competing obligations and loyalties. They were torn between a commitment to a personal and moral professional responsibility and the requirement to respond to strong external constraints. Certainly, then, there has been a shift from relative autonomy and a reliance on 'professionalism' to greater external accountability and control. The question is how far this has affected teachers' sense of professional identity.

3.3 CHANGES IN TEACHER ROLE AND IDENTITY

Over the course of the PACE project the impact of market forces in education and the growth of managerialism appeared to be pushing in the direction of a shift in teachers' professional identities in order to make them more responsive to client demand and external judgement. How far did this actually cause teachers to redefine what they saw as their central professional concerns? As Nias (1989) has shown, English primary teachers invest their 'selves' in their work, often merging their professional and personal identity so that the classroom may become a main source of self-esteem and fulfilment, but also for vulnerability. This is closely linked to the need to exercise professional skill, to act consistently with their beliefs and values and to how they define the nature of their work, its goals and priorities. It follows that external attempts to change the nature of their work without taking into account this self-investment and the importance of beliefs and values may have devastating effects for teachers' sense of fulfilment and professional identity.

In successive rounds of interviews with classroom teachers, we asked teachers to talk in an open-ended way about their role and how it might have changed as a result of the multiple innovations beginning with the 1988 Education Reform Act. As the reforms impacted on successive year groups through the primary school, there was a marked increase in the proportions of teachers who had experienced 'considerable' change in their role. For virtually all teachers there was a sense that there had been a significant intensification of their work without a corresponding sense of being valued in what they were being required to do. As one teacher of a mixed Year 5 and 6 class argued:

> There's so much pressure now from paperwork and record-keeping and from attending meetings after school. I have no time to myself. I live, eat, drink and sleep school. We are expected to give an awful lot more of ourselves than other professions yet we are not given any credit.

For many, these changes were profound and were experienced in a predominantly negative way, even though most teachers felt positive about the overall structure provided by the National Curriculum. Overwhelmingly, teachers were experiencing an increasing sense of constraint and loss of freedom to do what they felt was best. They mentioned a loss of spontaneity and enjoyment in teaching, an increased feeling of stress, and a sense of priorities being imposed on them from outside. It was noticeable that this stress and sense of imposed priorities were particularly marked in the year groups in which external assessment took place (Years 2 and 6). An increase in time spent planning and on paperwork was particularly marked at Key Stage 1, although it was still mentioned by a significant proportion of teachers at Key Stage 2.

In 1992 a Key Stage 1 teacher had said to us:

It's just a different pace. There's a pressure and a feeling that you're never doing enough ... You look at the documents and you think, 'How can I possibly fulfil all these demands? How can I fit all this in?' It's just overwhelming sometimes. You feel you're just going through a wheel. You're desperately covering stuff because you must give an assessment for it, and you think, 'This is just not what it's about. Learning is not about this and this is not what it should be like.'

In 1995–6 when we interviewed the Year 6 teachers this feeling of intensification was expressed just as strongly by some. One Year 6 teacher said:

I think that more and more paperwork has meant that my role has changed. When I was at college and we discussed sort of what we would be expected to do and whatever, it seems that there is so much extra now because on top of teaching and assessing and reporting, you've got, I mean at the moment in school we've got all the policies that we are sorting out for OFSTED, so a lot of my time is taken up – well, a lot of my time has been taken up doing those. And just keeping abreast of things, like with Dearing.

She went on to say that she had just written the school policy on special needs and then, as a result of the Dearing Review of the National Curriculum, it had to be rewritten, which created 'extra work on top of what you have got to do in a normal school day'.

At the end of the day I really feel that the most important role I have is to give the children the best that they can get, and sometimes I feel that I am not actually doing that because of things like, perhaps being up late doing other school work and not being prepared and having to fit extra things in. For example next week, with the sports, having to fit that into – on top of – whatever else you have got to do, I sometimes feel that perhaps we don't spend enough time on things because there is so much to get through.

For many teachers, then, there had been an intensification of their work and a corresponding loss of satisfaction in their role.

These strongly negative feelings were counterbalanced to a limited extent by the positive feelings of those who saw the changes as having the effect of focusing and confirming their role. However, this sense of an 'emergent professionalism' was more marked at Key Stage 1, where the reforms had impacted first, than at Key Stage 2. It was particularly noticeable in 1994 when we re-interviewed Key Stage 2 teachers.

One of these teachers felt that she had emerged from the difficulties of the past four years with a new sense of clarity and focus about her role and her practice. She was feeling positive about the way in which she was using the National Curriculum and assessment practices. She recognized that her approach to teaching had changed considerably and that it had become 'slightly more formal than it was before'. Although she couldn't be sure whether the results for the children were any better, she felt:

I'm more focused when I plan an activity and because of the National Curriculum – this is a positive thing – I definitely do specify now what I'm intending the children to learn, whereas I think before, I planned an activity and was open to see what the children learned. Now of course you still do have exciting situations where children do learn all sorts of things that you didn't expect them to and they show all sorts of things that you didn't expect them to and they show all sorts of knowledge, skills etc. that you didn't know they had, which is good, and honestly I'm still looking for this. But I think that I'm far more able now to explain to somebody else in more concrete terms what I'm doing, which I think is a good thing.

Even at Key Stage 2, however, where the reforms impacted later, there was evidence of this emergent confidence about the place of professional judgement even within the new regime, albeit with more reservations. One teacher of a mixed Year 5 and 6 class argued:

> If I am honest, I haven't let the changes affect my work. They have made me focus on different things, but I still feel I am prepared to follow the needs of the children at certain times, and to take risks. But part of me believes in the National Curriculum anyway. We have got to plan and think as a group with other teachers about the needs of the children.

Throughout the primary school, but most markedly in the upper years, teachers mentioned an increase in close collaboration with colleagues as part of the change in their role. Initially most experienced this as a largely positive development, but there was some sense of dissatisfaction in the upper years with the amount of time spent on meetings and on formal, imposed 'contrived' collegiality, which was perceived as closely connected with an unwelcome increase in managerialism. See also Menter *et al.* (1995) and Webb and Vulliamy (1996b). Chapter 5 discusses this in more depth.

3.4 WHAT DOES IT MEAN TO BE A PRIMARY TEACHER? WHAT IS IMPORTANT?

From the 1930s onwards, if not before, many researchers and writers have argued that the affective and emotional dimensions of teaching are central to being a good primary teacher. Waller (1932), for example, argued that human relationships were vital in schools, arguing, 'Let no one be deceived, the important things that happen in schools result from the interaction of personalities', a theme which was echoed in D. H. Lawrence's portrayal of Ursula's first experiences of teaching in *The Rainbow*.

The teachers studied by Lortie (1975) and Jackson (1968) accepted the legitimacy of the prescribed curriculum but saw their role as more than just implementing this. They were 'moral agents' as well, emphasizing the social and personal development of children and the importance of making emotional connections between the children and their learning. For these teachers, and those studied more recently by Nias (1989) the main rewards and key professional 'satisfiers' in teaching came from the affective dimension of classroom events, from students responding well and from being influenced by their teaching. It is clear that these values have been deeply held by teachers. Yet at a time when school systems are being restructured to meet ever-increasing demands for accountability, for greater rationality and for technical competencies in teaching, these sources of professional satisfaction may be under threat as never before (Hoyle and John, 1995).

The reforms in England have paralleled moves towards greater control of teachers and greater accountability in many other Westernized countries. In England, with the introduction of the National Curriculum and national assessment and of a system of teacher appraisal and school inspection by OFSTED, as well as by the infiltration of the values of the marketplace into education, it became apparent that teachers were being required to have an increasing range of more technicist, cognitive and managerial skills. It was unclear how far these requirements would allow teachers to continue to hold on to their affective concerns. To the extent that they did, they were likely to suffer an even greater intensification of their work and a resulting stress as they struggled to resolve competing concerns. On the other hand, without them they were likely to suffer an increasing sense of loss and were to feel that they were no longer able to teach as they might wish.

Over the six years of the PACE study, teachers were asked in successive rounds of interviews what they saw as the qualities of an outstanding primary teacher (Table 3.2). It was striking that, far from relinquishing the notion of the importance of the personal and social dimension of teaching and the qualities perhaps most closely connected with the 'emotions' of teaching (Nias, 1999a), teachers saw these as becoming more important, even though, by 1995, we were interviewing teachers at the top end of primary school rather than infant teachers, who we might have suspected would particularly value the personal and affective side of teaching. Thus, by 1995, 85% of Year 4, 5, and 6 teachers thought personality and personal qualities to be vital in a primary teacher and 78% highly valued affective-related skills compared with 66% and 68% respectively of infant teachers in 1990.

Table 3.2 Qualities of an outstanding teacher (percentages)

	KS1		KS2	
	1990/1 R/Y1	1992/3 Y1/2	1993/4 Y3/4	1995/6 Y4/5/6
Personality and personal qualities	65.9	73.1	83.7	84.4
Affective-related skills	68.2	87.1	75.0	78.1
Cognitive-related skills	26.1	54.8	30.4	48.4
Management-related skills	44.3	51.6	35.9	59.5
Professionalism	15.9	3.2	30.4	24.2
	$n = 88$	$n = 93$	$n = 92$	$n = 128$

Source: PACE 1, 2, 3 teacher interviews
Sample: 48 schools in eight local education authorities
Date: Summer 1990, Summer 1992, Autumn 1993, Autumn 1995
Note: Totals do not equal 100 per cent since questions were open-ended, and multiple coding was used

Yet a whole range of more technicist skills were also seen to be more important at that time than in the years immediately following the ERA. In 1995 nearly 50% of Year 4, 5 and 6 teachers mentioned cognitive-related skills as important for an outstanding teacher and 60% mentioned management-related skills, compared with 26% and 44% of infant teachers in 1990. These findings reinforce the earlier point about an increasing network of obligations taken on by English primary teachers. They suggest that while the emotional and affective side of teaching is seen as even more important than in the past, a good primary teacher now is perceived as needing an increasing range of more technicist, cognitive and managerial skills as well.

Overall, the range of qualities needed by a 'good' primary teacher have increased and become more demanding.

When teachers were asked what they saw as their own teaching strengths, throughout the primary school and throughout the years of the study most teachers mentioned affective skills (Table 3.3).

Table 3.3 Teachers' perceptions of their teaching strengths (percentages)

	KS1		KS2	
	1990/1 R/Y1	**1992/3 Y1/2**	**1993/4 Y3/4**	**1995/6 Y4/5/6**
Classroom management skills	34.1	36.6	–	33.6
Cognitive-related skills	23.9	58.1	–	21.9
Affective-related skills	75.0	68.9	–	74.2
Curriculum-related skills	46.8	41.9	–	21.1
Assessment-related skills	1.1	2.2	–	6.3
Life experience	3.4	5.4	–	5.5
Hard work and enthusiasm	12.5	18.3	–	33.6
Enjoyment of teaching children	36.3	28.0	–	43.8
Open to new things/continue learning	–	–	–	17.2
Confidence to take risks/know what is important	–	–	–	7.8
Other	–	–	–	11.7
	$n = 88$	$n = 93$	$n = 92$	$n = 128$

Source: PACE 1, 2, 3 teacher interviews
Sample: 48 schools in eight local education authorities
Date: Summer 1990, Summer 1992, Autumn 1995

The enjoyment of teaching children was seen as particularly important in 1995. Forty per cent mentioned this, together with enthusiasm and hard work (34 per cent), all qualities bound up with the personal and perhaps more emotional side of teaching. Although half or more of Year 4, 5 and 6 teachers had mentioned the need for a good primary teacher to have cognitive and management-related skills, much smaller proportions of teachers actually saw themselves as having strengths in these areas, and only 21 per cent saw themselves as having particular strengths in curriculum-related areas, a considerable decline as compared with the earlier years of the study. It is likely that this is related to the much greater demands of curriculum coverage at a relatively high level which are now placed upon teachers at the upper end of the primary school compared with in the past.

Clearly, then, concerns bound up with the emotional and affective dimensions of teaching were as strongly important for Year 5 and 6 teachers at the end of the PACE study as they had been for Key Stage 1 teachers earlier on. The enjoyment of teaching children still appeared to be a major satisfier for most teachers (Nias, 1989), yet the evidence suggested that such enjoyment was harder for teachers to obtain as they struggled to get through the curriculum, even after its revision as a result of the Dearing review (Dearing, 1993). Most teachers felt that their relationships with children had been affected as a result of lack of time and the pressure for curriculum coverage, and from the assessment requirements.

When we first interviewed Key Stage 1 teachers, this feeling emerged strongly. One teacher in an inner-city school, interviewed in 1990, argued:

> There are social and economic difficulties here. You can't start where you would hope to. You have to start building up closeness to the child first. If you don't do that you might as well not bother. I'd hate to get to the point where I think, 'I must do that today and I'm sorry if Emma comes in crying, but she's just got to sit and do it, because the law says I must be doing it.'

Amongst Year 5 and 6 teachers interviewed in 1995 and 1996 this feeling was still in evidence. One Year 5 teacher, working in a school on a council estate, described her feelings that her teaching had been adversely affected by the demands of an overloaded curriculum and the loss of time for affective concerns:

> I think it's awful. I think it's one of the most destructive things I've ever had the misfortune to deal with. I actually feel that my teaching's a lot worse now than it's ever been because it takes out the spontaneity that you can have. I have a timetable that I now have to work to, I have so many hours a week that I have to fulfil certain things. There is no flexibility and it doesn't allow for either the child who's distressed or they've got a problem. And I now feel that I pressurize my children into finishing their work ... A lot of my children, especially in the first term, get very, very worried about it.

These feelings were particularly marked amongst teachers working in disadvantaged areas, a theme to which we return later in this chapter.

This PACE evidence suggests that teachers cared as strongly as ever about the affective and expressive dimension of their teaching. In fact, this was seen as more important than ever and teachers were struggling to maintain it in spite of the increasing intensification of their work. For some teachers this was harder than for others. Yet theirs would perhaps be an easier job if they were to focus less on this aspect of their pupils' development and limit their concerns to children's cognitive development. Comparative research has shown that teachers in some other countries do not take such a comprehensive view of their responsibilities (Poppleton, 1999). French primary teachers, for example, see their responsibility towards their pupils as limited, clearly delineated and largely cognitive. They focus their activity on academic goals and are expected by their pupils to adopt this largely instrumental role (Broadfoot *et al.*, 1993; Osborn *et al.*, 1997a, b). Similarly, Nias (1997, p. 11) quotes a German primary teacher visiting an English school as remarking, 'The trouble with English teachers is that they care too much and perhaps about the wrong things. I care if my pupils do not learn as they should. That's enough!'

3.5 DESKILLING OR RESKILLING?

The Bristaix research (Broadfoot *et al.*, 1993) suggested that before the 1988 Education Reform Act, although teachers in England were becoming increasingly constrained on all sides, they nevertheless saw it as central to their role that they would be able to define and decide for themselves both what they would teach and how they would teach it, in other words that they would be able to 'behave professionally' (Helsby, 1999). Following these reforms and the restructuring of the education system in a number of countries, it is arguable that concepts of professionalism and even of behaving professionally may not still be valid in relation to a discussion of teachers and their work.

It has been argued that teachers' work has not only intensified but also become deskilled. As a result of public discourses centring on a new work order, new public management, marketization and managerialism, the bureaucratized professionalism which developed so strongly in education and in other parts of the welfare state is being systematically dismantled (Helsby, 1999). These dominant discourses create particular images of schooling and of the role of teachers within it. Thus teachers' work is seen as increasingly dependent on an externally imposed apparatus of behavioural objectives, assessment and accountability, leading to a proliferation of paperwork and administrative tasks, chronic work overload and the loss of opportunities for more creative work and for developing caring relationships with pupils (Apple, 1986; Densmore, 1987; Lawn and Ozga, 1981).

All these developments have tended to emphasize an 'employee' rather than a 'professional' perspective for teachers' work (Ball, 1990). Yet embedded in all this are contradictory and competing discourses about teachers' work. Views of the 'new teacher' range 'from the innovative and competitive "petit-professional" to the harassed reactive teaching technician' (Ball, 1990, p. 214). Teachers can be seen as deskilled but they can also be seen to have developed new skills and to have extended their professional behaviour into new areas. It is possible to focus too much on the 'intended consequences' of policy change and to ignore the possibilities of 'unintended consequences', in particular the gap between central policy and the way it is interpreted and implemented in schools and by individual teachers. Above all, it is easy to underplay the role played by teachers' beliefs in interpreting, accommodating or resisting state policy. It is likely that structure and agency interact to produce new interpretations of teachers' work. Indeed, a number of researchers have shown how some teachers have developed creative responses to working within imposed frameworks (Osborn *et al.*, 1997b; Troman, 1995; Woods and Wenham, 1995). In the chapter that follows, we unpack these issues and some of these responses in more detail. Here we examine one particular facet of the deskilling argument, the extent to which teachers felt their skills to have been eroded by the National Curriculum and national assessment.

Table 3.4 shows that a considerable proportion of teachers throughout the study felt that the reforms had eroded their particular strengths as a teacher. In 1990, when we first interviewed Key Stage 1 reception and Year 1 teachers, only 22 per cent of teachers felt this and an equal proportion felt that their strengths had been complemented, whilst the majority had experienced no influence either way. By 1992, when we interviewed Year 1 and Year 2 teachers after the first experience of national assessment at Key Stage 1, almost half the teachers could be said to have been feeling deskilled in the sense that they felt their strengths to have been eroded by the changes, while only 18 per cent felt reaffirmed. In 1994, however, when these Key Stage 1 teachers were interviewed again after a two-year gap, perceptions of deskilling had become less. The proportion who felt that their skills had been complemented and re-affirmed had increased to 30 per cent compared with 21 per cent who felt deskilled in the sense that they had experienced erosion of their skills. Forty-two per cent still saw 'no change'. These teachers had gained in professional confidence in other ways as they had time to develop a more reasoned and measured response to the changes, as Chapter 5 shows.

Table 3.4 Teachers' perceptions of the influence of the National Curriculum (NC) on their strengths (percentages)

Perceived influences on strengths	KS1		KS2	
	1990/1 R/Y1	**1992/3 Y1/2**	**1993/4 Y3/4**	**1995/6 Y4/5/6**
Complemented by NC	21.6	18.3	–	26.6
Eroded by NC	21.6	49.5	–	35.9
No influence from NC	42.0	25.8	–	22.7
Possibly an influence in future/mixed improved and eroded	11.4	5.4	–	8.6
Other	3.4	1.0	–	0.0
	$n = 88$	$n = 93$	$n = 92$	$n = 128$

Source: PACE 1, 2, 3 teacher interviews
Sample: 48 schools in eight local education authorities
Date: Summer 1990, Summer 1992, Autumn 1993, Autumn 1995

This new-found professional confidence had not fully extended to the Year 3, 4 and 5 teachers at the upper end of Key Stage 2 who had experienced the strongest impact of the reforms later, with the introduction of Key Stage 2 national assessment in 1995. Thirty-six per cent of these Key Stage 2 teachers felt their skills to have been eroded. However, a larger group (36 per cent) felt that they had been reaffirmed, while fewer teachers (23 per cent) now saw no influence from the reforms. This suggested that the reforms had impacted very differently on different groups of teachers, a notion which we explore further later in this chapter and in Chapter 5. For the teachers at the upper end of Key Stage 2 in particular, the issue of subject confidence was likely to be particularly salient in making some of them feel deskilled. They were now required to teach a wider range of subjects at a depth not previously required. Sixty-five per cent of teachers in Years 4, 5 and 6 expressed lack of confidence in some areas of the curriculum. Chapter 6 looks in more detail at this issue. It was striking, however, that it was very new teachers (those with under five years' experience) and very experienced teachers (those with over twenty years' experience) who felt least confident about being able to teach all the National Curriculum subjects. About 75 per cent of these two groups felt less confident, compared with about 50 per cent of those with between six and twenty years of experience.

As we show in the detailed case-study material reported in PACE 2 (Osborn, 1996a; Osborn, 1996c) and also in Chapter 4, the issue of confidence lies at the heart of an explanation of primary teachers' changing perspectives in recent years. Both in terms of what united them as groups and in terms of what distinguished them as individuals, the successful mediation of change required both that teachers felt sufficiently confident in their knowledge, skills and abilities to be able to adapt and that they were able to develop practices that accorded with their values and individual situations. The data reported above suggest that this issue was particularly salient for teachers of Years 4, 5 and 6.

3.6 PROFESSIONAL AUTONOMY AND PERSONAL FULFILMENT

Most societies expect that teachers will exercise authority by virtue of their knowledge and skills and, as a result of their early socialization and training, it is central to most teachers' beliefs that being in authority and being in control is a key dimension of their work. In a review of recent studies of teachers in Belgium, North America and England, Nias (1996) has shown that loss of control is linked to a sense of loss of self, and as a result it may arouse profound and hostile emotions. She argues that when teachers cease to feel in control of their jobs and their working lives, they surrender a core part of their identity, a form of 'bereavement' that has emotional consequences for them. It follows that teachers who feel that they have lost part of their professional autonomy may experience a profound sense of loss which has serious consequences for the personal fulfilment they derive from teaching, and possibly for their willingness to remain in the job.

We noted earlier that the PACE teachers were experiencing an increasing sense of constraint and a loss of freedom to do what they felt was best. Seventy-three per cent of the PACE Year 4, 5 and 6 teachers felt more constraint and less professional autonomy than in the past. Forty-three per cent felt 'less enjoyment and fulfilment'. Thirty-three per cent felt more stress and 44 per cent reported 'less enjoyment than in the past'.

A Year 1 and 2 teacher with 26 years of experience reported that she derived far less satisfaction from teaching than she had felt before the changes, and saw her role as a teacher as having changed for the worse. This was closely bound up with a sense of loss of enjoyment, of creativity, and of children's individuality in learning:

> For me the National Curriculum has narrowed my outlook as much as I have tried for it not to. There is still so much to get through and I still feel in a straitjacket. I do smashing work with the children and then I find it doesn't cover the Attainment Targets so I realize that I still have all that to do ... it takes a lot of enjoyment from me. For me, teaching has always been a creative outlet. Now I'm constrained. I've lost a lot of creativity.

This was closely bound up with loss of a sense of fun:

> I've tightened up but also narrowed down. We are really missing the fun of the extra bits. As someone said in one of our staff meetings, 'It's like walking through a wood and keeping to a pathway, not seeing the interesting things on either side.'

A Year 5 teacher reported a sense of loss in her relationship with children and consequently in her own sense of satisfaction:

I don't have as much time for them as I would like. I don't feel as relaxed as I used to be. I don't feel ... I feel pressured that I have to get through so much work, a set amount of work, and there are times, especially during my day when I'm constantly interrupted, that I know that I haven't taught them properly. What I've actually done is given them a worksheet and said 'Get on with it', and that, I am guilty of that quite regularly, and I don't like it. That's not the way I work. And I think if you talked to several members of staff, we would all say we feel our standard of teaching has actually dropped. Because, again I keep going back to it, there isn't the flexibility and there isn't the time for us even to step outside of our doors and just be ... human beings.

This same teacher felt that she had lost much of her personal fulfilment in teaching, since this was so closely bound up with the rewards derived from working with children in a relaxed, unpressured way.

I would like to leave tomorrow if I could. I used to *love* teaching. I can genuinely say I used to love teaching, and now I don't feel that I'm actually communicating with the children in the way that I was when I went into teaching in the first place.

However, a teacher of a mixed Year 5 and 6 class described considerable loss of freedom and loss of fulfilment *except* for the satisfaction she still derived from working with children:

My workload has increased enormously and the paperwork. I have not trained as a secretary, but sometimes I feel like one. I spend an hour after school every day on paperwork, another hour on marking and planning. When I'm down I really do feel it's taking time away from children. My enjoyment is not so great. I'm tired all the time. I feel I'm doing a bit of everything, not doing anything properly ... I still get satisfaction from working with the children. I wouldn't go for a job out of the classroom.

Thus whilst as we show elsewhere, teachers accepted some of the reforms as improving the overall situation for children, they nevertheless experienced a sense of loss on their own behalf as well as that of children. This sense of loss was strongly bound up with another strong emotion in primary teaching – a 'commitment to caring' (Acker, 1999; Jackson, 1968; Lortie, 1975; Nias, 1999b) – and with teachers' sense that they could no longer take time to care about all aspects of children's development as they wished.

In the last report of the PACE findings on teachers in the earlier years of Key Stage 2 (Osborn, 1996a; c), we reported that there was an increase in teachers' sense of pessimism about the future of primary education and a sense that constraints on teachers would increase still further, together with a further loss of autonomy and a narrowing of role.

Our data suggest that in 1995 teachers of Years 4, 5, and 6 were marginally more optimistic than their colleagues had been in 1993 about the future of primary education. Twenty per cent, the highest proportion for any of the rounds of data collection, said that they were optimistic about the future. Twenty-eight per cent had mixed feelings and 17 per cent were pessimistic. In some of the earlier rounds of interviewing, half or more of teachers had been pessimistic about the future. A higher proportion of Year 4, 5 and 6 teachers than of those teachers interviewed in the past were unsure and were reserving judgement (34 per cent). Specifically, they expected teachers' work to change in the direction of more constraint and further loss of autonomy (23 per cent), but this was counterbalanced by those who felt that there would be a clearer framework and structure within which to work (21 per cent). Twenty-one per cent also predicted further subject specialism in the future (Table 3.5).

Table 3.5 Changes predicted by teachers in the nature of their work (percentages)

Type of change	1990/1	1992/3	1993/4	1995/6
More teacher stress/drop out	66.7	55.8	9.8	14.8
More constraints/loss of autonomy	25.9	79.2	33.7	23.4
Less personal fulfilment	17.3	35.1	4.3	8.6
More collaboration amongst teachers	11.1	7.8	4.3	11.7
More reflection, review of practice	6.2	7.8	5.4	10.9
New subject specialism	–	–	–	21.1
Clearer framework/more structure	–	–	–	21.1

Source: PACE 1 teacher interviews
Sample: 88 Key Stage 1 teachers
Date: Summer 1990, Summer 1992
Note: Totals do not equal 100 per cent since teachers could predict more than one change

Other data also suggest a slightly greater degree of optimism since the years immediately after the ERA. When asked whether, if they had the chance to choose again, they would still choose to be a teacher, 56 per cent of Year 4, 5 and 6 teachers in 1995 said 'yes' compared with 46 per cent of Reception and Year 1 teachers in 1990. Twenty-seven per cent said 'no' and 17 per cent were undecided. Most of those who responded positively when asked if they would still choose to stay in teaching cited the pleasure they still derived from successful work with children as the main reason for staying. One Year 5 teacher was fairly typical in her response:

> I have very mixed feelings. I am revising my position. I am always shattered and I have no social life. But it has given me so much. I have thoroughly enjoyed *teaching*, not meetings and record-keeping. Sharing children's successes is still very fulfilling.

However, these findings may need to be examined carefully. Many said they would choose teaching again because they couldn't imagine what else they could do, but that they would never recommend teaching to a daughter or son. Menter *et al.* (1997) point to a gap between the model of a responsible and accountable professional and teachers' private experiences of bitterness, anxiety and overload. They argue that the discourse of the new managerialism may structure the range of acceptable responses that teachers feel able to give to researchers, so as to minimize feelings of alienation and deskilling. The qualitative data from PACE teacher interviews seem to suggest a disjuncture between some teachers' discourse, which emphasizes their identity as accountable, competent and skilled professionals, and their beliefs, which continue to value the emotional and affective side of teaching. Feelings of a loss of fulfilment, anxiety and overload often coexist with the expression of an emergent profession-alism. Some teachers may be 'living out the consequences of change in terms of fractured and fragmented identities' (Menter *et al.*, 1997). However, we are aware of the need to avoid notions of 'false consciousness' which see teachers as the passive victims of imposed change who are unable to understand the implications of their situation as well as those who are researching them.

3.7 DIFFERENTIAL IMPACT OF CHANGE ON DIFFERENT GROUPS OF TEACHERS

As Jeffrey and Woods (1996) assert, there appear to be many contradictory forces at work, some moving towards deskilling, some towards reskilling and a feeling of re-professionalization for some teachers. The outcome of these may depend on a number of variables, including school history, ethos, and strategy for change, experience and determination of staff, strength of local resources, amount and nature of retraining, and school leadership (Bowe *et al.*, 1992). The evidence from the earlier phases of the PACE study (Pollard *et al.*, 1994a; Osborn, 1996a, b) also indicated the variety of variables at both institutional and individual level that might influence a teacher's stance towards change. These include all the factors mentioned above plus the socio-economic catchment area of the school, the teacher's values and previous beliefs about teaching, as well as the teacher's gender, age and years of teaching experience. In the earlier phases of the study we found in particular that younger teachers and new entrants to teaching felt more positively towards the changes being introduced and more ready to internalize them and develop their practice from them.

The teachers in the PACE 1 and 2 samples working in schools in different types of socio-economic catchment areas experienced very different pressures as a result of the changes, and consequently expressed a different set of concerns and anxieties. Teachers working in schools in areas of disadvantage felt the National Curriculum to be particularly inappropriate for their pupils' needs and were no longer able to provide a differentiated pedagogy in the way they felt appropriate.

There was also some evidence of gender differences in response to the changes, with younger males initially feeling the most positive about the changes and about the growth of managerialism, and older women who had perceived themselves as strongly child-centred, creative and spontaneous in their approach feeling that they had the most to lose as a result of the reforms. Conscientiousness and feelings of guilt were an issue here too. The strong feelings of responsibility and conscientious-ness of women primary teachers are well documented (Acker, 1990, 1999; Hargreaves, 1994; Nias, 1999b). This internalized commitment to high personal standards was a gender-based factor in teacher stress and consequent demoraliza-tion, because it made it difficult for teachers to limit their workloads, a necessary condition to enable them to make a positive, creative response to the National Curriculum by exercising choice and rationing and prioritizing the workload (Campbell and Neill, 1994).

Our most recent round of interviews with teachers of Years 4, 5 and 6 show the trends noted above continuing and becoming more marked. We found that, not surprisingly, it was the older, more experienced teachers who felt that their role had changed most markedly (Table 3.6). Teachers with under five years' experience had been trained within a National Curriculum framework and generally felt well prepared to work within it, although they had concerns about subject expertise in some areas of the curriculum (Chapter 6). However, there were striking differences between teachers with six to ten years of experience, 48 per cent of whom said that their role had changed considerably, and teachers with over ten years of experience, 77 per cent of whom had experienced 'considerable' change.

Table 3.6 Changes in role as a teacher, by experience (percentages)

	1995/6 Years 4/5/6			
	Years of experience			
	0–5 yrs	6–10 yrs	11–20 yrs	Over 20 yrs
Less freedom	39.3	69.0	84.0	91.3
More freedom	3.6	3.4	4.0	0.0
Closer cooperation between teachers	28.6	69.0	76.0	73.9
More careful planning	25.0	41.4	44.0	43.5
More bureaucracy	7.1	20.7	48.0	37.0
Increased accountability	10.7	17.2	16.0	17.4
Imposition of priorities	10.7	37.9	48.0	39.1
More focused/confirmed role	25.0	20.7	12.0	6.5
Loss of spontaneity	14.3	31.0	48.0	37.0
Increased stress/anxiety	10.7	34.5	48.0	37.0
More emphasis on product/less on process	3.6	10.3	16.0	8.7
Less enjoyment/fulfilment	14.3	34.5	48.0	65.2
Less informal contact with colleagues	3.6	13.8	4.0	15.2
Other	3.6	6.9	4.0	2.2
	42.9	3.4	0.0	0.0
			Total *n* = 128	

Source: PACE 3 teacher interviews
Sample: 48 schools in eight local education authorities
Date: Autumn 1995
Note: Totals do not equal 100 per cent since questions were open-ended and multiple coding was used

Our data suggest that older, more experienced teachers felt a loss of autonomy in teaching more strongly than those with under ten years of experience. They were more likely to feel that priorities had been imposed on the teacher from outside, that bureaucracy and paperwork had increased and spontaneity in teaching had decreased. Older, more experienced teachers were more likely to have experienced increased stress and anxiety and a loss of enjoyment and fulfilment in teaching. This loss of enjoyment and fulfilment appeared to become more pronounced the longer a teacher had been working. In view of all this, it is not surprising that more experienced teachers were the least likely to feel that the National Curriculum and its associated changes had focused and confirmed their role (Table 3.6).

Similarly, when asked whether, if they had the chance to choose again, they would still choose to be a teacher, it was the longest-serving and most experienced who were most likely to say 'no' or to be undecided, and the newest teachers who were most likely to answer in the affirmative (Table 3.7).

Table 3.7 Would you still be a teacher? (answers by experience) (percentages)

	1995/6 Years 4/5/6			
	0–5 yrs	6–10 yrs	11–20 yrs	Over 20 yrs
Yes	89.3	58.6	60.0	30.4
No	7.1	17.2	32.0	43.5
Undecided	3.6	24.1	8.0	26.1
%	100	100	100	100
	$n = 28$	$n = 29$	$n = 25$	$n = 46$
				Signif. 0.0009

Source: PACE 3 teacher interviews
Sample: 48 schools in eight local education authorities
Date: Autumn 1995

There were no significant differences between teachers working in different socio-economic catchment areas as regards the *extent* to which they felt their role to have changed. However, as Table 3.8 shows, there were striking differences in *how* they felt their role to have changed. The data indicate the extent to which the introduction of the quasi-market into education has impacted differently on teachers working in schools in different socio-economic catchment areas. For example, in schools of low socio-economic status, teachers felt a greater loss of freedom to do as they thought best in their teaching. They were more likely to have experienced an increase in stress and anxiety, and considerably more likely to feel that priorities had been imposed on their teaching from outside. Interestingly, however, some teachers working in these areas were slightly more likely to feel that the changes had given them more focus and confirmed them in their role. It was some of the teachers working in schools in inner-city areas who were particularly likely to feel this new focus, and they tended to be newer entrants to teaching, some of whom had relinquished other jobs to retrain as teachers. Chapter 9 explores some of these differences between teachers in the light of case-studies of three very different schools.

3.8 CONCLUSION

The findings presented in this chapter suggest that amongst teachers in the upper years of primary school there were increasing feelings of priorities being imposed upon the teacher from outside and a loss of fulfilment and autonomy. External accountability had increased, and although personal and moral responsibility was

Table 3.8 Change in role as teacher, by socio-economic status of school (percentages)

	1995/6 Years 4/5/6	
	Socio-economic catchment area of school	
	High SES	Low SES
Less freedom	68.8	76.3
More freedom	6.3	0.0
Closer cooperation between teachers	68.8	60.0
More careful planning	35.4	41.3
More bureaucracy	31.3	27.5
Increased accountability	12.5	17.5
Imposition of priorities	25.0	40.0
More focused/confirmed role	10.4	17.5
Loss of spontaneity	31.3	33.8
Increased stress/anxiety	29.2	35.0
More emphasis on product/less on process	12.5	7.5
Less enjoyment/fulfilment	14.6	16.3
Less informal contact with colleagues	6.3	12.5
Other	6.3	2.5
No comment	8.3	11.3
	Total n = 128	

Source: PACE 3 teacher interviews
Sample: 48 schools in eight local education authorities
Date: Autumn 1995
Note: Totals do not equal 100 per cent since questions were open-ended and multiple coding was used

still seen as highly important, there was some evidence of a shift in climate from a covenant based on trust to a contract based on the delivery of education to meet external requirements and national economic goals. Some teachers expressed fragmented identities, torn between a discourse which emphasized technical and managerial skills and values which continued to emphasize the importance of an emotional and affective dimension to teaching. The evidence suggested that older, more experienced teachers found it more difficult to reconcile their beliefs with the new technocracy. A new professionalism seemed to be emerging amongst some newer teachers, who were more likely to find satisfaction within a more constrained and instrumental role without losing their commitment to the affective side of teaching. The issue of professional confidence was important to all teachers, and lack of confidence to cover all the National Curriculum subjects may have contributed to the loss of fulfilment and enjoyment experienced by some teachers.

Overall, the PACE research suggests that primary teachers are neither passive victims of imposed change nor openly resistant to education reform. There is still evidence of the influence of both structure and agency as important influences on professional practice. In the next chapter we examine how many teachers managed to work within the framework of the new requirements but nevertheless to interpret the policies in the light of their own values before translating them into practice (Osborn, 1996c). To the extent that different teachers actively and creatively mediate change in similar ways, they may in practice be transformed into policy-makers in their own classrooms.

Chapter 4

Teacher Stances and Strategies in Response to Change

4.1 INTRODUCTION

In this chapter we identify key features of teachers' response to change and discuss the extent to which this response has shifted and developed over time and between different groups of teachers.

As the previous chapter highlighted, the requirement to implement a national curriculum and to carry out national assessment imposed changes which were in fundamental conflict with the values and deeply held beliefs of many English primary teachers. The 1988 Education Reform Act was followed by processes of multiple change. These included the introduction of new forms of management into schools, new forms of evaluation of teachers' work, and the infiltration of the values of the marketplace into education. These changes highlighted particularly strongly the debate over the professional role of teachers with regard to the formulation and implementation of educational policy. There were fears that the changes would deskill teachers and reduce them from being professionals exercising judgement to mere classroom technicians (Lawn and Ozga, 1981; Apple, 1986; Densmore, 1987). The notion of teachers as passive 'victims' forced to implement educational policy in a largely uncritical way was placed in opposition to accounts of teachers' ability to resist or to contest policy change (Croll *et al.*, 1994).

However, the main argument of this chapter is that, on the whole, the majority of English primary teachers have adopted neither of these extreme positions. Although there has been some resistance and contestation of policy, notably the action of the teachers' unions over national assessment, in general there has been neither strong resistance nor passive acceptance of government policy by teachers. The previous chapter concluded with a focus on the loss of fulfilment, sometimes shading into feelings of stress and burn-out experienced by many of the PACE teachers. In this chapter the main focus is on the ways in which, in spite of the pressures, some teachers have had the confidence to mediate change in creative ways which may not necessarily represent the intended consequences of government policy. First, however, we outline the PACE teachers' initial responses to change.

4.2 TEACHERS' INITIAL STRATEGIES IN RESPONSE TO CHANGE

In the book reporting the first phase of the PACE project (Pollard *et al.*, 1994a) we argued that teachers' response to change at that point could be categorized in terms of five strategies. These were:

- *compliance*: acceptance of the imposed changes and adjustment of teachers' professional ideology accordingly, so that greater central control was perceived as acceptable, or even desirable;
- *incorporation*: appearing to accept the imposed changes but incorporating them into existing modes of working, so that existing methods were adapted rather than changed and the effect of change was considerably different from that intended;
- *creative mediation*: taking active control of the changes and responding to them in a creative, but possibly selective, way;
- *retreatism*: submission to the imposed changes without any change in professional ideology, leading to deep-seated feelings of resentment, demoralization and alienation; and
- *resistance*: resistance to the imposed changes in the hope that the sanctions available to enforce them would not be sufficiently powerful to make this impossible.

These stances were not intended to be seen as static or unshifting typologies of teachers. Rather, they represent role configurations or strategies which individual teachers might adopt and move through at different times and in different ways. Teacher strategies may have varying features at different moments and in response to differing situations. Thus teachers may sometimes adopt the position of creative mediators and sometimes that of retreatists or resisters. As we suggested in the previous chapter, the notion of 'fragmented identity' may be relevant in analysing the discourse of some of the PACE teachers, who were often torn between conflicting obligations and priorities. Thus teachers' discourse could sometimes illustrate a shift to greater instrumentalism yet at other times suggest a focus on creativity outside National Curriculum requirements.

In general, the PACE data suggest that outright *resistance* was not a predominant response amongst primary teachers. For many primary teachers this stance was made difficult by their strong 'commitment to caring' and to their deeply held values about the importance of their relationship with pupils. The moral order of most primary schools was one in which conscientiousness, loyalty and an ethic of care was reinforced (Evetts, 1990; Campbell and Neill, 1994, Acker, 1999; Nias, 1999b), sometimes making outright resistance difficult because of the effect it might have on pupils or on colleagues.

On the other hand, neither was unquestioning *compliance* a common response, although a readiness to accept the imposed changes was most noticeable amongst young teachers who had newly entered the profession, most of whom had never experienced teaching before the Education Reform Act (ERA). It was also evident amongst older returners to teaching who had been out of the profession for a number of years.

There was considerable evidence of *retreatism* amongst older teachers who were about to take early retirement or were strongly considering it. These teachers felt an overwhelming sense of loss at all the things they had valued most about teaching, and many were looking for a way out as a result. Our evidence, and that of Woods *et al.* (1997), suggests that for some of this group who did not leave, the feelings of loss, alienation and demoralization they continued to experience, as they struggled unsuccessfully to reconcile the way they had to work currently with their beliefs and values, resulted in feelings of stress and burn-out. As their values and personal sense of identity became more and more out of line with their working environment, so they adopted a retreatist position, often pursuing the option of early retirement where this was a realistic possibility. The impact of OFSTED inspections on some schools (Woods *et al.*, 1997, and next chapter) has since offered central government a 'powerful tool' for increasing control over the nature and direction of teachers' work (Robertson, 1998), and has increased this stress considerably, leading more teachers to adopt a retreatist position.

An overview of teachers' stances over the eight years of the study suggests that a predominant response was one of *incorporation*, in which many teachers were able to adapt the changes into existing ways of working – at least to some extent. The research evidence from PACE and from a number of other studies (Campbell *et al.*, 1993; Cox and Sanders, 1994; Osborn and Black, 1994; Woods, 1995; Woods and Jeffrey, 1996) consistently suggests that many of those who stayed as primary teachers accepted and adapted to the National Curriculum, but that they worked with it in a way that suited their beliefs and values so that, as one teacher put it, 'I'll accept the changes, but I won't allow anything I consider to be really important to be lost.' Our study revealed that what was 'really important' to many teachers was a strong moral commitment to the children, expressed by one teacher as 'I'll never sacrifice the children. I'll go on doing what I think best for them.' These teachers could be seen as operating as 'street-level bureaucrats' (Lipsky, 1980) developing their own means of reconciling the conflicting demands made upon them. Nevertheless, it may be that even for those who adopted this strategy and were 'incorporators' some of the time, the emotional costs of constantly adapting to the situation might have been almost as high as for those who 'retreated', since incorporation cannot always be successful and deeply held values may sometimes have to be betrayed (Nias, 1996a; Woods *et al.*, 1997).

A smaller but nonetheless highly significant group of teachers (which varied over time) were able to respond more actively to changes. These teachers managed to preserve what they consider to be best about their practice, and to protect children to some extent from what they consider to be the worst effects of change. They were able to be very creative in their response, even though they had to work within a prescribed framework. We have suggested that such a response may be seen as '*creative mediation*' (Osborn, 1996c).

In addition to this strategic response of creative mediation from some older and more experienced teachers who were in post before the 1988 Education Reform Act, there have been further developments as a new generation of teachers has entered schools since 1988. Some of these teachers who were trained within the National Curriculum, and who have accepted this as their 'taken-for-granted' way of working, are developing their own forms of practice which have a National Curriculum framework as an initial starting-point, but which go beyond this to produce innovative and creative ways of teaching. As we show elsewhere in this book, the majority of teachers have had to adapt to new demands by becoming more instrumental in their approach, paralleling a greater instrumentalism on the part of pupils (Pollard *et al.*, 2000). As some of the case-studies in Chapter 9 suggest, this may be particularly the case for new teachers, who may have more to risk in trying out new ideas of their own. Such instrumentalism may sometimes be in conflict with any possibility of creative mediation, but at other times it may run in parallel with it.

This chapter therefore draws upon an alternative model of teachers' work which presents them not only as having the potential to become creative mediators, but also in some instances as having the ability to transform themselves into 'policy-makers in practice' in the classroom (Croll *et al.*, 1994). In this view, teachers have the ability to mediate educational policy in the light of their own beliefs about teaching and the constraints that operate on them in the classroom.

This model of teaching suggests that as teachers attempt to reconcile external demands with their belief in professional autonomy and with the practicalities of the working situation, they must make choices about the way in which they carry out their work. Where numbers of individual teachers faced with a similar situation mediate change in similar ways and take communal action (i.e. similar individual action), even though it may not be collective action, they effectively become makers of policy in their own classrooms as well as implementers of policy (Croll *et al.*, 1994).

This view of teachers acting communally to make policy parallel to that intended by government is one suggested particularly by the evidence from the PACE study. Other researchers have written of stronger or weaker versions of teachers' actions as subverting, resisting, transforming or appropriating government policy. However, all the accounts have in common a notion of the filtering of policy through teachers' values before it is translated into classroom practice. For example, Bowe *et al.* (1992) describe how secondary teachers successfully appropriated the Technical and

Vocational Education Initiative (TVEI) to 'very different purposes to those intended by the policy', and Vulliamy and Webb (1993) write of new policies having 'to be mediated through teachers'. Woods (1995) gives case-study examples of 'creative teaching' within the National Curriculum. Troman (1995) talks of 'new professionals', teachers who largely accommodated to the reforms but nevertheless, in some instances, contested and resisted them. Bowe *et al.* (1992), quoting Barthes, talk of 'writerly' and 'readerly' responses to policy reform. 'Writerly' responses are those where teachers make use of the gaps and ambiguities in policy texts and seize a margin of manoeuvre in order to assert their own priorities and beliefs. Whereas a 'readerly' approach implies an unquestioning acceptance of the texts as prescriptions for action, a 'writerly' approach involves critical scrutiny, interpretation and selectivity.

Although teachers in England have traditionally believed more strongly in their professional autonomy than teachers in many other countries (Broadfoot *et al.*, 1993), the research evidence suggests that the ability to mediate is a feature of teaching as a profession which transcends national and cross-cultural differences. When confronted with change, and in particular with reform imposed from above, a proportion of teachers in many countries, even those working in highly prescriptive, centrally controlled systems, will respond by subverting, mediating, reinventing, or developing an innovative response. Darmanin (1990), for example, demonstrates how Maltese teachers subverted some aspects of educational change. There is evidence of some teachers in Greece ignoring a rigid, over-prescriptive curriculum in selective ways (Krespi, 1995), while Hargreaves's study of Canadian primary teachers and the introduction of 'preparation time' suggested that although there was evidence for the intensification of teachers' work, this could not account for the whole range and complexity of teachers' response (Hargreaves, 1994). In a recent study comparing the response of primary teachers in France and England when confronted with reform imposed from above, some French primary teachers in France talked of the need to 'internalize the changes, to be selective', and of the importance of 'taking the best from the reforms, but using their own judgement in the end' (Broadfoot *et al.*, 1994; Osborn, 1996c).

Of course, not all teachers are able to adopt this strategy when confronted with change. Just as the teachers in the PACE sample sometimes adopted alternative responses of 'compliance', 'incorporation' and 'retreatism' as well as 'creative mediation' and 'resistance' (Osborn *et al.*, 1992; Pollard *et al.*, 1994a) the evidence suggests that this can equally be true of those in other countries (Menlo and Poppleton, 1999). Webb and Vulliamy's study of curriculum change in Finland and England shows how effectively some teachers could avoid change. Troman (1995), in a case-study of one English primary school, writes of the 'old professionals' who stuck to what they felt worked, regardless of policy directives. There were many such teachers in the French study cited above, carried out by Broadfoot *et al.* (1994), who justified their refusal to change by arguing that the reforms were inappropriate and that they lacked the necessary training and resources to change.

However, the concern of this chapter is particularly with those teachers who (for at least some of the time and in response to some events) have had the confidence, and also the support from within their school, to be enabled to become creative mediators, to be selective in how they implement National Curriculum policy, to prioritize, and to develop new forms of practice in pedagogy and assessment. Four strategies of creative mediation, which we have termed 'protective', 'innovative', 'collaborative' and 'conspiratorial', will be identified, drawing upon the PACE data. Whilst some of these represent teachers acting solely at an individual level, it will be argued that most of the examples suggest that either because of similar structural and situational constraints or because of similar ideologies teachers have acted in similar ways, taking common actions in response to the realities of their working situations (Croll *et al.*, 1994). In so far as this is the case, these actions can be seen to have systematic effects and may effectively redirect educational activities in a way that transforms teachers into policy-makers. First, however, we want to identify some key features in the development of primary teachers' response to change over the eight years of the PACE study.

4.3 DEVELOPMENTS IN TEACHERS' RESPONSE TO CHANGE

Initially, most Key Stage 1 teachers interviewed by the PACE team in 1990 welcomed at least some aspects of the National Curriculum, particularly the curriculum clarification and focus it provided. However, there were strong feelings about many aspects of the reforms, in particular the standardized assessment tasks (SATs), the amount of paperwork involved, and the sheer pace and extent of change. Whilst many argued that some of the National Curriculum equated with good practice and was what good teachers were doing already, it was striking that a majority of all teachers interviewed felt that they had to make substantial changes to their teaching approach, to their working day and to their role as a teacher as a result of the ERA. However, most teachers continued to hold strong personal value commitments and felt responsible and accountable in many, often conflicting, directions. Overall, teachers' work was perceived to have intensified following the reforms, but many Key Stage 1 teachers were unwilling to give up their expressive commitment to children and their 'extended' sense of professional responsibility.

Nevertheless, they experienced their work as far more stressful and regretted the decrease in their professional autonomy and the loss of spontaneity in their work with children as a result of the time constraints imposed by the need to cover an overloaded curriculum. In general, the level of stress, intensification, and sense of deskilling experienced, and the corresponding loss of fulfilment and enjoyment in teaching, increased and became more marked between 1992 and 1994, when we reinterviewed the same cohort of teachers. There were considerable differences in response between older and younger teachers and between teachers working in different socio-economic catchment areas. Older, more experienced teachers were more depressed about the changes than younger, newer teachers. Many felt close to burn-out and argued that the nature of teaching was now such that it could no longer be a job for life. Levels of drop-out through stress and early retirement increased dramatically. Teachers of special needs children and those working in inner-city schools felt the National Curriculum to be particularly inappropriate for their pupils' needs.

However, by 1994 when the Dearing review was already under way, some Key Stage 1 teachers in particular began to feel a decline in pressure and an increased sense of optimism about the future. These teachers argued that they now experienced an increased sense of focus and clarity about their role. Perceptions of deskilling had become less, and a considerable proportion of those who had remained in teaching and had become 'survivors' (Woods, 1977) of the changes thus far, saw themselves as having acquired new professional skills and having developed creative ways of working and assessing within the National Curriculum. There was an increasing sense that it was possible to maintain their own beliefs and good practice and even to enrich their work within a prescribed curriculum. Table 4.1 illustrates this shift by showing a comparison of the attitudes of these Key Stage 1 teachers between 1990 and 1992 in the extent to which they felt their skills to have been complemented or eroded by the National Curriculum.

Table 4.1 Teachers' perceptions of the influence of the National Curriculum (NC) on their strengths (percentages)

Perceived influence on strengths	1992/3 Y1/2	1994/5 Y1/2
Complemented by NC	18.3	29.6
Eroded by NC	49.5	20.9
No influence from NC	25.8	41.9
Possibly an influence in future – positive	3.2	–
Possibly an influence in future – negative	2.2	–
Other	1.0	–

Source: PACE 1 teacher interviews
Sample: 88 Key Stage 1 teachers
Date: Summer 1990, Summer 1992

Key Stage 2 teachers, who by 1995 were experiencing the pressure of national assessment at the upper end of the primary school, felt, on the whole, somewhat less reassured by the Dearing review and subsequent report. Dearing had argued that the content and prescription of the curriculum would be reduced and the professional judgement of teachers increased by the freeing of one day per week for discretionary, non-curricular activities (Dearing, 1994). However, after the first term of the revised National Curriculum, many Key Stage 2 teachers interviewed by the PACE team argued that they had experienced no perceptible difference in curriculum overload. When pressed, some did say that more time had been released for catching up, for activities which had previously been squeezed out such as art, music, a school or class production which might not otherwise be possible, or for concentrating on children with particular needs. Some also argued that they now felt 'freed up' to do those things which they thought were important, or 'released from a feeling of guilt' at taking time out to digress from National Curriculum topics. For others, it had made them more 'relaxed about time' and put them 'in a more legally tenable position'.

Overall, the evidence suggested that teachers at both Key Stage 1 and Key Stage 2 had adopted coping strategies in response to change ranging from compliance (complete acceptance), through incorporation (fitting the changes into existing means of working), mediation, and retreatism (dropping out of teaching or submission to change without any fundamental change in values) to resistance (Osborn *et al.*, 1992; Pollard *et al.*, 1994a). Many had managed, to varying degrees, to incorporate the changes into existing ways of working. Most of those who remained in teaching after an unprecedented level of drop-out had adopted strategies which enabled them to mediate the pressures of change imposed from above through the filter of their own particular values in relation to teaching. For many of the teachers studied, this produced a particular, personal response to change which was evident in their professional ideology and their classroom practice (Osborn, 1996a). As a result, they had been able to work with the National Curriculum in a way that suited their beliefs, and enabled them to preserve what they considered to be most important about their practice. In some cases they felt that having guidelines and a framework to work within had left them free to develop creative ways of teaching.

We have argued that such teachers may be seen as 'creative mediators' filtering change through their own values, which are in turn influenced by gender, social class, previous experience in the classroom, professional training, and other historical and biographical factors (Osborn, 1996c). However, the argument may be taken a stage further. In this mediating role, teachers may well act in similar ways, so that the effect on classrooms and schools is much greater, and more powerful, and in so doing they may effectively be seen to have become makers of policy in their own classrooms as well as implementers of policy (Croll *et al.*, 1994). This model of teachers as 'policy-makers in practice' implies action in common rather than collective action by teachers. Collective action would imply that teachers deliberately adopted this strategy in common, whereas this is not necessarily the case with communal action.

The PACE research suggests several different strategies of creative mediation adopted by teachers which may contribute to policy-making in practice. These are 'protective mediation', 'innovative mediation', 'collaborative mediation' and 'conspiratorial mediation'. Although these strategies are often adopted at an individual level, they have been used in common by many teachers to the extent that they form a particular pattern of response which may have far-reaching implications for primary practice.

4.4 PROTECTIVE MEDIATION

As protective mediators, teachers have been particularly concerned with the effect of external directives such as the SAT requirements, the time pressure to cover a vast curriculum, and the pressures of more rigorous assessment procedures on children, and have striven to protect the children from what they deem to be the worst effects of these.

For example, right from the outset of the implementation of the National Curriculum, teachers were determined to protect the good relationship they had with children from the pressures on teachers' time resulting from the need to cover a broad and prescriptive curriculum. They emphasized the need to maintain spontaneity and the ability to respond to children's interests even where this did not involve the coverage of an Attainment Target. Many teachers made a deliberate and sustained attempt to maintain this freedom to respond in spite of the pressures.

Examples such as this became more prevalent from 1994 onwards when more teachers gained the confidence to follow their own instincts and to feel, as one Year 2 teacher put it, 'far more in control now, feeling "Yes, I can do this again. It is possible, and I'll be able to gradually get back to focusing on maths and English, and the other things being a very important enrichment."' By resisting the pressures to stick closely to a prescribed curriculum, such teachers were taking a common action which had consequences unintended by government policy, and were, in effect, making parallel National Curriculum policy in the classroom.

One Year 5 teacher felt that her relationship with the children had deteriorated as a result of outside pressures initially but that later she had been able to reassert her priorities more and ensure that she protected the children from some of these pressures:

> My relationship with the children? Yes, it's bound to have been affected. I would say I push them more than I used to. I've relaxed a lot more but at the beginning, the first year of operating the National Curriculum, with the children that I knew were going to do SATs or trial SATs, I was very conscious of this and I think I missed out a lot of the nice things. So I kept them hard at it really. But that isn't the case now. I've relaxed more and I'm operating more like I used to do.

Similarly, another Year 5/6 teacher in a rural school described her relationship with the children in her class as initially affected but now reasserted in a way which ensured that the children did not suffer:

> I think it's settled down now [the relationship] ... But that's because we feel we've come to grips, as far as we are able, with what we've got to do. And I still work in a lot of things, in the same way that I've always worked, which I feel is successful in terms of teaching skills. So I've never lost sight of those things. I think I've probably maintained it all the way through but I have developed some new things as well.

Another Year 6 teacher described the National Curriculum as 'manageable if you choose to interpret it that way':

> It depends what you read into it. I don't follow the letter of the law. I still feel you need to take risks and not follow the prescribed course all of the time. I often go with the flow of children's interest. Occasionally you *have* to take risks to motivate children.

Examples of protective mediation were particularly striking in the area of assessment, where teachers throughout the primary school mediated the impact of assessment on the children in a way which accorded with their beliefs and concerns about children's needs. The common action taken by many teachers was a response not to a collective decision but to the similarity of the situation in which teachers found themselves and the ideas which informed their actions.

Key Stage 1 teachers were deeply concerned about the stress and anxiety which the Standard Assessment Tasks (SATs) might cause 7-year-olds and were striving to counteract any sense of pressure, tension and awareness of failure by a variety of subterfuges. Teachers' strategies included making no overt reference to national assessment in the children's presence, asking parents to avoid mentioning the SATs, and presenting the tasks as 'fun' and a normal part of classroom life, in some cases turning the SATs into games and competitions, in which the teacher played the role of a quiz show host or master of ceremonies (Pollard *et al.*, 1994a). The PACE interviews with children after the SATs had taken place suggested that these strategies were largely successful, since few 7-year-olds were aware that testing had taken place and many had actually enjoyed the activities. In St Anne's, an inner-city primary school in the north of England, for example, the Key Stage 1 teacher responsible for SATs said:

> We had many parents saying to us at the end of it [the SATs], 'When are they going to do their SAT?', thinking that it was all sitting in the hall at separate desks! I'm sure the children have no idea they've done one. We just introduce them as puzzles or challenges or mysteries – 'We'd like to know what you know about etc. etc.'

For teachers, the central issue was to normalize the SATs and to integrate them as far as possible into day-to-day teaching, as the following extract from the same teacher's interview suggests:

> I found that the way we approached it and tackled it and we built it into our emergent work on multiplication, use of calculators ... the basic maths – addition, subtraction – were already there anyway. That was fine. The children just treated it like another activity which I regularly give them. Perhaps that was why it worked so well, when I think about it, is because I do take them off the textbook almost on a weekly basis to give them activities that we've created, or I've made, or which are parallel to how they're learning or what they're learning, and they just saw it as something else like that.

At Key Stage 2, protective mediation in relation to the SATs took a rather different common pattern. After the first full-scale SATs at Key Stage 2 in the Summer Term of 1995, many Year 6 teachers were dismayed to find how ill-prepared and ill-equipped children were to face a high-stakes test situation. Given the age of the children and the pencil-and-paper test nature of the majority of the SATs, it was no longer seen as possible or appropriate to try to disguise the purpose and nature of the assessments. Many children experienced the SATs sitting in the school hall or in the classroom at separate desks in what was quite clearly a test situation and, in the Autumn Term of 1995, Year 6 teachers often reported that at least some of their children had become anxious and stressed during the SAT period. In order to help children to deal with this in future, many argued that they planned to carry out regular mock tests during the year in order to teach the skills required, such as reading the questions carefully, allowing adequate time for each question, but also simply to provide general practice in taking tests in order to routinize the test situation.

Whereas some would limit this practice to Years 5 and 6 only, others argued that such practice needed to start lower down the school. As one teacher of a mixed Year 5 and 6 class put it:

> The SATs *are* affecting teaching and learning. We are having to start preparing for the SATs at the beginning of the year. We will be doing SAT-like tasks regularly and making

them aware of how to organize their time in the SATs; be aware of time limits. It all needs to start further down the school.

Another argued, 'The children need training for tests now. The situation is too foreign to them. The tests have implications for teaching in Year 5 as well as Year 6, and probably earlier on.' Some were reluctant to accept this but nevertheless felt that training for tests would be inevitable. As one Year 5 teacher put it:

> If you deliver the National Curriculum, you should have no need to do extra SATs work, but they do have an influence. There's a pressure to prepare the children for it – it's not teaching but training to take tests. It will be expected of me.

In one village primary school, the children had themselves asked for more formal testing to help them prepare for the SATs. Teachers were coming under pressure not only from their own desire to do their best for the children, but in some cases from the children themselves, from the parents, and from school policy and the need to protect the reputation of the school when league tables of SAT results were published.

At both Key Stage 1 and 2 it was clear that a central concern of the teachers was to routinize the SATs so that they would be seen by the children as part of everyday practice. This common pattern of response adopted by teachers is of a kind which is clearly making assessment policy and changing classroom practice on a relatively large scale. Although each teacher is operating this protective mediation at an individual level or, at the most, at a school level, it will nevertheless have systematic effects as similar actions by teachers aggregate across many primary schools.

It is ironic that this strategy operated by teachers at the upper end of primary school with the aim of protecting the children and enabling them to do their best was likely to result in increasing the climate of instrumentalism already developing. As Year 5 and 6 teachers became more instrumental, in part out of a desire to protect children, so too, as the parallel PACE book on pupils (Pollard *et al.*, 2000) shows, pupils in Years 5 and 6 were becoming increasingly instrumental and unwilling to take risks.

4.5 INNOVATIVE MEDIATION

A second central concern of many teachers following the implementation of the National Curriculum and assessment was to develop creative and innovative ways of working within a National Curriculum framework and of interpreting statutory requirements, as well as maintaining the freedom to go outside these when they felt it appropriate. In making these judgements about appropriateness, they often felt it necessary first to internalize the statutory requirements and make them part of their thinking, or, as one Year 5 teacher argued, 'let it sink into the skin and come out as a professional judgement'.

Once again, this common concern when faced with a similar situation led numbers of teachers to respond by taking the aspects of the National Curriculum which most closely accorded with their beliefs and values as teachers and by introducing creative ways of covering the attainment targets with children. Thus a Key Stage 1 teacher argued:

> We've worked very hard at taking the National Curriculum and looking at our beliefs and philosophy and what we believe is good early-years practice and marrying the two. So we've worked very hard at not being swamped and panicking and rushing. For us to step outside our beliefs would be to rush into worksheets and have the children sitting at tables all day trying to cover attainment targets, but we've tried to make it part of our philosophy to give the children first-hand experience and the chance to discover things, and everything's kept very lively. We don't feel we've lost out.

These teachers often felt that the National Curriculum complemented and enhanced their skills, providing them with a focus and allowing them to concentrate on creative methods of covering the content. Sara, a Key Stage 1 teacher, whom we describe in more detail later in this chapter, felt in 1994 that she had emerged from the changes with a new sense of clarity and focus about her role and her practice. She could be seen as an innovative mediator who had taken active control of the changes in a creative, albeit selective, way (Osborn, 1996c). Several other researchers have written detailed accounts of creative teaching taking place within a National Curriculum framework (Galton, 1995; Woods, 1995). Common to all these accounts of creative teaching is the ability to make choices, to be adaptable and flexible, to see alternatives, although working within constraints, and to have the confidence and motivation to put values into practice. These teachers were able to resist pressures to become technicians carrying out the dictates of others. They had also managed to avoid the trap of over-conscientiousness referred to by Campbell *et al.* (1993). They worked hard to create new ways of working with children which were exciting and lively and yet covered what were perceived as important parts of the National Curriculum.

As a teacher of a mixed Year 5 and 6 class put it in the Autumn Term of 1995, being creative involves being able to take risks and to have the courage of your own convictions:

> You have to accept that you never know it all, be open to new things and go on learning. You need to be prepared to take risks and have confidence to do what you see is necessary in your class. A few years ago I had a very disruptive class and in that context my main priority was to create a happy work environment where learning could take place. It's that skill to have the power of your own conviction, to create the right environment and know where you want to go. What I got at the end of that year was phenomenal in terms of children's response, but I had to take risks, not just stick to papers and worksheets, and be prepared to follow the needs of the children at certain times.

As Woods (1995) also found in his study of creative teachers, such teachers often had in common holistic perceptions of children, of learning and of the curriculum, and were concerned with the affective as well as the cognitive. They 'possessed the ability and flair to formulate and act upon hunches, to "play with ideas", but within a disciplined framework' (Woods, 1995). To the extent that the teachers in the PACE sample were acting in common or similar ways as innovators and risk-takers, developing new forms of pedagogy, it could be argued that they were making policy in the classroom.

New teachers who had been trained within a National Curriculum framework and had come into schools in the past few years were also contributing to this process. Many saw the guidance and framework provided by the National Curriculum as a distinct advantage, although there was anxiety created by the 'shifting of goalposts' created by frequent changes in government policy, particularly in relation to assessment. However, many new teachers in the PACE sample had quickly gained confidence to experiment and adapt the National Curriculum framework, using it as a tool, rather than letting it govern their approach. As one Year 5 teacher, in her third year of teaching, put it, 'It's good to have a format to follow. Within that there is a lot of freedom. The curriculum can be personalized to suit the teacher and the class.' A Year 4 teacher in his first year of teaching pointed out that like most new teachers he was adapting his approach all the time as he gained experience. He argued that he felt 'very free' within the National Curriculum: 'It's easy to plan. I can plan around the National Curriculum, use it and work within it.' He did not feel, as some more experienced teachers did, that the National Curriculum had an effect on his relationship with the children: 'I'm still close to my class. We have good fun and have a laugh. I get loads of satisfaction. I have a smile on my face at the end of the day.'

4.6 COLLABORATIVE MEDIATION

One of the unintended consequences of National Curriculum implementation was the unprecedented level of collaboration which emerged amongst primary teachers. This has been seen by teachers, as a mainly positive outcome although they have some reservations (Acker, 1990; Nias *et al.*, 1992; Pollard *et al.*, 1994a). Chapter 5 discusses the nature of this collaboration more extensively and distinguishes between relatively contrived, top-down and managed forms of collaboration and more informal modes of working together adopted by teachers themselves. However, its significance here is that there is a particular sense in which collaboration by some groups of teachers has emerged as a practice which makes policy in the classroom. A major concern of teachers in Years 5 and 6 has been with the difficulties of covering the curriculum in the breadth required, and a lack of confidence in covering some of the subject areas in depth (Bennett *et al.*, 1992; Osborn and Black, 1994). A study of Year 5 and 6 teachers in 1993 found that some classroom teachers had made their own informal arrangements to mediate the effects of the overloaded curriculum (Osborn and Black, 1994). This involved teachers swapping and sharing the teaching of certain activities and subject areas where one felt confident or had a particular expertise in an area where the other felt less confident. In one school a Year 5 and a Year 6 teacher made an informal arrangement which they saw as building on each other's weaknesses and strengths, whereby one taught science for the other's class whilst the other taught physical education (PE) and gymnastics. In another school it was higher language and reading skills which were swapped with maths by teachers who felt particularly strong in one area and weak in another. These arrangements, although supported by the headteacher, were largely instigated by the teachers themselves when they recognized that they had complementary skills and acted upon this, using their own initiative.

In the Autumn Term of 1995, the first term in which the revised National Curriculum was implemented, a number of Year 5 and 6 teachers interviewed as part of the PACE sample reported that they had similar arrangements with colleagues. In spite of the 'slimming down' of the curriculum they found a greater degree of satisfaction in teaching what they knew they were good at, and leaving a colleague to do the same, although this in no way extended to a desire to give up responsibility for teaching the majority of subject areas to their own class. Collaboration for many of the PACE teachers was a strategy of creative mediation because it helped them to survive and to reduce feelings of stress and burn-out which might otherwise result from an overloaded and demanding curriculum. It also helped to protect teachers' confidence and hence their personal identity as people who were able to cope and to continue to feel like successful teachers. As Nias comments: 'Appropriate collegial relations provide teachers with a moral reference group and with a social environment that may protect them from burnout or, at the least, alleviate the ethical conditions which make it likely.' (Nias, 1999a, p. 223).

4.7 CONSPIRATORIAL MEDIATION

In a few schools in the PACE sample, collaboration had taken a more subversive form, where teachers had worked together and supported one another to resist aspects of the National Curriculum that were felt to be particularly inappropriate for the children. This type of collaboration which we have termed 'conspiratorial mediation', can be distinguished from outright 'resistance' by its partial nature. It was a response by groups of teachers who normally accepted that they had to work within the National Curriculum framework or to accept other implications of reform such as OFSTED inspections, but who felt so strongly about a certain issue or a particular practice that they decided to adopt a group strategy in opposition. This was strongly evident in one inner-city school where teachers, with the tacit support of the head, saw themselves as 'conspirators' working together to implement the National Curriculum selectively in a way they felt would protect the children and avoid overload. In this school a decision had been made in 1992 to ignore the history and geography programmes of study, except where they 'fitted naturally' into topics planned for the core subjects.

In the same school in 1995, Year 2 teachers had decided, again with the support of the headteacher, not to carry out the SATs, although they had agreed to use SAT materials in their teaching and in their own teacher assessment of children. On this occasion they had the added support of their wider cluster of schools, all of which had 'conspired' to refuse to implement the SATs in the same way. This form of mediating the SAT materials to what were deemed more acceptable professional ends, making use of them in their own teaching and assessment but not as the government had intended, could also be seen as a common action by a group of inner-city teachers which, if more widely adopted, would have a systematic impact on assessment policy.

In another cluster of five primary schools, two of which were in the PACE sample, a decision had been made not to release the SAT results for publication to the local education authority so that the schools would not be forced into competing with one another in the marketplace in order to attract new pupils based on their SAT results.

There is evidence to suggest that some teachers may have adopted a form of conspiratorial mediation in relation to school inspections by OFSTED. While the form and content of such inspections represent one of the most stringent attempts to control teachers' work, teachers in some schools have 'conspired' to mediate inspections by strategic compliance and impression management both before and during the visit in order to be seen by the inspectors to be complying with OFSTED criteria (Troman, 1995; Woods *et al.*, 1997).

4.8 FACTORS INFLUENCING CREATIVE MEDIATION

We make the assumption in this chapter that the ability to 'creatively mediate' external reforms will increase the involvement and commitment of teachers in their work and consequently enhance the teaching and learning process. A central factor in determining teachers' ability to adopt a creative response to the imposed reforms was their level of professional confidence. As Helsby (1999, p. 173) argues,

> Teachers who are professionally confident have a strong belief not only in their capacity but also in their authority to make important decisions about the conduct of their work ... In order to be able to do this, the teacher needs to feel 'in control' of the work situation. Thus professional confidence also implies that the teacher is not overwhelmed by excessive work demands that can never be properly met. The confident teacher has a sense of being able to manage the tasks in hand rather than being driven by them. Instead of crisis management, corner-cutting and ill-considered coping strategies, they are able to reflect upon, and make conscious choices between, alternative courses of action and can feel that they are doing 'a good job'.

The key question here is to be able to identify and foster those factors which contribute to a teacher's level of professional confidence. We have shown previously that, to some extent, teachers' personal biographies, their previous experiences and the values they have developed as a result influenced their level of professional confidence (Osborn, 1996a, c). In our report of phase 2 of the PACE project we drew upon the examples of Sara and Elizabeth, two Key Stage 1 teachers of roughly the same age and level of teaching experience who worked in the same school. A comparison of these two teachers over the first few years of the reforms, from 1990 to 1994, showed how personal biography and career trajectories can affect the level of professional confidence and a continued sense of satisfaction with the teaching role.

Both Sara Wilson and Elizabeth West were highly experienced teachers who had been working in the same infant school on the outskirts of a large southern city for well over ten years. Sara had been a teacher for 22 years and Elizabeth for 26 years. In 1990 both were feeling overloaded, stressed and anxious about the effect of the National Curriculum on the children in their class. They had considerable fears about how primary education would develop in the future and about the effect of national assessment on the quality of teaching and learning in their school. During the course of the study, Sara, who was responsible for a Year 2 class, had become deputy head. Elizabeth, who taught a mixed Year 1 and Year 2 class, had a point of responsibility for special needs. Strikingly, in spite of many similarities in terms of their experience in teaching, their commitment to the children, and the same school context, the changes impacted quite differently upon them during the course of the four years.

By the end of the four years, Sara felt she had emerged with a new sense of focus and clarity about her role and her practice. She saw the gains and rewards from teaching post-National Curriculum as clearly outweighing the losses, and was particularly confident that she had acquired improved skills in assessment. As she described it, 'I'm more focused now when I plan an activity.' Sara felt that a key factor in helping her to adapt to change was the support she derived 'from being in a school with a strong, stable staff', and from her own temperament, which she defined as calm and practical, enabling her to 'get hold of the changes and do them in the least damaging way, keeping hold of children's happiness and enthusiasm'. However, perhaps the key point in Sara's response to the changes, and the one which most differentiated her from Elizabeth, was the emphasis she placed on the importance of taking control of the changes, and finding ways of making them part of her thinking rather than simply seeing them as external targets which had to be met. She described this in the following way: 'I think that what I hope to do is to internalize myself as a teacher, internalize all this detail and to then be able to use it in good infant practice etc.' This striving after internalization, taking control, and integration of new demands into what she defined as good infant practice was a hallmark of teachers whom we have described as 'creative mediators', those who feel able to take active control of educational changes and to respond to them in a creative, but possibly selective, way.

Sara's emergence as a confident post-ERA professional who had successfully integrated the new requirements into her own identity as a teacher contrasted with the unhappiness and sense of loss expressed by Elizabeth four years into the reforms. Although she also saw gains from teachers having a clearer idea and more awareness of what they were aiming for in their work with children, for her the losses outweighed the gains. She did not feel that she had been able to hold on to the creativity she had before:

> I've tightened up but also narrowed down. We are really missing the fun of the extra bits ... As someone said in one of our staff meetings, 'It's like walking through a wood and keeping to a pathway, not seeing the interesting things on either side ... For me the National Curriculum has narrowed my outlook, as much as I have tried for it not to. There is still so much to get through and I still feel in a straitjacket. I do smashing work with the children and then I find it doesn't cover the Attainment Targets, so I realize that I still have all that to do ... It takes a lot of enjoyment from me. For me, teaching has always been a creative outlet. Now I'm constrained, I've lost a lot of creativity.

Her own identity as a teacher, her confidence and her ability to be creative were perceived by her to be under threat. A key difference between Elizabeth and Sara seemed to be in their ability to take control and make choices about how to implement the changes. Elizabeth was, by her own description, a perfectionist. She felt that she must conscientiously cover every Attainment Target with every child no matter what the cost. Sara, on the other hand, saw herself as able to say 'no' to new demands. She was able to avoid the over-conscientiousness which has been a characteristic of many committed primary teachers (Campbell *et al.*, 1991).

Another key difference was in the new roles taken on by both teachers in the course of the study. Sara had been able to move on to a new role as deputy head which arguably gave her a broader view of the reforms, new challenges and new motivations. Rather than feeling deskilled, she had been able to make the new demands build upon her strengths. Huberman (1993) argued that a key factor in the professional satisfaction of teachers was a feeling of 'upward mobility and social promotion'. This characterized the career trajectories of many teachers in his sample of middle- and high-school teachers who had remained the most energetic and committed throughout their careers.

Another factor in these teachers' continued satisfaction was the continuation of an enjoyable and good relationship with pupils. Whereas Sara had certainly gained a new role which involved 'upward mobility and social promotion', Elizabeth had lost her key 'satisfier', her relationship with the children, which she perceived to be increasingly under threat. Her post of responsibility for special needs children was particularly significant here and may have exacerbated this sense of loss. Of the Key Stage 1 teachers in the 1994 PACE sample, 44 per cent saw the National Curriculum as particularly disadvantaging children with special needs. It was clear from Elizabeth's responses that she shared this view. In primary teaching there is a close link between a teacher's self or sense of identity as part of the professional role and the 'self' as a person (Pollard, 1985; Nias, 1989; Cortazzi, 1991). In Elizabeth's case it appears that the changes threatened not only her professional identity, but also her sense of 'self' as a person, since for her it was the emotional response of the 'personal self' reinforced by her relationships which made teaching worth while.

Both these teachers had been working under many constraints, not the least of which were large classes. The strategies that they evolved to cope with the constraints imposed by multiple change were influenced by their level of professional confidence, which in turn appeared to be influenced by their personal biographies and career trajectories and the level of satisfaction they continued to derive from their work.

Another key factor in the development of professional confidence, even within the constraints imposed by multiple change, is the context and culture within which a teacher works. As Chapter 3 suggested, the socio-economic catchment area of the school may lead to teachers experiencing very different pressures and consequently adopting different strategies for change. Research also suggests that the ability to adopt a response of 'creative mediation' to the National Curriculum is heavily influenced by the presence of a supportive school climate, in particular where a collaborative culture flourishes which gives teachers the confidence to assert their own interpretations upon situations (Helsby and McCulloch, 1997). In the case-study drawn upon above, Sara commented upon the importance of the supportive environment provided by the head and the school in which teachers were encouraged to make their own decisions about how they selectively implemented change. Most of the teachers we identified as 'creative mediators' worked within a strong, collaborative school culture where they were given confidence that they could benefit from the structure and guidelines of the National Curriculum without letting it drive them or destroy what they knew to be good about their practice.

4.9 CONCLUSION

In this chapter we have identified some areas where teachers can be seen to have mediated policy through professional practice in ways that may amount to policy creation. We have outlined four strategies of creative mediation – protective, innovative, collaborative and conspiratorial – by which teachers can be seen to have formulated classroom policy by acting in common, although not necessarily collective, ways.

More recent evidence suggests that even with the imposition of the national literacy and numeracy strategies on schools, many schools and the individual teachers within them are seizing the potential for a margin of manoeuvre between such centralized policies and their implementation. Thus some teachers are finding creative ways of working within the guidelines imposed by these recent strategies and gaining a 'new professional discourse' (Woods and Jeffrey, 1997) as a result. The evidence presented here suggests that creative mediation by teachers is an important strategy that may have system-wide effects on policy and which will continue as long as there are teachers who feel sufficiently confident to adapt and develop practices that accord with their values and working situations.

Professional confidence may depend upon many variables at both institutional and individual level, including personal biographies and career trajectories; the gaining of an overview through moving to a new level of responsibility and a consequent sense of being revalued and reskilled; school context; and, perhaps most significantly of all, the existence of a supportive and collaborative school climate and culture. In the next chapter we explore the implications of such collaborative cultures more fully and discuss the extent to which teachers have moved towards a more collaborative professionalism or alternatively had imposed upon them a form of 'contrived collegiality' (Hargreaves, 1994).

Chapter 5

Teachers' Working Relationships: Becoming a Collaborative Professional?

5.1 INTRODUCTION

In this chapter we examine the changing relationship of English primary teachers with colleagues, including the headteacher and senior staff, and with OFSTED inspectors. In particular we investigate the apparent growth of teacher collaboration and what this means for an understanding of teachers' work. On the one hand, it has been argued that teachers' working lives continue to be characterized by privacy, autonomy and individual initiative (e.g. Little, 1990). Yet on the other hand it has been suggested that the evidence points to teachers becoming more collaborative professionals and that it is possible to identify collaborative cultures in primary schools with a supportive school ethos (Nias *et al.*, 1989). A third strand of this debate suggests that the policy changes of the past few years, including the 1988 Educational Reform Act (ERA) itself and the requirement to teach nine or ten subjects to a high level of competence at the upper end of the primary school, together with the impact of OFSTED inspections, league tables of schools, and teacher appraisal, have impacted on the way in which teachers work with colleagues in such a way that informal collaboration has been forced to give way to a more imposed or 'contrived' collegiality (Hargreaves, 1994).

This chapter first considers these arguments in more detail and then reviews them in the light of data from the PACE study. We consider the evidence for change in teacher relationships with colleagues, headteachers and senior staff, the extent and nature of collaboration within and across schools, and teachers' relationship with OFSTED. What are the implications of this for an understanding of the changing nature of teachers' work?

5.2 TEACHER RELATIONSHIPS WITH COLLEAGUES

Certainly, until relatively recently it was possible to represent teachers' work as relatively isolated, and autonomous. As lone adults, isolated behind the classroom door, teachers who chose to do so could avoid the staffroom altogether and limit most of their contacts with other adults to superficial exchanges with colleagues and to occasional parent evenings. Teachers' work was described as being characterized by individualism, presentism and conservatism (Lortie, 1975) or by immediacy and privacy (Jackson, 1968).

Recent policy reforms have brought dramatic changes to this picture not only in North America, where Lortie and Jackson were writing, but also in some European countries. In England and Wales teachers are required to attend frequent meetings to discuss school policies relating to assessment, special needs, recording and reporting, and school inspection, to name but a few. Increased teacher collaboration or collegiality has also taken many other forms, ranging from planning curriculum topics and sharing resources to sharing teaching and exchanging expertise. In the typical English primary school of the late 1990s, teachers are in frequent contact with one another before, during and after the school day about many matters relating to planning, teaching and administration (Nias *et al.*, 1989; Osborn and Black, 1994; Webb and Vulliamy, 1996b). Often teachers are also expected to plan together and share ideas across schools in cluster groups or federations within one local authority area.

These developments can present a dilemma for teachers which can be characterized as a tension between the need to cooperate with colleagues, pupils and parents for mutually agreed benefits as against the pressure to compete in the marketplace for resources and a clientele which are no longer guaranteed. Thus the marketization of education obliges teachers and heads to compete with each other for places in a league table and for pupils by selling their school to prospective parents. This sense of competition may increase with the introduction of performance-related pay for teachers. Yet at the same time there is a pressure for whole-school cooperation and for schools to work closely together with other schools nearby.

As Helsby (1999) points out, collaboration between teachers can potentially be an empowering experience, not only providing support in times of change and uncertainty, but also drawing upon shared thinking and alternative ideas to widen and improve the range of possible solutions teachers may adopt in response to imposed change. The 'solidarity that comes from being part of a wider group tends to enhance confidence and encourage experimentation'. At the same time, 'exposure to different perspectives and participation in joint development work within a supportive context can challenge taken-for-granted ways of seeing and doing things and thereby broaden professional knowledge and enhance professional skills' (Helsby, 1999, p. 97). For this reason, collaboration and collegiality have been seen as 'pivotal to current orthodoxies of change' (Hargreaves, 1994, p. 186), and are commonly promoted as a means of improving the quality of schooling.

However, not all forms of collaboration are empowering. Hargreaves (1994) has also demonstrated how, when imposed from above, collaboration may shade into 'contrived collegiality' in which teachers may feel that they have lost autonomy and control, are 'over-managed' and are no longer free to teach as they would wish. Evidence of positive outcomes for collegiality are sometimes contrasted with claims of a growing fragmentation of the teaching force (Lawn, 1995) and increasing divisions between classroom teachers and those with managerial responsibilities (Evetts, 1994; Webb and Vulliamy, 1996b). Evetts (1990, p. 48) has demonstrated that at times there can be consequences for the working lives of teachers in terms of their closeness and constant proximity to colleagues, which can sometimes result in irritation and professional disagreements: 'It is almost impossible ... for teachers to avoid or distance themselves from other teachers ... an outcast teacher would find life intolerable in the close confines of the primary staffroom.'

The term 'collegiality' is in itself an amorphous idea. 'Weak' and 'strong' forms of collegiality or collaboration have been delineated by Little (1990). There have been many benefits claimed for teacher collegiality ranging from improved teacher morale, improved pupil achievement, support and informal mentoring for new teachers, and support for change. However, the evidence for this link has been seen by many commentators as tenuous.

Little (1990) argues that teacher collegiality can be seen on a continuum from independence to interdependence, ranging from storytelling and scanning for ideas to sharing to joint work in the classroom. In Figure 5.1 we have adapted Little's model to include a significant feature of teachers' work in English primary schools since the advent of the National Curriculum: joint planning in year groups or across year groups as a whole school. In the 'weakest' form of collegiality, teachers collaborate through storytelling and scanning for ideas. It is opportunistic, takes place during fleeting moments in the staffroom and enables teachers to gain information and assurance in the quick exchange of stories or ideas.

This portrait of teachers' work has altered little over decades. It was described vividly by Acker in her portrait of an English primary school on the brink of educational reforms at the end of the 1980s as a culture in which collaborative and participatory discussions over major and minor matters took place over coffee, in break times and lunchtimes:

> Hillview's traditional way of working was casual, flexible and warm. Staff meetings and other breaks served as occasions to unwind from a demanding daily job, as well as ways of making decisions and discussing curricula. Values of caring for one another; warmth expressed through rituals of sharing food and drink (especially following a major effort

such as a Christmas production, or at the end of term); overt expressions of thanks from the headteacher to her hard working staff; humour, camaraderie and reassuring expressions of the school's commitment to children and to a caring ethos all were evident.

(Acker, 1990, p. 263)

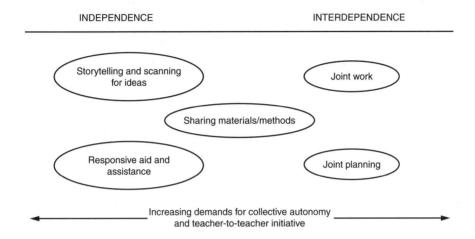

Figure 5.1 A provisional continuum of collegial relations
Source: Adapted from Warren-Little (1990)

In contrast, teacher collegiality, in its strongest form, may involve a far greater level of interdependence between teachers, one that might mean joint work in the classroom, collective conceptions of autonomy, joint planning of work in teams which teach closely together even if not actually in the same classroom. Consistently, Little and other commentators have argued that there is little evidence of the widespread acceptance of this stronger form of collegiality or of substantial signs of school improvement resulting. Much that passes for collegiality, according to these researchers, 'does not add up to much'. Classroom autonomy with the occasional exchange of views is seen by them to be the predominant mode.

Yet other researchers have argued that even before the ERA there was real evidence of teachers' collaborative cultures in the context of English primary education. Nias *et al.* (1989) have described teachers' collaborative cultures in the setting of four English primary schools as characterized by strong leadership, and a valuing of openness as well as sense of collective responsibility. In such schools both individuality and interdependence are valued:

> Collaborative cultures are built upon a belief in the value of both the individual and the group to which he/she belongs. In schools with such cultures, people habitually praise, thank, appreciate, help, support, encourage one another and welcome the differences between them as a source of mutual learning and enrichment. (Nias *et al.*, 1989, p. 73)

Other research also suggests that the culture of many English primary schools has progressed beyond the storytelling and idea scanning stage so that collaboration between teachers is now a central element of the 'new professionalism' (Hoyle, 1986;

Woods *et al.*, 1997). However, this institutionalized collaboration is not without cost, as we show later in this chapter and in Chapter 10. Cooperativeness between teachers is no longer 'a possible quality a teacher may embody, but a necessary technical requirement in the teaching and management of the curriculum proposed for schoolwork' (Lawn, 1987, p. 162). This means that teachers are often 'collaborating under constraint' (Woods *et al.*, 1997) and may be forced into a 'contrived collegiality' (Hargreaves, 1994) in which the teacher's strong sense of moral and professional responsibility to the children in his or her class is threatened by the requirement to attend constant meetings and by the imposition of 'managed collaborative cultures' (Webb and Vulliamy, 1996b; Woods *et al.*, 1997). According to Hargreaves (1994), whereas the informal collaboration described by Nias, Acker and others is characterized by spontaneity and by voluntarism, and is development oriented, contrived collegiality is compulsory, fixed in time and space, predictable, and administratively regulated.

In the section which follows we go on to consider how the evidence from the PACE study can illuminate this debate about the changing nature of teachers' work and the significance of this for English primary schools. To what extent did the PACE teachers see themselves becoming genuinely 'collaborative professionals'? How did they view any such changes to their individualism and autonomy?

5.3 WORKING WITH COLLEAGUES WITHIN THE SCHOOL

In Chapter 3 we saw how the PACE teachers were feeling greater accountability to more people, and particularly to colleagues, than ever in the past, so that sometimes they were caught up in a network of competing obligations. The evidence suggested that over the eight years of the PACE study there was a steady increase in the proportion of teachers identifying closer collaboration and cooperation with colleagues as an important dimension of their changing role (from 34% in 1990, 44% in 1992, to 52% in 1994) (see Table 5.1) Of course, this may have reflected increases in collaboration amongst teachers of older children as well as increases due to the impact of reforms. This evidence of more intense collaboration continued in the final phase of the research. By 1995, 63 per cent of teachers in the upper years of primary school identified closer cooperation with colleagues as an important feature of their work.

During the earlier phases of PACE it was certainly clear that this collaboration represented a limited form of collegiality since it mainly took the form of meetings and joint planning rather than joint work at the level of classroom practice. However, there were significant changes in the upper years of the primary school. Teachers of Years 4, 5 and 6 identified the form that their collaboration took as shown in Table 5.2.

It was clear that *planning* together in year groups or bands of year groups, rather than actually teaching together was still the most important form of collaboration. Fifty-nine per cent of teachers reported joint planning of this type as a regular activity, and 28 per cent reported planning together as a whole staff. Forty-seven per cent regularly attended staff meetings. However, increasing numbers of teachers

Table 5.1 Importance of teacher relationships with others (percentages)

	KS1			KS2	
	1985/6	**1990/1**	**1992/3**	**1993/4**	**1995/6**
Relationships with colleagues	23.1	47.3	43.0	25.0	
Relationships with parents	19.0	29.1	29.3	7.0	
Relationships with pupils	15.0	30.0	28.7	33.0	

Source: PACE 1 teacher questionnaires and Bristaix questionnaires
Sample: 94 Key Stage 1 teachers, 360 English Bristaix teachers
Date: Summer 1985, Summer 1990, Summer 1992

Table 5.2 Ways of working with other teachers (percentages)

Plan with year or broader age groups	58.6
Curricular planning as whole staff	28.1
Whole-staff planning: non-curricular	10.2
Exchanging/combining classes with other	31.3
Meetings as part of senior management team	8.6
Shared resources	3.9
Meetings with year group/KS stage teacher	27.3
Regular staff meetings	46.9
More formalized, less informal interaction	4.7
Curriculum coordinator role: resources and planning	34.4
Curriculum coordinator role: teach with class teacher	15.6
Other	6.3
No comments	0.8

Total *n* = 128

Source: PACE 3 teacher interviews
Sample: 128 Key Stage 2 teachers, 48 schools in eight local education authorities
Date: Autumn 1995, Spring 1996
Note: Totals do not equal 100 per cent since teachers could identify more than one change

reported actually teaching with colleagues either by combining classes or exchanging classes. Thirty-four per cent of teachers of Years 4, 5 and 6 did this for some lessons, compared with a much smaller proportion of teachers in lower age groups in earlier years.

A Year 5 teacher in the north of England described what Little would call a 'weaker' version of collegiality, which nevertheless was a source of considerable of support.

> Well, because it is a very small school, we have always supported each other but I do think we have had far more discussions. If another teacher has a problem, she will come to me. If I have a problem, I will go to someone else. It is a very supportive atmosphere here. You don't need to worry at all about going to someone else or admitting, 'I can't do this', or 'I don't know what to do next', because nobody thinks any the worse of you and if they can help you sort it out, they will, but I think we have relied on each other a lot more since the National Curriculum has come in. With our strengths and weaknesses really.

Most of the PACE teachers, apart from those in their probationary year, were also curriculum coordinators with a well-defined responsibility for particular areas of the curriculum and/or for cross-curricular themes such as assessment, special needs or equal opportunities. Often such teachers were responsible for more than one subject area or cross-curricular area, which could amount to a heavy burden of work, as the following quotation illustrates. A Year 6 teacher in a middle school who was also a Key Stage 2 curriculum coordinator and coordinator for maths and religious education (RE) described a well-organized system of joint planning which she operated with colleagues:

> Our Year 6 team meets regularly to plan. We do this in a fair amount of detail. There is a lot of informal chat as well. They [the other Year 6 teachers] are all NQTs [newly qualified teachers]. We discuss individual children and the mentoring meetings. For maths, the Key Stage 2 team meets once a term. We also have an RE meeting each term with teachers from each year at the start and the end of the module. There are meetings where all Key Stage 2 teachers meet. I go to them all. There are also working parties on endless policies. I would say I spend about five hours a week on meetings and liaison with other schools.

Collaboration was particularly important for new and more inexperienced teachers. Young teachers may suffer badly when the rest of the staff are overburdened and lack the time to give the help new teachers need. Darling-Hammond (1990, p. 289) emphasized the vulnerability of newly trained teachers and the need for their 'supportive and sustained induction' but argued that ironically this is unlikely to be forthcoming when it is most essential: in conditions of high staff turnover or of continuous change. For some of the newer PACE teachers, however, this support was available. A young Year 6 teacher described how she had gained in confidence from being able to talk about work with more experienced colleagues:

> I haven't been in other schools so I don't know what relationships are like between heads and staff. I have only been in as a student and that is a different situation, but I do feel that I can talk to other members of staff about virtually anything and I never really feel that I am being damned. If I can't do something, I never feel that I can't ask and they are going to think 'she can't do it'. I don't feel in any way like that. They do try and boost my confidence. They are aware that I don't really feel I do my best, and very often they will say 'I saw something really good going on in your classroom today.'

Where this help from other teachers was less forthcoming, new teachers sometimes worked together to support one another. Two newly qualified teachers we interviewed early in the study in an inner-city first school described how they supported each other in the difficult early years of teaching by planning together informally, by sharing work in the areas they found most difficult and by taking each other's class.

For many PACE teachers these developments in collaboration were seen as a welcome and largely positive move. Increased collegiality and interdependence was not simply something imposed upon them from above, but an added source of job satisfaction. In Chapter 4 we described this informal, teacher-inspired collaboration as a form of teacher mediation of the impact of the National Curriculum on their work. It was not imposed by a top-down management strategy but inspired by the teachers' own diagnosis of their needs and building on their own strengths.

For many, collaboration and increased interdependence was also a survival strategy. It was no longer possible to cope with current demands working as a relatively autonomous individual. One older, more experienced teacher of a mixed Year 5 and 6 class argued:

> If someone likes doing something or has a particular interest you should give them a chance. There is no place in teaching now for prima donnas. You must work with others. If you don't share ideas, planning and practice you will go under. The teacher who can't share is no longer a good teacher.

Many other teachers described the positive features of working together, seeing it as a lifeline which had helped them to cope during a time of extreme turbulence. As one teacher described it,

> We have to be really aware to help each other out when we're feeling low about it, and really put the effort in to talk to your colleagues and console them and say, 'Look, I feel the same way', and 'Yes, it's not just you'. 'If you can't do it, well, hard luck, don't do it.'

There is evidence here that appropriate collaborative cultures may provide teachers with what Nias (1999a) has called 'a moral reference group' as well as a social environment that may protect them from burn-out.

However, there was sometimes a downside to these changes. Inevitably there is a tension between professional autonomy and increased interdependence. Sometimes the cost of the latter can be very high. Indeed, some researchers have argued that some teamwork and joint planning, particularly where it is imposed by school policy, may be limited in its effect, 'contrived', and an obstacle to teacher creativity, suggesting, for example, that when teachers tried to implement topic work planned on a whole-school basis, they found increased difficulty in presenting such curriculum ideas in a creative and interesting way (Stone, 1993). Some teachers in the PACE study identified this as a problem. One teacher of Year 5 and 6 children, with 23 years of experience, argued:

> Part of me believes in the curriculum. We have to plan and think as a group with other teachers about the needs of children. But I can't accept over-prescription. It can be narrowing. One young teacher here said, 'When can I actually choose what I am doing?' It's sad when teachers don't feel they can follow their enthusiasm. When someone else plans you don't have the same enthusiasm, the same creativity. Too much prescription can deaden.

This experience of loss was described by many teachers who regretted the disappearance of the kind of informal and unplanned interchange with other colleagues which was not always about work, but which often led to a spontaneous sharing of ideas and the sort of storytelling and scanning described by Little. Another Year 6 teacher with 22 years of experience said, 'There is no time for social chat now. We now only talk about school issues. There are too many meetings. The classroom is no longer your domain. I find it awkward going into other classrooms.' As a Year 5/6 teacher with 32 years of teaching experience argued,

> You can't just chat and enjoy colleagues' company. It's all very structured activity now. It's taken the fun element out of teaching. There is less time to talk about issues that come up. There are meetings and clubs every day after school. It's all pressure from the minute you arrive. I do at least two hours extra per day compared with the past. It's all go ... meetings and courses. We have year group meetings, whole-school meetings. I relate to all the staff as deputy head and am curriculum coordinator for science and IT. I would like to spend more time with the children.

In a sense, then, this lack of time to socialize and build relaxed relationships with other teachers paralleled the lack of time to build relationships with children which many teachers described. Indeed, a key feature of this managerially imposed or 'contrived' collegiality was that it was perceived as detracting from the time which teachers had to focus on teaching, in particular on preparing and planning their work as individuals. It is a process identified by Woods *et al.* (1997, p. 32) as the 'institutionalising of the informal discourse'. Although only a small group of teachers in previous years had identified the loss of informal relaxed contact (such as that described by Acker) with colleagues as a source of concern, it was significant that the proportion of teachers mentioning this increased in the last years of the study as teachers' work intensified. More experienced teachers (those with over twenty years' experience) were more likely to express this sense of loss, as the quotation above and Table 5.3 demonstrate. To some degree this loss of an emotional dimension to teachers' relationships can be seen as part of a wider shift in schools, documented throughout this book and its companion volume (Pollard *et al.*, 2000), from an emphasis on human values and an affective dimension towards greater rationalism and instrumentalism.

Although there was no great difference in the emphasis on loss of informal contact between teachers working in areas of higher and lower socio-economic status, it was noticeable that those in more disadvantaged schools were significantly more likely to have to plan the curriculum on a whole-school basis, which might be perceived as more constraining since it considerably lessened teachers' individual autonomy (Table 5.4).

For most of the PACE teachers, it appeared that collaboration with colleagues was becoming a significant focus of their work and a major support in coping with the consequences of change. At the same time, increased managerialism was seen as imposing more and more meetings and taking away from teaching (see also Webb and Vulliamy, 1996b), thus threatening this positive response to working with colleagues. Collaboration imposed from above was sometimes seen as an intolerable burden on already over-extended teachers. Sometimes individuals felt required to take their colleagues into account more than was reasonable. At times like this, for some teachers collaboration was perceived as taking precious time away from their work with their own pupils and consequently seen as an exploitative and intolerable burden (Nias, 1999a). For these teachers, maintaining an increased level of support was tiring and an extra strain. The PACE teachers talked of 'forever throwing lifelines to your colleagues' and of exhaustion at the end of a day spent sharing colleagues' worries as well as one's own.

Over the course of the study, teachers' discourse shifted somewhat from an initial welcoming of the benefits of increased collaboration to a tendency to see aspects of

Table 5.3 Ways of working with other teachers, as affected by number of years of experience

	1995/6 Yrs 4/5/6			
	Years of experience			
	0–5 yrs	6–10 yrs	11–20 yrs	Over 20 yrs
Plan with year or broader age groups	60.7	55.2	56.0	60.9
Curricular planning as whole staff	21.4	31.0	24.0	32.6
Whole-staff planning: non-curricular	3.6	10.3	8.0	15.2
Exchanging/combining classes with other	28.6	31.0	32.0	32.6
Meetings as part of senior management team	7.1	10.3	8.0	8.7
Shared resources	3.6	3.4	4.0	4.3
Meetings with year group/KS stage teacher	28.6	27.6	32.0	23.9
Regular staff meetings	50.0	55.2	40.0	43.5
More formalized, less informal interaction	3.6	0.0	0.0	10.9
Curriculum coordinator role: resources and planning	21.4	34.5	44.0	37.0
Curriculum coordinator role: teach with class teacher	14.3	24.1	28.0	4.3
Other	21.4	0.0	0.0	4.3
No comments	0.0	3.4	0.0	0.0
	$n = 28$	$n = 29$	$n = 25$	$n = 46$
			Total $n = 128$	

Source: PACE 3 teacher interviews
Sample: 128 Key Stage 2 teachers, 48 schools in eight local education authorities
Date: Autumn 1995, Spring 1996
Note: Totals do not equal 100 per cent since teachers could predict more than one change

this colleagiality as 'contrived' and managerially imposed. Nevertheless, the overall evidence from the PACE study supported the view that, with all the caveats mentioned above, both willingly and unwillingly teachers were behaving increasingly as collaborative professional workers. The PACE teachers on the whole supported the thesis of Nias (1999b, p. 74) that

> working together in a school which unequivocally accepts the interpersonal basis of education and carries this emphasis through into adult relationships can be a positive experience in several ways . . . It may lead to the giving and receiving of practical assistance and emotional support, to the acceptance and remediation of weakness and failure (in oneself and others), to shared laughter, to mutual appreciation, gratitude and praise. Second, it helps the development of a sense of collective endeavour and shared accountability . . . Third, by providing emotional security and a climate of open communication, it facilitates both risk-taking and the constructive resolution of personal or professional conflict. Fourth, it contributes to professional learning.

The following section describes a further pressure which has led teachers to develop for themselves new ways of working together which lend both moral support and practical assistance when confidence is lacking. It is distinguished from the

Table 5.4 Ways of working with other teachers according to socio-economic status of school catchment area (percentages)

	Yrs 4/5/6	
	High SES	**Low SES**
Plan with year or broader age groups	62.5	56.3
Curricular planning as whole staff	18.8	33.8
Whole-staff planning: non-curricular	10.4	10.0
Exchanging/combining classes with other	31.3	31.3
Meetings as part of senior management team	10.4	7.5
Shared resources	4.2	3.8
Meetings with year group/KS stage teacher	29.2	26.3
Regular staff meetings	41.7	50.0
More formalized, less informal interaction	4.2	5.0
Curriculum coordinator role: resources and planning	29.2	37.5
Curriculum coordinator role: teach with class teacher	14.6	16.3
Other	12.5	2.5
No comments	2.1	0.0
	n = 48	*n* = 80
		Total *n* = 128

Source: PACE 3 teacher interviews
Sample: 128 Key Stage 2 teachers, 48 schools in eight local education authorities
Date: Autumn 1995, Spring 1996
Note: Totals do not equal 100 per cent since teachers could identify more than one change

imposed, top-down managerialism or contrived collegiality sometimes referred to in the previous section by the spontaneous and teacher-initiated way in which it has arisen and is directly related to a coping strategy adopted by teachers to deal with an overloaded curriculum and competing demands for their time.

5.4 ISSUE OF SUBJECT CONFIDENCE AND SHARED TEACHING

In Section 4.6 we referred to the issue of teacher confidence to teach the National Curriculum to the level required for all ten subjects in Years 5 and 6. Many of the teachers in the PACE sample, like those in the studies of Bennett *et al.* (1992) and Moses and Croll (1990), said that they did not feel confident in some areas. In the upper years of primary school 65% of teachers expressed a lack of confidence. Eighteen per cent specifically mentioned music; 15% specifically mentioned science and 14% mentioned technology; 14% said they needed support and more resources in some areas. As a teacher of a mixed Year 3, 4 and 5 class with 32 years of teaching experience argued:

> I don't feel totally confident about teaching all the National Curriculum subjects. Teachers are demoralized by all the negative things said about them. It hasn't helped

teachers. Many have dropped out. We try to divide up subject responsibility to keep us informed and help us. We are not experts in everything. We try to help each other.

Another Year 4 teacher who had been teaching for 23 years felt

not totally confident especially at the levels that are expected now. For example in music and art. I get a lot of help from the curriculum coordinator in music but achieving any depth is difficult. I am fairly confident in the three core subjects including science.

A Year 5 teacher who had taught for seventeen years, twelve of them at one school, was

not confident teaching all the National Curriculum subjects. Previously we had a system in which specialist teachers took some subjects. Now I know, yet I don't know. It puts incredible pressure on us. I'm not a musician nor a scientist. I can't give children exactly what they need. I definitely think there is a place for some subject specialism.

As a result of this lack of confidence, especially in the curriculum areas mentioned above, 49 per cent of Year 4, 5 and 6 teachers felt that there was some place for specialist subject teaching in the upper years of primary school. It was the newest teachers (with under five years of experience) and the most experienced (with over twenty years of experience) who were most likely to feel this.

Table 5.5 Does subject specialism take place in school (percentages)?

	1995/6 Yrs 4/5/6
Yes, in one or some subjects	35.1
No	13.5
Individual agreements with teachers	31.0
Occasionally with curriculum coordinators	17.0
Middle school, timetabled subject specialisms	3.5
	Total *n* = 128

Source: PACE 3 teacher interviews
Sample: 48 schools in eight local education authorities
Date: Autumn 1995

As Table 5.5 shows, 35 per cent of Year 4, 5 and 6 teachers already had some degree of subject specialism taking place in their schools. This parallels the findings of OFSTED (1997), which explored the use of subject specialism in schools and suggested that some specialist teaching might 'promote high standards at Key Stage 2'. Some of these teachers (17%) were in middle schools where a degree of specialism was automatic in Year 5 and 6, but a further 31 per cent of teachers experienced some subject teaching done by their curriculum coordinators and in 14 per cent of cases the specialist teaching was a result of individual informal agreements between teachers.

This was not necessarily confined to teachers of Years 5 and 6. One Year 4 teacher felt that subject specialism, especially in music and physical education (PE) would be beneficial and would help to cut down on teachers' preparation time. Another newly qualified Year 6 teacher described the downside of having no specialist input:

> Well, there are some things that I personally don't take an interest in and I still have to teach them to the children and I find that difficult because I am trying to enthuse them to be motivated to do work that perhaps myself I don't feel. And I sometimes find it very hard to try and think up a really good way of getting a message across. We did some work last term on land formation and to me it was quite a boring subject. Personally, I wasn't too interested in sediment rock and igneous rock and whatever, and it was really hard, and when I was actually teaching it I had this aura of 'Yes it is really good to learn about rock like this', but really in the back of my head it wasn't something that was an interest, and I find that difficult, some of the contents of what I am expected to teach. Also, with the Year 6s, maths is not my strong point, and sometimes I do feel that I am being stretched to understand it myself and yet I have got to teach it to a child, and I do find that difficult sometimes.

For those PACE teachers who worked in middle schools rather than primaries, a degree of subject specialism was timetabled and taken for granted in Years 5 and 6. Most welcomed this arrangement and found it hard to understand how other teachers coped without this degree of interdependence.

One Year 5/6 middle school teacher thought that the children would get 'fidgety' with the same teacher all day. In her view a change of teachers made them more alert and helped with the problem that every teacher had areas of the curriculum where they felt less confident. She described how specialist teaching operated for some subjects in her school:

> We have specialist teaching for music. There is a technology specialist and a PE specialist. You can choose which subjects you are not comfortable with. I take health throughout Year 5, but my class does not have me for maths. The coordinator for maths takes them.

In primary and junior schools, arrangements were far more variable, but those teachers who had reached informal agreement with colleagues to share and exchange teaching felt very positive about the arrangement. These informal arrangements were made by the teachers themselves, usually with the approval and support of the headteacher. However, they were rarely instigated by the head and did not necessarily reflect the working patterns of other teachers in the same schools. It seemed that most of these arrangements largely happened when two teachers recognized that they had complementary skills and acted upon this, using their own professional initiative.

One Year 3 and 4 teacher who was also a Deputy Head described the way in which she worked with the other Year 3/4 teacher in her school:

> We swap teaching on a regular basis. This term we have chosen to swap geography and science. We may choose to vary the subjects; for instance, we will probably change to art and music in the spring. In the summer we may split the English work into two specific areas and cover one each.

Possibly the very success of this type of collaboration depended upon the fact that it belonged to and was initiated by the teachers themselves and lay within their own control. Teachers become accustomed early in their training and careers to the notion that being in control is essential to being a professional. As Nias (1996a) has shown, recent studies of teachers in North America, Belgium and England suggest that loss of control is linked to a sense of loss of identity and sense of self. It is when teachers no longer feel in control of their working lives that collegiality can become a destructive, rather than potentially a creative, force.

5.5 COLLABORATION ACROSS SCHOOLS

For teachers in small schools there were often severe limits to the collaborative activity which they were able to undertake with colleagues since there were often no other teachers of the same year groups within the school and the pool of subject expertise and advice on which to draw was more severely limited. However, while teachers might lack some of the benefits of collaboration open to their counterparts in larger schools, they often benefited from the more informal approach to planning and working together which was possible in a small school where teachers were naturally together at break and lunchtimes, as several heads and teachers pointed out:

> Because we are a small school we have always worked closely together but we are doing so even more now. But it's very easy for us because, with only four teachers, you can't miss each other and it's easy to grab someone for a quick chat in the staffroom.

For many of the PACE teachers, not only those working in small schools, collaboration with teachers in other local schools was becoming an increasingly important aspect of their work through cluster groups, local federations made up of a number of neighbouring primary schools and often one or more secondary schools into which the primary schools 'fed' pupils.

The cluster group notion constitutes a dilemma for schools in the current market-oriented climate in primary education. They have to choose whether to work for cooperation with other schools in the face of challenges or to compete for resources and clientele. Almost without exception, the PACE teachers and heads tended to prefer cooperative to competitive modes of relationship with colleagues in and between schools. They acknowledged the need for greater staff cooperation whilst at the same time recognizing the ambiguity inherent in cooperating with other schools when the market obliged them to compete for position in a league table, and in selling their school to prospective parents.

As a Year 3/4 teacher who was also a deputy head argued:

> I have changed over the years. I was more insular before, now I am more involved in management and collaboration. I need to see the detail but I see the need to let others contribute as well. I am involved in the Frome federation [a cluster group of teachers across schools]. All levels of teachers [Key Stage 1, Key Stage 2 and secondary schools] get together to coordinate children's progression. We have formed curriculum working parties to look at specific areas.

In one of our case-study schools, Orchard, located in a small village, the Year 5/6 teacher collaborated extensively both within and beyond the confines of her own school. Apart from her responsibilities as special needs coordinator, maths coordinator and IT coordinator, she also acted as administrative coordinator for the cluster of primary schools of which Orchard was one. Teachers across the cluster worked together for maths, sports, science and art in order to share expertise. In art they had organized a range of activities based in a local secondary school for all the children based in a particular year group in the cluster of schools. They had developed joint policies in special needs, the arts and PE, and for able children and equal opportunities. The cluster schools had also collaborated by issuing a joint statement opposing the publication of the SATs and by refusing to release the results to the LEA, although reporting them on an individual basis to parents.

One teacher made it quite clear how important it was to her to have this leadership role in working with colleagues from other schools: 'I value the time I spend discussing the curriculum areas and communicating with other teachers. Teaching was quite isolated in the past and in this sense [in terms of her leadership roles, although not in other ways] I get great satisfaction.'

For many of the PACE teachers, collaboration with other schools appeared to be a creative means of mediating the competitive force which derived from the marketization of education.

5.6 TEACHER RELATIONSHIPS WITH HEADTEACHERS AND SENIOR STAFF

Much of the research evidence on teacher relationships with the head and senior staff shows that teachers are experiencing an increase in managerialism and managerial discourse which focuses more on the systems of organization in place than on actual teaching and learning in the classroom (Webb and Vulliamy, 1996a; Woods *et al.*, 1997). Heads and senior staff were seen by the Conservative government which introduced the Education Reform Act as the prime agents in the implementation of the reforms. It was almost inevitable, then, that teachers would experience changes in their relationships with their headteachers. There was a danger of what Hargreaves (1994) referred to as 'balkanization' occurring, where the culture of schools becomes split into small sub-groups which are isolated and cut off from each other. In the case of primary schools there was often a fundamental division between, on the one hand, classroom teachers and, on the other, headteachers and the senior management team, who had access to knowledge and power not possessed by 'ordinary' classroom teachers.

Certainly the PACE evidence suggests that over the course of the study, teachers perceived a marked decrease in collegial management emphasizing democratic participation within their schools and an increased emphasis on 'top-down management styles'. Early in the study a Year 2 teacher in one of the case-study schools, St Anne's, argued:

> Things have changed considerably. I mean the head seems more like a manager now. Quite against his will he's had to devolve responsibility into subject meetings and management teams and department groups, and there are times when one just longs for the old days when the boss would come in and say, 'Look, we're going to do this, we're

going to do that'... because that's what he's getting paid for. He's had the role of accountant and manager, and chairman of the board, as it were, thrust upon him and he's not trained for it . . . It is becoming a business, which is, I suppose, what the government wanted.

The majority of teachers, in the earlier phases of the study, argued that there had been no change in the relationships between the head and the staff, although roughly one-fifth felt that relationships had worsened. Many heads were perceived by their staff to be under more strain and, reciprocally, some had adopted an increasingly protective role towards their staff, attempting to organize things so as to put the least possible strain on classroom teachers. As the reforms progressed this became increasingly difficult for heads, as Chapter 10 will show. Most were forced by external demands to become increasingly managerial. There was evidence from the qualitative data in the later phases of the study that teachers felt far more distance between themselves and the head than they had experienced in the past. A Year 5 teacher in the north of England argued:

> She's [referring to the headteacher] far more busy. At one time she would always be in the staffroom with us. We knew every single little thing. You didn't have to wait for a staff meeting to be told anything, but now I think we get more information at staff meetings because she has to make notes of what we want to know because she has so much more work and so much more to do. So, although we've got a good relationship, we're a bit more distant. And that is not because her character's changed. I think it's because of the workload of everyone.

There were many examples of headteachers using the National Curriculum as a means of facilitating managerial changes that they had wanted to implement in any case. As one head put this: 'It's a powerful lever for me in getting things done in school. It would be a harder struggle without the National Curriculum in getting any change. I use it as an enhancer for what I want to do anyway.'

Although there is no doubt that the externally imposed changes had resulted in a considerable diffusion of the power of the head (see Black, 1996, and Chapter 10), many teachers were nevertheless aware of an increased managerialism emanating from the headteacher. As one Year 4/5 teacher put it, 'If you don't agree with your head you might as well change your school.' In a different school another Year 5 teacher who was accustomed to using social constructivist approaches in her teaching, and had found them valid and rewarding, was now being required by her headteacher to return to the transmission mode which he felt more appropriate to deliver improved SAT results. She felt managed and controlled by the headteacher, as the following remark she made illustrates: 'We are being pushed along a path we don't like [by the head]. We are being treated like a machine. Quite a lot of people don't respond to that. I prefer to take responsibility for myself. It's tough if you're conscientious.'

Yet in some schools headteachers continued to take a protective role, and, aware of the culture of overwork and conscientiousness existing in primary education, urged their staff to ease up on themselves. A new Year 6 teacher described how this happened in her school:

> I don't like to feel that I walk into the classroom unprepared, although I do perhaps sometimes feel that I haven't quite done enough preparation, and we have actually discussed this as a staff and the headteacher, Ken, was saying that perhaps sometimes you can just give 95 per cent rather than 100 per cent.

There were also examples of teachers feeling empowered by a new headteacher who had brought with him or her a change of culture and had created a climate of confidence as the case study of Orchard School in chapter 9 suggests.

Campbell (1996) has suggested that the power imbalance between head and staff may be redressed by the introduction of subject specialism into primary schools. This, he argues, will push more power over decisions about curriculum and pedagogy away from the head down to the staff as a whole. Thus if a teacher is, for example, a science specialist and the head is not, that teacher will become more powerful in defining good practice for herself and her colleagues in respect of that subject area, consequently offering the possibility of restraint upon the headteacher's exercise of professional control. He argues that in a situation where many primary school heads are male and many of the other staff are female, changing the distribution of power in primary schools may be a particularly important objective. However, it is possible that the opposite could also be true: that such specialism could lead to 'balkanization' in larger primary schools, splitting up the united front of the staff into smaller sub-groups and leaving the head that much more powerful as a result. This is an issue on which we have relatively little research evidence in PACE. Certainly, the case-study of Greenmantle School in Chapter 9 suggests some of the tensions inherent in attempts to embrace a subject specialism model.

In summary, over the course of the study, teachers were feeling increasingly managed and directed by the head and less able to ignore the pressures to change which were being mediated by the headteacher.

5.7 TEACHERS AND OFSTED

In 1992 a new form of school inspection under OFSTED (the Office for Standards in Education) was instituted which was designed to include all schools in a pattern of rigorous and systematic inspection every four years by new teams of specially appointed inspectors. This was intended to be seen as a further step in the Conservative government's drive to raise standards in schools. It was a significant change in that it reduced that margin of manoeuvre that schools and teachers had previously been able to exercise in the implementation of policy change. To the extent that it was another step in the reduction of control that teachers had over their working lives, it was likely to be a source of further stress and tension for teachers.

Woods *et al.* (1997), in their analysis of the impact of OFSTED inspection on three individual teachers, distinguished between three criteria of influence: the nature and degree of intensification experienced by teachers in preparing for the event; the realities of the event as it was constructed by teachers; and the meanings of the event for teachers' identity and professional selves. They identified very different responses in each of the three teachers they studied, ranging from enhanced confidence to negative trauma which led to a redefinition and reconstruction of self by the teacher concerned, a deputy head.

How did the PACE teachers respond to this further challenge? In the autumn of 1995 when we interviewed Year 4, 5 and 6 teachers, 22 per cent had already experienced an OFSTED inspection and a further 29 per cent were preparing for one later in that school year. A further 52 per cent were anticipating an inspection the following year. We asked the teachers, depending on the point their school had reached in the process, what impact they felt that undergoing an OFSTED inspection, preparing for one, or awareness of an OFSTED inspection in the future had on teaching and learning in their class. Seventeen per cent of teachers identified a clearly negative impact, mentioning the stressful effect it had, the sense of demoralization that resulted even where the outcome of the inspection was favourable. They reported incidences of teacher stress, illness and drop-out as a result of the experience of inspection itself. Twenty-two per cent mentioned the endless preparation of documents before the inspection, and 25 per cent talked of the work involved afterwards in terms of preparing an action plan for the school and addressing areas identified as weak by OFSTED.

A teacher in a school which had received an unfavourable OFSTED report argued that the effect had been 'completely negative'. As a result of the outcome, the head had taken early retirement because of 'stress'. The collaborative atmosphere amongst the staff had been totally destroyed. 'Now, nobody will do anything for anyone else. There was giant apathy prior to the appointment of the new head. The paperwork was endless.'

It was clear that for nearly all teachers the workload associated with an inspection was very high, both in terms of preparation for the event and in terms of developing an action plan afterwards. In a school which had recently been inspected, a Year 4 teacher felt that there had been no real impact on children's learning, either positively or negatively. The main impact was on teacher energy:

> I don't think it has affected learning. It's just that there was such a peak of pressure just before and during the inspection. It's difficult afterwards to maintain energy. The oral feedback we received was good but people just experienced it as anticlimactic.

The stress and anxiety experienced before the event was seen as very damaging to morale and resulted in a loss of professional confidence for many teachers. One teacher of a Year 5 and 6 class in a school which was still awaiting inspection felt that awareness of OFSTED had caused

> tightening up of teaching and more stress for all of us. It's worrying that OFSTED has such a demoralizing effect on schools. Teachers are not being made to feel that they are good at their job. Many are leaving the profession, or have gone sick long-term. It has wrenched the school in two in some places.

As this quotation illustrates, an established mythology about the effect of OFSTED on others was evident even where the school in question had not even been informed of an inspection. This in itself was damaging to teacher confidence and morale.

In a middle school awaiting inspection later that year, the Year 5 and 6 teacher reiterated a similar point:

> Planning is tightening up. I can see the paperwork mounting up. The staff are getting perturbed and worried about it. No one knows what to expect. You hear such horrendous stories. In one school two people have resigned even before OFSTED came. That's two out of sixteen people.

Nevertheless, 34 per cent of teachers identified a positive effect of OFSTED as a focus for getting things done in the school, and 22 per cent identified a positive effect as a focus on particular classroom issues. One teacher of a mixed Year 4, 5 and 6 class in Valley, one of our case-study schools, talked of the focus she felt OFSTED could give in enhancing teaching:

> I think OFSTED in its own way has actually been quite useful because it's made us focus on the continuity and progression and quality of learning, as well as the quality of teaching – in a useful way, in a positive way. And I wish more people felt more positive about it. I think the OFSTED, the new framework, is actually quite useful for planning by. So, in those terms I think OFSTED has been quite useful.

There is further discussion of the impact of OFSTED on one case-study school in Chapter 9.

Overall, the evidence suggested that most PACE teachers accepted the need for inspection but at the same time they found it too costly personally and professionally. The cost was high in terms of time, effort, loss of self-esteem and threat to professional identity. What was most striking was the experience of demoralization and destabilization which resulted in burn-out for some, even where the inspection was successful. OFSTED inspections, as Woods *et al.* (1997) argue, can hold different meanings for different teachers and 'can have variable and contradictory effects'. However, even where teachers experienced some positive effects, there was no doubt that the inspections contributed greatly to the intensification of their work, and certainly, for many, to the loss of a sense of professional control and confidence. Teachers were forced to work even more closely together in order to prepare for OFSTED and for its aftermath, but this often took the form of a 'contrived collegiality' that lessened the time and energy available for developing other learning opportunities. As documented throughout this book, the issue of control emerged as vitally important for teachers in how they responded to OFSTED.

5.8 CONCLUSION

There was no doubt from the PACE evidence that isolation and independence in teachers' work was being replaced by interaction and interdependence. It is important to differentiate between the very distinct attitudes to collaboration that are evident in the PACE teachers. On the one hand, there are the closer relationships brought about by the 'wartime crisis' or siege mentality in response to denigration by central government, publication of league tables or the threat of an OFSTED inspection. On the other hand, there are the teams formed in response to the demands of the National Curriculum, such as Key Stage planning groups, cluster groups which are expanding in different although usually supportive ways, curriculum coordinator roles and limited subject specialism. In the first, close relationships are derived largely from the individual beliefs of teachers; the second are more of a professional strategy to meet new goals. In both these types of collaboration, but particularly in the second, the growth area for teacher teamwork, the PACE data show that when collaboration is genuine and 'bottom-up', or democratically constructed and genuinely concerned with improving teaching, it can produce real benefits for the teachers concerned and their classes. When it is top-down and managerially imposed, and more concerned with producing documentation and paperwork, it is more likely to be perceived as a threat to good and focused teaching, taking away from preparation time, and from good relationships with children.

In some PACE schools professional relationships are being reconstructed as 'managed collaborative cultures' and teachers are being reconstructed as 'teacher-managers' (Woods *et al.*, 1997, p. 47). In others, collaboration is not only a survival strategy but a genuinely creative response to change, and teachers feel able to see themselves 'reprofessionalized' as interdependent colleagues, not only effective team members and good organizers, but also with a continued sense of interpersonal involvement and a moral responsibility to their colleagues. The overall evidence suggests a considerable shift from the informal collaboration that characterized primary schools in the 1980s to a more imposed and contrived collegiality, but still points to the existence of opportunities for more creative collaboration. In the future, it is possible that further competitive forces may still further reduce this narrow window of opportunity for genuine collaboration. For example, the recent government plans for the selection of some teachers for 'fast-tracking', leading to greater career opportunities and higher salaries (DfEE, 1999), could lead to a greater sense of divisiveness between colleagues in the same school and pose a threat to genuine collaboration. As we suggest in the conclusion to the book, in the new millennium success may depend on the extent to which it is possible to manage collaboration so that teachers can maintain a sense of professional and personal control over what they do in a climate of confidence and trust in colleagues.

Part 3

Teacher Experience

Chapter 6

Teachers and the Curriculum

6.1 INTRODUCTION

In this part of the book (Chapters 6, 7 and 8) we examine more closely that component of primary education which is central to the process of effective teaching and learning: the classroom teacher and pedagogic practice. It is clear that the nature of educational priorities and the different ways of conceiving the task of achieving these priorities are, ultimately, the responsibility of individual classroom practitioners. In an effort to unravel the complicated context of interactions between teachers and their pupils, we have used the framework of what Bernstein has referred to as the 'three message systems': curriculum, pedagogy and assessment. These, he suggests, are used by teachers to convey the existing 'education codes' of a particular society, and for this reason their conception and application conveys far more than the ideologically free set of skills, knowledge and understanding which is often claimed for them (Bernstein, 1975, 1990a, 1996). From this it follows that different ways of understanding knowledge and the learning process have implications for different perspectives on curriculum organization, teaching methods and evaluation techniques. The values that practitioners hold will influence decisions they make about the curriculum they devise, the teaching approaches they employ and the outcomes that they intend from the education process. As Chapter 4 has shown, classroom teachers have a vital role to play, for practitioners are rarely the passive implementers of policy but will inevitably become 'policy-makers in practice' (Croll, 1996) through a process of 'creative mediation' (Osborn, 1996a).

Through the 1988 Education Reform Act (ERA), primary teachers had, for the first time in recent history, a statutory obligation to meet academic objectives in each of nine, and later ten, subject areas for each child, in each academic year. There was also a direct form of accountability through national testing (Standard Assessment Tasks, SATs) enabling not only the levels of achievement for each child to be measured, at ages 7 and 11, but also a direct comparison between schools, through the publication of national 'league tables'. We wanted to discover the extent to which these changes had impacted on the daily lives of pupils and teachers in their classrooms.

Each year from 1991 to 1996 members of the project team spent one week in each of the nine classroom study schools observing the daily routines of the classes in which the target pupils were situated. The data collected in this way gave detail and insight to the interview and questionnaire data collected from the larger sample of 48 schools. In interpreting these data, however, it must be recognized that as the target pupils progressed through the system, the sample of teachers altered. It must also be recognized that the trends evidenced were the result not only of the National Curriculum and assessment but also the increasing maturity of the pupils as they progressed from Key Stage 1 to Key Stage 2.

In this chapter we consider teachers' perceptions of the curriculum changes over the course of the PACE study. We reported in PACE 1 (Pollard *et al.*, 1994a) and PACE 2 (Croll, 1996) that primary teachers at both Key Stage 1 and Key Stage 2 had initially accepted the National Curriculum in principle. They believed that it offered an entitlement to each child, which ensured a set of broad, structured experiences that, with good curriculum design, provided for progression and continuity. It was seen as a potential source of coherence and equity, and embodied egalitarian values that had previously been reflected in the relatively undifferentiated curriculum provision of primary schools. However, we also recorded a tension between the desire to engage with a 'broad and balanced' curriculum and the emphasis on 'basics' which was a necessary consequence of the assessment requirements, particularly national testing. Classroom observation showed the dominance of the core curriculum, especially English and mathematics, leaving foundation subjects to be squeezed in many schools, which in turn made achievement of curriculum breadth difficult. There was some evidence that subjects such as music and art had suffered as teachers felt their control of the classroom curriculum tighten as a consequence of overload. Teachers began to feel that it was too much, too soon, that it was constraining and that it did not allow for responses to pupils' particular learning needs. We also noted a considerable move away from combining subjects in pupils' classroom tasks and a move towards tasks based on single subjects, in line with the subject-based organization of the National Curriculum. To what extent had these early trends continued as the study progressed?

6.2 TEACHERS' EDUCATIONAL AIMS AND CURRICULUM PRIORITIES

Table 6.1 shows data from semi-structured interviews carried out with teachers in five successive rounds of data collection: 1990, 1992, 1993, 1994 and 1995. In reply to an open-ended question concerning their academic priorities, teachers spontaneously offered various responses that were later coded by the research team.

Table 6.1 Teachers' academic priorities (percentages)

	KEY STAGE 1			KEY STAGE 2	
	1990/1 R/Y1	1991/2 Y1/2	1993/4 Y1/2	1993/4 Y3/4	1995/6 Y4/5/6
Emphasizing basic skills	24.8	24.6	33.1	19.8	15.9
Developing individual potential	21.6	24.0	26.0	29.6	28.0
Matching work to children	18.3	11.7	14.9	24.1	13.3
Listening and communication skills	10.5	2.9	5.8	3.1	6.6
Broad, balanced curriculum	8.5	23.4	10.4	14.2	5.5
Affective, creative curriculum	3.3	4.7	2.6	1.2	1.1
Achieving NC Attainment Targets	1.3	7.0	0.6	3.1	7.0
Independence in learning	–	–	–	–	16.6
Other	6.5	–	4.5	1.2	3.7
Not mentioned	5.2	1.8	1.9	3.7	2.2
	n = 88	*n* = 93	*n* = 88	*n* = 92	*n* = 128

Source: PACE 1, 2 and 3 teacher interviews
Sample: Key Stage 1 and 2 teachers in 48 schools in eight local education authorities
Note: Priorities are listed in the order of importance in which they occurred in 1990. R = Reception class; NC = National Curriculum

It can be seen that whilst a similar emphasis is placed by Key Stage 1 teachers on the acquisition of 'basic skills' and the 'developing of individual potential', and that these both increased slightly during the study, Key Stage 2 teachers placed most emphasis on 'developing individual potential'. Teachers of the older children also began to mention 'independence in learning', which had been absent from the comments by teachers earlier in the study and may well have been linked more closely to the advancing age and maturity of their pupils. However, the declining emphasis on 'matching work to children' is common to both Key Stage 1 and Key Stage 2 teachers, which would suggest that the demands of the National Curriculum may have been making this more difficult. Governmental discourse emphasizing the 'broad, balanced curriculum' appears to have made an impact on teachers' discourse in 1992, when 23 per cent of the responses from Year 1 and Year 2 teachers made mention of this as an academic priority. This figure fell to a low of 6 per cent of the responses from Year 4, 5 and 6 teachers in 1995, suggesting a tension between maintaining a broad, balanced curriculum and the need to cover the core subjects in sufficient depth. These data also showed evidence of a reduction in the priority which teachers felt able to give to the 'affective, creative' curriculum, as spontaneous mentions of this had reduced to 1 per cent by 1995. The pressure to ensure that children achieved the National Curriculum Attainment Targets was most noticeable in 1992 and 1995, when Year 2 and Year 6 teachers had to prepare pupils for the statutory tests at Key Stage 1 and Key Stage 2 respectively, though mentions of this as an academic priority were lower than might have been expected.

Not all the responses from teachers could be coded against the notion of an 'academic' priority. Teachers considered their role to be broader and mentioned many priorities that could be classified as 'non-academic'.

Table 6.2 Teachers' non-academic priorities (percentages)

	KEY STAGE 1			KEY STAGE 2	
	1990/1 R/Y1	1991/2 Y1/2	1993/4 Y1/2	1993/4 Y3/4	1995/6 Y4/5/6
Happiness, enjoyment in learning	35.6	28.9	45.3	46.9	28.5
Social skills, cooperative attitudes	22.7	17.4	20.8	27.4	34.5
Independence, autonomy, confident	22.0	26.4	–	–	26.3
Moral, religious education	3.8	1.7	2.8	5.3	1.5
Other	3.0	2.5	6.6	2.7	1.5
Not mentioned	12.9	23.1	24.5	17.7	7.7
	n = 88	*n* = 93	*n* = 88	*n* = 92	*n* = 128

Source: PACE 1, 2 and 3 teacher interviews
Sample: Key Stage 1 and 2 teachers in 48 schools in eight local education authorities
Note: Priorities are listed in the order of importance in which they occurred in 1990

Table 6.2 shows that teachers of Years 4, 5 and 6 in 1995 placed less emphasis on the importance of children's 'happiness and enjoyment in learning', but more emphasis on the importance of developing 'social skills' and 'cooperative attitudes'. Emphasis was placed by both Key Stage 1 and Key Stage 2 teachers on building independence, autonomy and confidence in their pupils, though mentions of an emphasis on moral and religious education diminished as the study progressed. This could again reflect pressures of an overloaded curriculum. Although the recognition of 'non-academic' priorities diminished for Key Stage 1 teachers during the period of the study, only 8 per cent of Key Stage 2 teachers in 1995 failed to mention some aspect of the more affective dimensions of education as one of their priorities when teaching their children. This would point to a retention on the part of these teachers, to a commitment to the broader role of the teacher that extends beyond the purely instrumental.

6.3 TEACHERS' PERCEPTIONS OF CHANGES IN CURRICULUM CONTENT

The question of how far teachers shared fears, expressed when the National Curriculum was initiated (Haviland, 1988), that the balance of the primary school curriculum was likely to shift towards the 'core' subjects (English, mathematics, science) laid down by the 1988 Act and away from some of the more expressive and creative areas, such as art and music, was a major concern of the study. Evidence was collected by teacher interview and classroom observation, and these data were then triangulated through interview with the pupils.

Data in Tables 6.3 and 6.4 appear to support the thesis that time spent on core subjects had been increasing and that this could have been a result of the subject-orientated National Curriculum and its assessment requirements. The relatively high percentage of Key Stage 1 teachers (10 per cent, 22 per cent, 16 per cent, respectively) who perceived less time being spent on English also added weight to the fear of some teachers that the pressure to deliver a ten-subject curriculum was restricting their ability to ensure basic reading and writing skills for the youngest of the primary children.

Table 6.3 Curriculum changes as perceived by Key Stage 1 teachers (percentages)

	More			Same			Less		
	1990 R/Y1	1992 Y1/2	1993 Y1/2	1990 R/Y1	1992 Y1/2	1993 Y1/2	1990 R/Y1	1992 Y1/2	1993 Y1/2
Core curriculum									
Maths	9.1	20.4	23.9	79.5	66.7	48.9	11.4	12.9	9.1
English	20.5	14.0	22.7	69.3	64.5	43.2	10.2	21.5	15.9
Science	84.1	73.1	64.8	14.8	22.6	15.9	1.1	4.3	1.1
Foundation subjects									
Technology	69.3	68.8	60.2	29.5	25.9	12.5	1.1	5.4	9.1
IT	–	–	56.8	–	–	19.3	–	–	5.7
History	40.9	53.7	55.7	54.5	38.7	23.9	4.5	7.5	2.3
Geog.	43.2	57.0	60.2	51.1	37.7	19.3	5.7	5.4	2.3
Music	3.4	1.1	15.9	67.0	55.9	47.7	29.5	43.0	18.2
Art	2.3	1.1	5.7	68.2	45.2	45.5	29.5	53.8	30.7
PE	3.4	2.2	8.0	85.2	79.6	62.5	11.4	18.3	11.4
RE	7.9	4.3	18.2	84.1	73.1	52.3	8.0	22.6	11.4
Other	4.5	1.1	5.7	11.4	0.0	3.4	1.1	4.3	10.2
	$n = 88$	$n = 93$	$n = 88$	$n = 88$	$n = 93$	$n = 88$	$n = 88$	$n = 93$	$n = 88$

Source: PACE teacher interviews
Sample: Key Stage 1 teachers in eight local education authorities
Date: Summer 1990, Summer 1992, Spring 1994
Note: Totals do not equal 100 per cent in 1993 because approximately 18 per cent of the sample were newly qualified teachers. Totals do not equal 100 per cent in the category 'other' as a proportion of the sample did not respond – 1990, 83.0%; 1991, 94.6%; 1993, 62.7%. PE = physical education; RE = religious education (statutory but not part of the NC)

Table 6.3 also shows a marked perception, by Key Stage 1 teachers, that there had been an overall increase in the time spent on science. In 1990 a massive 84 per cent of teachers perceived an increase in time spent on science, although the rate of this increase fell over time. However, evidence from interviews with teachers suggested that this perceived increase may also have been a function of a clearer labelling of certain topics as 'science' that would have been covered in a more general way previously. Contrary to some fears that history and geography would suffer, our data show that this was not perceived by teachers to be the case. Again, many teachers explained that these areas had always been covered in topic work and that a more conscious labelling of the subject areas may have contributed to the perceived increase. The relatively new subjects of technology and IT showed a dramatic perceived increase in time spent on them, with over 60 per cent (technology) and 57 per cent (IT) of teachers in 1993 considering that these areas took up more curriculum time than before the introduction of the National Curriculum. At the same time, more creative subjects such as art, music and, to a lesser extent, physical education (PE) were perceived to have less curriculum time and to have lost ground to some extent. Time spent on religious education (RE) also appeared to have been reduced, although there were signs in the later rounds of data collection that the position here was changing.

Table 6.4 Curriculum changes as perceived by Key Stage 2 teachers (percentages)

	More		Same		Less	
	1993 Y3/4	1995 Y4/5/6	1993 Y3/4	1995 Y4/5/6	1993 Y3/4	1995 Y4/5/6
Core curriculum						
Maths	13.0	36.1	54.3	51.3	14.1	5.0
English	14.1	33.6	52.2	52.1	14.1	7.6
Science	70.7	60.5	9.8	26.1	2.2	6.7
Foundation subjects						
Technology	60.9	50.4	15.2	26.1	6.5	15.1
Infor. Technology	–	50.4	–	35.3	–	6.7
History	46.7	18.5	32.6	60.5	3.3	14.3
Geography	44.6	16.8	34.8	61.3	3.3	14.3
Music	19.6	21.0	44.6	53.1	17.4	18.5
Art	6.5	9.2	44.6	51.3	31.5	31.9
PE	7.6	10.1	62.0	56.3	13.0	25.2
RE	19.6	21.8	48.9	58.8	14.1	11.8
Other	26.1	9.2	3.3	3.4	8.7	5.9
	n = 92	*n* = 120	*n* = 92	*n* = 120	*n* = 92	*n* = 120

Source: PACE teacher interviews and questionnaires
Sample: Key Stage 2 teachers in eight local education authorities
Date: Autumn 1993, Autumn 1995
Note: Totals do not equal 100 per cent because approximately 18 per cent of the sample in 1993 and 7% of the sample in 1995 were newly qualified teachers. Totals do not equal 100 per cent in the category 'other' as a proportion of the sample did not respond – 1993, 44.6%; 1995, 74.0%. In 1995 74% of the sample did not respond to the 'other' category

In Table 6.4 there is a similar picture for Key Stage 2 teachers. In 1995 approximately one-third of teachers perceived there to have been an increase in mathematics and English, whilst almost two-thirds perceived an increase in science. Over half of the sample perceived an increase in technology and IT, but the evidence for history, geography and music is less easy to interpret. Again, art and PE continued to be squeezed, but there was some improvement in the case of RE, which might have been the result of governmental and media attention in this area. The fear expressed by some observers that work in classrooms would become restricted to the ten National Curriculum subjects had some support, as 74 per cent of the sample did not complete the 'Other' category.

Later interviews also revealed the feeling of many teachers that there were other, more subtle, ways in which the 'creative' side of the curriculum was being affected. Teachers considered that they were less able to give children free choice in areas such as creative writing and art, as everything had to be related to the National Curriculum Attainment Targets. This constraint on teaching meant that teachers felt unable to follow children's ideas and that there was less room for what many referred to as 'inspirational' teachers or teachers with special interests.

> You lose a certain amount of spontaneity. You lose the enthusiasm, to a certain extent. Children learn best when the teacher's really enthusiastic and some of the subjects you can't summon up any inkling of enthusiasm. (Year 5/6 teacher, 1995)

> I think a lot of the spontaneity has gone out of teaching. It was a job in which one could use one's imagination and flair and personal interest in certain specific areas. That's gone now. We feel compelled to find out more information, from whatever source, in order to deliver the National Curriculum, and sometimes that can be a bit tedious. (Year 5/6 teacher, 1996)

6.4 CLASSROOM OBSERVATION OF CURRICULUM CONTENT

As part of the data collection, during the middle three days of the week of observation, a systematic observation schedule was employed to triangulate the data collected through teacher and pupil interviews. In one sense this was likely to be a more objective source of data than the teacher interviews and surveys of teacher perceptions since it recorded how far teachers' perceptions were reflected in actual classroom practice. However, it must be recognized that the observations were restricted, in the main, to recording those activities taking place during classroom work in the middle three days of a particular week each year. Nevertheless, when the statistics were aggregated, as they have been over the entire six years of the PACE research, they did provide indicative information on curriculum content and balance.

In our observations the National Curriculum subject classifications were used to code each six-minute period of pupil–teacher activity by 'curriculum context'. This was by no means straightforward, and considerable researcher judgement was involved, though it was a mark of the extent of subject differentiation that this judgement became easier as the observations moved up the age range. Where there was uncertainty, the classroom teachers were consulted before coding was confirmed. Table 6.5 records the 'main' curriculum content coded at the end of each six-minute observational period, in relation to the curriculum context in which each observed teacher or pupil had been engaged.

Table 6.5 Main curriculum context (percentage of observed time)

	Key Stage 1		Key Stage 2				
	1990/91 Y1	1991/92 Y2	1992/93 Y3	1993/94 Y4	1994/95 Y5	1995/96 Y6	Av.
Core curriculum							
English	37.6	33.1	27.4	32.3	24.1	25.4	29.7
Mathematics	14.1	16.9	19.8	21.8	17.6	23.0	19.0
Science	7.1	9.0	9.4	6.1	16.3	12.9	10.2
Total core curriculum	*58.8*	*59.0*	*56.6*	*60.1*	*58.0*	*61.3*	*58.9*
Other foundation subjects							
Art	8.5	2.2	6.6	2.6	6.9	3.3	5.0
History	2.9	0.0	6.3	1.8	3.8	7.4	3.8
Technology	4.4	3.2	1.2	1.0	2.1	2.5	2.4
Physical education	2.6	3.2	2.3	3.3	0.6	1.9	2.3
Music	2.4	2.8	0.8	2.8	1.5	2.7	2.1
Geography	0.3	0.2	1.6	5.1	6.1	0.8	2.4
Total other foundation subjects	*21.1*	*11.6*	*18.9*	*16.7*	*20.9*	*18.4*	*17.9*
Religious education	0.7	3.8	1.5	4.0	2.5	1.9	2.4
No main curriculum subject	19.4	25.6	23.2	19.3	18.5	18.4	20.7

Source: PACE 1, 2 and 3 systematic observations of teachers and pupils
Sample: Nine teachers and 54 children in nine classrooms over each of six years
Date: Summer 1990 to Summer 1996
Note: The observational figure for physical education is low because sampling was classroom-based only. However, it does reflect some class lessons in school halls where data-gathering opportunities were constrained

As Table 6.5 reveals, the core curriculum of English, mathematics and science was dominant in the classrooms observed. Irrespective of the age of the pupils being observed, it took approximately 60 per cent of all observed time throughout the period. However, it is also apparent that an early emphasis on literacy gave way to a significant growth in the time spent on mathematics and science. This can be related to public pressures through the period and the schedule for the introduction of assessment in science, but it was to lead later to public concern that the teaching of reading was being undermined by the National Curriculum. Our sampling and data-gathering methods were not appropriate to record accurately the very small amounts of time taken up by the other foundation subjects. Indeed, as the main focus of the curriculum, they managed to secure only 18 per cent of observed classroom time throughout Key Stages 1 and 2. In the case of history and geography, evidence from teacher interviews suggested that these subjects were often dealt with as topic work and 'blocked' into one part of the term as part of a rolling programme to ease pressure on resources. It is therefore possible that none would have been observed in any particular week. Interestingly, despite the teachers' perceived increased importance of technology and IT, evidence from classroom observation suggested that these subjects still did not take up a large proportion of curriculum time. Religious education was similarly small in its impact, averaging 2 per cent of time. However, this was augmented by acts of collective worship and school assemblies that were not recorded by the systematic observation.

6.5 DEARING REVIEW OF THE CURRICULUM CONTENT

Evidence from the first two phases of the PACE study highlighted the increasing frustration of teachers unable to ensure adequate delivery of an overloaded curriculum of ten subjects when they were also under pressure to ensure proper coverage of the 'basics' in literacy and numeracy. Issues of 'work intensification' and a general feeling of overload began to show themselves more clearly in the final phase of the study:

> My teaching lurches from panic to panic. I very rarely finish what I start doing. With science, for example, time runs out before you get to finish a certain topic, before the next class comes. We're so timetabled we don't have time to say, 'OK, we've got half an hour now. Please finish the science that you started yesterday.'   (Year 5/6 teacher, 1995)

However, as time went on, many teachers began a process of 'creative mediation' to help make space for themselves, as this quotation from another Year 5 teacher in 1995 illustrates:

> I felt mainly constraint at first. I've made more freedom for myself now. I found that every time we went on a course we were always looking at Attainment Targets and looking at levels. I was conscious of getting all that in rather than expanding on things. But I do expand on things now. If I omit something, I'd rather do it properly than try and fit everything in because there isn't time to fit everything in.

Complaints of the speed of new initiatives, the amount of paperwork to be absorbed and the inability of teachers to get their voices heard above the general critical clamour of the politicians and media were also becoming more apparent, as this quotation from a Year 4/5/6 teacher in 1995 shows:

> I think there are lots of other things that I've been affected by as a teacher – press reports and ... I mean, what did I hear this morning on the radio? About how they've done this four-year study and the standards in education are no better. You know, I find that absolutely galling and every other day there's something. That's what affects me – far more. I find that soul-destroying. I really do.

However, by 1993 there had been official recognition of the overloading of the curriculum (NCC, 1993; OFSTED, 1993), and a major review under the direction of Sir Ron Dearing was set up to look at the curriculum and assessment procedures. The review proposed a slimming down of the existing curriculum and an allocation of 20 per cent of the timetable to be given over to a curriculum determined by the individual school. These changes came into effect in the autumn of 1995, and the reactions of class teachers were investigated by the study. The reactions of a sample of 128 Year 4, 5 and 6 teachers are shown in Table 6.6.

Table 6.6 Key Stage 2 – teacher responses to the Dearing review of the curriculum (percentages)

Initial reactions to curriculum revision	
Approved	39.8
Mixed feelings	25.0
Makes no difference	25.0
Neutral/don't know	7.0
Disapprove	3.2
Manageability at upper end of Key Stage 2	
Manageable	25.0
Manageable with experience	15.6
Manageable with careful timetabling	20.3
Manageable with superficial coverage	10.2
Unmanageable, still overloaded	28.1
Don't know	0.8
	$n = 128$

Source: PACE 3 teacher interviews
Sample: 128 Year 4, 5 and 6 teachers in 48 schools in eight local education authorities
Date: Autumn 1995

Though nearly 40 per cent of the teachers approved of the revised curriculum, opinions differed as to whether there had been any real reduction in content, and 25 per cent of teachers considered that it had made no difference to their increased workload. Concerns as to the manageability of the curriculum remained. Whilst 25 per cent of teachers considered the revised version of the curriculum to be 'manageable', 16 per cent considered that it would be manageable once they had got used to it, a further 20 per cent considered that it would be manageable only with careful timetabling and 10 per cent considered that it was still so crowded that coverage would be superficial, restricting the extent to which they could extend and deepen pupils' knowledge. Twenty-eight per cent of teachers continued to consider the revised curriculum 'overloaded'.

When asked what use they were able to make of the 20 per cent of unallocated time, two-thirds of the teachers considered that it had made no difference to their planning, as the whole of the time available was still needed to cover all that was required of them in the National Curriculum. In response to the question of whether or not this 20 per cent allocation of time for local initiatives had made a difference, one Year 5/6 teacher replied:

> No, I just think there's just so much to fit in that it's not physically possible to have 20 per cent. I'd *love* 20 per cent. I think they probably get about 5 per cent a week ... but having said that, it's usually a finishing-off time when they get any work that they haven't finished in the week and try and get it done.

When pressed, however, 32 per cent said that it allowed them more time to go into greater depth with National Curriculum subjects, 24 per cent said that the extra time was spent on 'basics' (English and mathematics) and 19 per cent said that it enabled them to continue with activities such as school plays, assemblies and swimming which had been under threat because of time constraints. In some cases it gave back to teachers a small amount of freedom to build upon the experiences and interest of their pupils, which they considered had been compromised by the constraints of an overloaded, prescriptive curriculum.

6.6 CHANGES IN CURRICULUM PLANNING

Since the beginning of our study in 1989, it had become clear that one feature of the introduction of the National Curriculum had been the way in which teachers began to plan jointly and to work together more closely, particularly in year groups and Key Stages. Interviews with Key Stage 2 teachers in 1993 and 1995 showed an increase in the numbers of those giving importance to 'closer co-operation with colleagues', from 52 per cent to 63 per cent, and a similar increase concerning 'more careful planning', from 24 per cent to 39 per cent.

This change had been brought about largely as a result of the introduction of 'curriculum coordinators' for each of the subject areas, coupled with the need for schools to produce documentary evidence of their curriculum planning for OFSTED inspections: 'Documentation, including the school's curriculum policy, guidelines and schemes of work, is a starting point for evaluating whether the whole curriculum makes broad, balanced and coherent provision for all aspects of pupils' development' (OFSTED, 1995, p. 76). Most primary teachers now had additional responsibilities outside their classrooms to ensure the appropriate delivery, across the school, of at least one curriculum subject. This led to cooperation in both planning and teaching, but brought with it additional workloads. The primary Subject Coordinator's role was not clearly defined compared with that of the Head of Department role of a secondary teacher. There was not the same access to rooms or resources and no opportunity to recruit a specialist team to work with them. Implicit in the arrangement was the idea that the subject coordinator would have specialist knowledge that could be brought to bear in advising on, and supporting, curriculum development within the school. However, this did not always work smoothly, as this experienced Year 6 teacher explains:

> Although he was the science coordinator, I mean you get this with people, because they know a lot and they've got a lot of knowledge, they can't understand people who haven't got it. And they're not sympathetic either, I mean in the nicest possible way. You know, you'd ask for an explanation or help and they'd just prattle on and you were still floundering! I used to think 'Oh gosh, what is he talking about?'

Teachers in small rural schools felt these pressures most acutely because individual teachers needed to take responsibility for the coordination of more than one subject area. This quotation from a Year 5 teacher in 1995 illustrates the concern:

At the moment in school we've got all the policies that we are sorting out for OFSTED, so a lot of my time is taken up doing those ... I had written the IT policy and then the IT policy changed because of Dearing and things were taken out and things were amalgamated, and it was just like extra work on top of what you have got to do in a normal day ... they seem to think that I am going to be the 'all-knowing one' about IT and that I can solve any problem that they have got, and it has meant that I have been on a lot of courses ... they do tend to come to me more when things go wrong ... and ask for advice, which ties me up in another capacity ... And then, at the moment I am in the middle of sorting out the music policy because I have also taken on music as a coordinator, and so I am liaising with Key Stage 1 to try and set up a scheme of work ready for next year.

Though this collaborative planning brought structure and cohesion for some teachers, there was also evidence that some of the time taken in planning was regarded as a diversion from the actual job of teaching, as these quotations from Key Stage 2 teachers show:

Yes, we have had a whole session of our Inset [in-service training] which was talking about assessment and recording and planning – short-term plans and long-term plans. The way I work I have had to alter because it wouldn't be suitable for OFSTED. The way I do my short-term planning has changed. I tend to write down what I am doing now, whereas before I held it in my head, and I knew in my mind what I was doing. My medium-term plans and all the schemes of work that we have done, that I might not even use again, have had to all be put down on paper. I have referred to them, but I really feel it was a lot of time spent when I felt I could have used it in better ways.

and again,

Yes, there's a lot more paperwork required, so the workload has increased a hundredfold, really. And, I mean, sometimes you almost feel as though you don't have enough time just to give the kids because you're having to record everything, you're having to plan everything . . . we have to plan, but I still find that because of my experience, I often find the plans are restrictive, and I like to be sort of intuitive, far more than the plans would allow me to be. And I think the kids prefer it as well, in a way.

The lack of support available from some local education authorities (LEAs), a result partly of their restricted powers and limited budgets, and the difficulty in finding time and money for appropriate in-service training to help teachers cope with the changes, were also becoming important issues that hampered the development of effective curriculum planning and review. Lack of clear guidance on curriculum planning issues caused more uncertainty for teachers, as this quotation from a Year 6 teacher in 1996 illustrates:

The science is on its upheaval again. We began at the beginning of the year with the LEA document; they'd done a long-term plan for science, based on the new orders, and we did start working from that. And only by pure chance we discovered that two classes (different year groups) were going to be doing exactly the same over. You know, as luck would have it, they'd both started it at the same time and someone came and said, 'Well, who knows where I can find such a thing?' And one of my colleagues said, 'Well, *I* need that – why do you need that?'

Researcher: So the document was faulty?

So we abandoned that and we tried again with our own, where we actually cut up [the science curriculum] – we photocopied and cut up and sectioned out ourselves as to what we would like to do, so there wasn't repetition. And then we decided that that's no good, so we're on our third upheaval of the year, really. So I think everybody's fed up of it.

Curriculum documents were increasingly being used by teachers in both short- and medium-term planning, as the following quotation from a Year 5 teacher in 1995 shows:

The school week is actually timetabled out at the beginning of the year according to, I think it's the Dearing report: how much maths we should be doing, how much English, how much science and so on. So we break each subject up and spread it around the week. Hopefully, looking at the timetable, we should be teaching the correct amount of music, say. Then we take the Attainment Targets, rather we take the programmes of study in, say, science, and we share them out between the teachers and that's how we know which science topic we are going to do.

This process of 'cutting up' the curriculum documents is illustrated by one school's plan in Figure 6.1 showing how the science, geography, history and religious education curricula were determined. In the case of small rural schools, where at Key Stage 2 there were mixed classes of Years 4, 5 and 6, an even more complicated schedule of rolling programmes had to be devised, as illustrated by Figure 6.2.

Although there were still some examples of topic-based curriculum plans, as shown in Figure 6.3, evidence from teachers suggested that these were becoming much more difficult to sustain:

We've changed from a topic web, and seeing where it fits in, to actually looking at where it fits in first of all. The idea, when it first came out, was, yes, you can still do it, you can still plan your topic and if you have varied enough topics, at the end you will have covered enough. But I believe you can't. That's an impossibility.

At the time we identified science as being an area that needed to be looked at within the school as regards the National Curriculum ... every topic was a science topic and we fitted in everything around science ... and I had started to realize myself that this wasn't the right way ... It was probably good for us, making us look at science in more detail. But, say, I'd get a topic and I'd find the things that I could include in that topic would be things that a colleague had covered the year before, when I knew that other things needed to be covered. But we did decide, as a school, later on, that things needed to be altered, but I did find that year very hard, struggling against what I believed in and what I had to do.

6.7 CONTINUITY AND PROGRESSION

This closer cooperation of teachers in curriculum planning had also emerged because of the need to evidence the progression of pupils through the curriculum. This extract from the OFSTED handbook (1995) illustrates the pressure that had been brought to bear on schools through the new inspection process:

AUTUMN TERM – YEARS 5/6

SCIENCE

Pupils should be taught: **1. Electricity** c ways of varying the current in a circuit to make bulbs brighter or dimmer (D) d how to represent series circuits by drawings and diagrams, and how to construct series circuits on the basis of drawings and diagrams (E)	**2. Changing materials:** d that dissolving, melting, boiling, condensing, freezing and evaporating are changes that can be reversed (D) e about the water cycle and the part played by evaporation and condensation (D) f that the changes that occur when materials, *e.g. wood, wax, natural gas*, are burned are not reversible (E)
5. Living things in their environment Micro-organisms e that micro-organisms exist, and that many may be beneficial, *e.g. in the breakdown of waste*, while others may be harmful, *e.g. in causing disease*; (D/E)	**3. Separating mixtures of materials** d that solids that have dissolved can be recovered by evaporating the liquid from the solution (E) e that there is a limit to the mass of solid that can dissolve in a given amount of water, and that this limit is different for different solids (E)

GEOGRAPHY

THEME IV Environmental Change. **A** Work on geographical themes should be at local and national scales, including UK and European Union. These themes can be taught alone, in combination with other themes, or as part of studies of places. Thematic work should be set in the contexts of real places and use topical examples and geographical skills.	• how people affect the environment, *e.g. by quarrying, building reservoirs or motorways;* • different methods of environmental management or the special protection of specific environments by combating river pollution, by organic farming, by conserving landscape features of specific scientific value or beauty.

THE LOCAL AREA

		SOUTH WALES	
• human features, *e.g. housing* **A1** *estates, reservoirs;*	• recent/proposed **A1** changes;	• human features, *e.g. housing estates,* **A1** *reservoirs;*	• recent/proposed **A1** changes;
map skills, 4 figure grid co-ordinates, keys and symbols for weather and direction; OS maps and roads;	simple instruments: rain gauges, clinometers, compasses, questionnaires;	geographical vocabulary relevant to the understanding of features and places, *e.g. temperature, transport industry*	

A1 HISTORY 1995–6

In outline • The Roman conquest and occupation of Britain • The arrival and settlement of the Anglo-Saxons • Viking raids and settlements	**ANGLO-SAXONS:** outline • The arrival and settlement of the Anglo-Saxons and their impact on England • everyday life • the legacy of settlement

A2 HISTORY 1997–8

LIFE IN TUDOR TIMES: – Major events and personalities – The ways of life of people at different levels of society

RE CHRISTIANITY

Features of worship   Codes of conduct

Figure 6.1 An example of a Year 5/6 curriculum plan based directly on National Curriculum guidelines

Terms	1	2	3	4	5	6
KS2 Year a	GREEKS	LIGHT & SOUND B2	LANGUAGE	EARTH & BEYOND B1 B3	BRITAIN SINCE 1930	MAJOR ORGAN SYSTEMS A1
	Signs and Symbols	1a DT ELEC. CONTROL	Islam and Judaism 1d TEXTILES DT		Ourselves and the Community	1c FOOD DT
KS1	Ourselves MATERIALS	DT MECHANISMS Festivals and Celebrations TOYS	DT MOULDABLE MATERIALS Milestones in Family Life PIRATES/IRON AGE	Our World VARIETY OF LIFE	DT STRUCTURES People from Other Faiths HOUSES AND HOMES	Stories from the Hebrew Bible HOLIDAYS/THE ENVIRON. AREA
KS2 Year b	ANCIENT EGYPT	PATTERNS incl. MAGNETS	LANGUAGE	SOLIDS, LIQUIDS, GASES A3 A1 B3	PLANTS AS ORGANISMS A2	WELLS
	Life Stories 1b DT STRUCTURES		Writings 1f MECHANISMS		The Arts in Religion	1e MOULDABLE MATERIALS
KS1	DT FOOD Our Family OURSELVES	Jesus' Life LIGHT, SOUND AND COLOUR	DT MECHANISMS Special Books ON THE MOVE	Spring GROWING THINGS/ VICTORIAN VALLEY	Places of Worship JOURNEYS	DT TEXTILES Special Things ANIMAL HOMES/ FARMING
KS2 Year c	TUDORS	FORCES A2 A3	LANGUAGE	INDIA	WEATHER AND CLIMATE B3	PSE B1
	Life and Teachings of Jesus	1a ELEC. CONTROL	Hinduism	1d DT TEXTILES	A Religious Community	1c FOOD DT
KS1	Ourselves MATERIALS	DT MECHANISMS Festivals and Celebrations TOYS	DT MOULDABLE MATERIALS Milestones in Family Life PIRATES/IRON AGE	Our World VARIETY OF LIFE	DT STRUCTURES People from Other Faiths HOUSES AND HOMES	Stories from the Hebrew Bible HOLIDAYS/THE ENVIRON. AREA
KS2 Year d	TRANSPORT	SETTLEMENT	LANGUAGE	INVADERS AND SETTLERS	HABITATS AND MINI-BEASTS B2	HOME STUDY (LOCAL)
	Celebrating and Remembering 1f MECHANISMS		Christianity 1e DT MOULDABLE MATERIALS		The Natural World	1b STRUCTURES
KS1	DT FOOD Our Family OURSELVES	Jesus' Life LIGHT, SOUND AND COLOUR	DT MECHANISMS Special Books ON THE MOVE	Spring GROWING THINGS/ VICTORIAN VALLEY	Places of Worship JOURNEYS	DT TEXTILES Special Things ANIMAL HOMES/ FARMING

Figure 6.2 An example of a curriculum plan used in a small rural school with mixed-age classes, which is based around a four-year cycle

Language	AT	Lv	Mathematics	AT	Lv
Listening/speaking – Greek myths and legends, retelling/drama/puppet shows etc.	1	3–4	Geometry – angles, measurement, Pythagoras	1, 3	3–4
Understanding of genre – legend, myth, fable etc.	2	3–4	Number bonds – use of abacus	1, 2	3–4
Creative writing – urban myths, hero/heroine stories, poetry	3	1, 2, 3, 4	Money – decimals, multiplication and division, algebra	1, 2	3–4
Research skills – use of thesaurus	2	3–4	Shape – all aspects	1, 3	3–4
Spelling – Spelling Made Easy	3	3–4	Data – revision of all aspects	1, 4	3–4
Handwriting – Charles Cripps and poetry anthology	3	3–4	General revision in preparation for SATs	1	3–4
Personal topics	1, 2, 3	All			

Science	AT	Lv			Geography	AT	Lv
Materials – properties and their uses.	3	2–5	**TOPIC** **ANCIENT GREECE**		Location of ancient Greece – in place and time		
• investigations	1	2–5			Climate, agriculture, economy		
• collections					Trade, sea etc.		
• comparisons			**Visits/Visitors**		Describe features of life in		
• fair tests					Athens, Sparta – compare		
• changing state					town to country		
• solids, liquids, gases					Collection of pictures		
					Map to show journeys of		
See separate sheet					heroes and heroines		

IT and Technology	AT	Lv	Art and Design	History	AT	Lv
Continue and develop LOGO skills.			Look at Greek art and practice silhouette designs	Time-line of ancient Greece and main events		
• make own program, simple design.			Understand symbolism in Greek art – idea of pictures telling stories	Understand and describe features of the ancient Greek period		
• simple design for Greek structure.			Create modern-day version (with urban myth?)	What do we know about the ancient Greeks? Significance		
Design and produce puppets and show for myths			Pottery – make figure of mythical hero/heroine – plate or goblet?	How do we know? Sources of evidence		
Design a poster for tourism, Olympics etc.				Explain causes of events		
				Influence of Greeks on other civilizations and modern world		

RE	AT	Lv	Music	PE, Movement and Drama
Beliefs and symbolism of the ancient Greeks			Sing songs from memory	Continue – ball skills – cricket, rounders etc.
Compare with contemporary religions			Develop breathing, pitch and rhythm	Olympic games – in teams, devise and plan a mini-Olympics
Festivals, customs, sacrifice			Rehearse and share music-making	Dance – focus on folk dancing
Bible aspects for Christian input			Compose music for puppet shows and perform to it.	Gymnastics – focus on coordination and balance
				Athletics
			PHSE	
			Drug awareness evening	
			Personal hygiene and fitness	
			Transfer to secondary school	
			Reflection on primary school	
			Areas of friendship	

Figure 6.3 An example of a Year 6 curriculum plan based around a single topic

Inspectors should evaluate whether curriculum planning takes account of what has gone before and what will follow. The need for continuity and progression applies between years, between key stages and between schools. Evidence is needed of whether, as pupils move through the school, the curriculum builds systematically on existing knowledge, understanding and skills.   (OFSTED, 1995, p. 77)

When Key Stage 2 teachers were asked in 1993 and 1995 which elements were important in ensuring continuity and progression they highlighted the themes shown in Table 6.7. These data point to an increase in whole-school planning through a 'planned sequence of topics', 'pupil portfolios of work' and 'structured schemes of work'. They also point to an increase in communication between teachers when pupils moved classes, from 16 per cent to 24 per cent. This combination of information helped schools provide evidence of individual, as well as year group, continuity and progression, which is what OFSTED inspectors were looking for.

Table 6.7 Key Stage 2 – continuity and progression between classes as perceived by teachers (percentages)

	1993/4		1995/6
	Y3	Y4	Y4
Planned sequence of topics – school-wide	24.4	22.5	29.5
Discussions with previous/next teacher	19.3	15.5	23.8
Pupil portfolios of work	8.9	8.5	12.4
Structured schemes of work	6.7	5.6	13.3
Mixed-age classes	3.7	9.9	13.3
Continuity difficult	11.1	4.2	2.9
Other	0.7	3.5	4.8
No response	25.2	30.3	0.0

Source: PACE 2 and 3 teacher interviews
Sample: 92 Year 3 and 4 teachers, 46 Year 4 teachers in 48 schools in eight local education authorities
Date: Autumn 1993, Autumn 1995

Evidence from teacher interviews also confirmed a more systematic approach to ensuring continuity and progression in the curriculum, which had previously been difficult to establish:

I would definitely look at another teacher's records before I started, and use those. I'm not saying I wouldn't look before, but now I look at them in more detail and think about them for my planning. Because, before, I would perhaps think it doesn't matter if they do the same thing twice, if they're experiencing it in a different way and getting something from it. But now, in order to get everything in, I try not to do anything twice unless it's a child who's not achieved and needs more experience.   (Year 5 teacher, 1995)

6.8 CLASSIFICATION ISSUES: SINGLE SUBJECTS AND INTEGRATED TOPIC WORK

The issue of single-subject teaching in preference to integrated topic work had been the focus of considerable public debate and became an increasingly important issue for teachers as the age of the children in the study increased. In an epistemological sense, the question concerns the degree to which the curriculum can be 'classified' under separate subject headings. Differing views of the extent to which knowledge can be divided into discrete subject areas creates different 'education codes', which in turn make concrete a particular ideological view.

In the late sixties, the Plowden Report (CACE, 1967) had been instrumental in moving practice towards a more integrated, 'topic work' approach to knowledge within primary schooling. However, by the nineties, after sustained criticism from ministers and many in the media, the report of Alexander *et al.* (1992) presented the most direct challenge to teachers' established practice by asserting that 'a National Curriculum conceived in terms of distinct subjects makes it impossible to defend a non-differentiated curriculum' (p. 17). Again, an implied pressure from inspection also had an influence in this area:

> Many primary schools use topic work as a major mode of curriculum organization. Topics may be broad-based or have one subject as the major focus, particularly at KS2. If topics are broad-based, inspectors should evaluate how effectively they are planned to cater for the intended programmes of study and whether they provide a clear structure and sufficient progression.   (OFSTED, 1995, p. 77)

Evidence gathered in the early part of the study suggested that, as a result of the implementation of the National Curriculum, teachers were beginning to move to a more subject-based form of delivery, building on what was regarded as 'common practice' in the case of mathematics and English. In the latter part of the study, teachers were asked for their reactions to the balance of single-subject and integrated topic teaching which they currently employed (Table 6.8). These data point to a major increase in single-subject teaching at the top end of Key Stage 2 and a dramatic fall in the incidence of integrated work, from 41 per cent in 1993 to 5 per cent in 1995. Again, this was probably the result of a combination of factors: both the introduction of a subject-orientated curriculum and the advancing years of the pupils. During interviews, teachers described this change as partly a function of their planning processes, which originated in the subject-specific schemes of work. It also helped to ensure that all attainment targets were covered for all children, which was becoming increasingly important so that pupils would be able to perform as well as possible in their SAT tests. However, the following quotation from a Year 5 teacher in 1995 illustrates the tension that remained for teachers:

> Yes, I think it's the National Curriculum that's forced us to look at subject teaching. Can I take geography, for example? It's very, very difficult to integrate some of the geography into anything else. It's totally separate so you have to teach separate little units. I don't think that's the school's choice. I think the choice has been made for us. I suppose I got away with it when I first started working here because people weren't that fussed about

Table 6.8 Balance of single subjects and integrated topics as perceived by teachers (percentages)

	Key Stage 1	Key Stage 2	
	1993/4 Y1/2	1993/4 Y3/4	1995/6 Y4/5/6
Mainly integrated	40.7	27.8	5.3
Basics only as single subjects	25.4	21.3	6.7
Even mix	17.8	15.7	8.2
Mainly single subjects	15.3	26.8	42.3
Some topic/integrated work planned	0.0	0.0	36.1
Other	0.8	1.9	1.0
No comment	0.0	6.5	0.5
	$n = 88$	$n = 92$	$n = 128$

Source: PACE teacher interviews
Sample: 88 Year 1/2 teachers, 92 Year 3/4 teachers, 128 Year 4/5/6 teachers in 48 schools in eight local education authorities
Date: Autumn 1993, Spring 1994, Autumn 1995

> the National Curriculum but as time's gone on it's become more and more pushed to the forefront of things.

Again:

> Some things I like formally teaching, so there are certain things, and I think the children like knowing which subject they're doing. But, on the other hand, it's taken a lot of enjoyment out of it. It's very much more prescribed and, before, I used to sort of ... if the children were enjoying something, I would continue it, bringing in other subjects into it, and if they looked bored I would give it up and tackle it from a different view.

However, there was also some evidence that history and geography, in particular, continued to be dealt with in an integrated, topic-based way, often as a result of limited time and lack of resources, though the balance here varied from school to school.

6.9 SUBJECT CONFIDENCE

The majority of teachers interviewed were happy with the increased emphasis on single-subject teaching. However, it did begin to raise questions of confidence and ability in relation to the depth of subject knowledge needed by teachers at the top end of Key Stage 2. These findings were supported by other studies such as those of Wragg *et al.* (1989), Moses and Croll (1990), Osborn and Black (1994), which also raised concerns over the increasing depth of subject knowledge required. In our sample a high proportion (65 per cent) of teachers of pupils in Years 4, 5 and 6 said that they were 'not confident' in some areas of the National Curriculum, while only 14 per cent declared themselves to be 'very confident'. The subjects where teachers had least confidence were music (30 per cent), science (26 per cent) and technology

(23 per cent). A further 23 per cent of teachers considered that they required more resources and support in certain areas of the National Curriculum.

When teachers of pupils in Years 4, 5 and 6 were asked, in the Autumn Term of 1995, whether they thought that there was a place for subject specialist teaching in primary schools, 48 per cent agreed and an additional 30 per cent agreed in the case of certain subjects. Not surprisingly, the subjects where teachers considered that subject specialist teaching would be most helpful were technology (34 per cent), music (30 per cent) and science (19 per cent), as this quotation from a Year 5 teacher in 1995 illustrates:

> I think that the subjects that we've been teaching for ever, like English and maths, they're OK. I'm thinking more of the newer subjects like design and technology. I'm supposed to be the IT coordinator and I don't know how to work half of the computers when they go wrong. In the States they have specialist peripatetic teachers who come in to do drama, PE and art. Although I'm not asking for drama, PE and art, I think we could have the same thing in perhaps design technology and IT. Those two subjects would help enormously if we had ... and perhaps music as well. Yes, music definitely.

However, 24 per cent of teachers were concerned about the loss of contact with their class which a move to subject specialist teaching would entail. To this end, 23 per cent of teachers preferred a system of supportive subject specialist teaching, where subject coordinators came into the class to teach alongside the class teacher. This was in preference to a system where individual teachers specialized in a particular subject and moved between the classes as they do in secondary teaching. Issues to do with size, location and pupil intake, together with the type of initial training of staff, were found to be crucial in creating differences between schools. Overall, 47 per cent of Year 4, 5 and 6 teachers interviewed in 1995 reported some subject specialist teaching taking place in their schools. This seemed to occur largely as a result of individual agreements between teachers and was not a specific policy decision made by the school.

Generally speaking, however, teachers were largely resistant to a move towards a secondary model of organization for the curriculum, which agrees with the findings of other studies (Osborn and Black, 1994). The only exceptions to this were the five middle schools in the sample, where a combination of class teaching and subject specialist teaching was used to great effect, with teachers being able to draw on the additional resources available to them. The case study of Greenmantle School in Chapter 9 illustrates how one school was handling the issue of subject confidence through increased specialization.

6.10 DIFFERENTIATION AND EFFECTS ON DIFFERENT GROUPS OF CHILDREN

It is clear from Table 6.9 that the groups of children which teachers considered to have benefited most from the introduction of the National Curriculum had been girls, high attainers and average attainers – though it is interesting to note that a lower percentage of teachers felt this to be so as the study progressed. In the early stages of the study, teachers had felt children with learning difficulties and emotional difficulties to be disadvantaged. However, this feeling diminished as the study progressed, possibly owing to related changes in the provision for special educational needs. The number of teachers who considered that children with learning difficulties had particularly benefited from the National Curriculum actually went up from 20 per cent in 1993 to 33 per cent in 1995. Teachers in the study were unsure about the benefits or otherwise for children from ethnic minorities, and this might be a reflection of the lack of schools in our sample with significant ethnic minority populations.

6.11 CONCLUSION

The values that underpinned the creation of the National Curriculum also had a fundamental influence on the changing role of the teacher. There was a tension between an understanding of education as the inculcation of established knowledge and its definition as a process of helping learners to construct their own insights and understanding. A view of curriculum knowledge as being 'strongly classified' and 'established' tends to devalue the professional pedagogic skills of the teacher by implying that the 'delivery' of the curriculum is largely unproblematic, giving rise to a heavily prescribed, 'teacher-proof' curriculum. In contrast, however, a view of the curriculum as being 'weakly classified' and 'constructed' by the learner emphasizes the teacher's professional skills, judgement and understanding, and places the focus on the quality of the learning experience.

With the introduction of the National Curriculum came concerns that it would result in a more restricted conception of the curriculum. Teachers feared that they would be forced to adopt a narrower set of objectives for the children, centred on academic goals rather than those of personal and social development. In other words, there were concerns that there would be a shift from the 'expressive' to the 'instrumental' (Bernstein, 1975). Whilst the discourse associated with the introduction of the National Curriculum had emphasized the provision of a 'broad and balanced' curriculum, and specialist subject working parties had created detailed programmes of study for each subject, there was some evidence that primary school teachers felt constrained by the core curriculum. National debates focused on 'basic skills', and public tests of pupil performance, through which teachers and schools were to be held accountable to parents, constantly drew teachers back to English and mathematics.

However, the structure of the curriculum and the emergence of 'subject coordinators' also increased the incidence of joint planning found in our sample schools. Despite the fact that this often resulted in 'work intensification' and consequent frustration, it also enabled teachers to be more systematic about the way they approached continuity and progression for both individual pupils and year groups. The Dearing review of the curriculum, though welcomed, was considered not to have gone far enough, and teachers continued to be concerned about the superficial coverage of much of what they did.

Integrated topic work became increasingly difficult to sustain and the pressure of

Table 6.9 Which groups of children have benefited/been disadvantaged by the National Curriculum?

	Particularly benefited			No particular benefit			Disadvantaged			Not sure		
	1994 Y1/2 KS1	1993 Y3/4 KS2	1995 Y4/5/6 KS2	1994 Y1/2 KS1	1993 Y3/4 KS2	1995 Y4/5/6 KS2	1994 Y1/2 KS1	1993 Y3/4 KS2	1995 Y4/5/6 KS2	1994 Y1/2 KS1	1993 Y3/4 KS2	1995 Y4/5/6 KS2
Girls	28.4	47.8	23.5	59.1	42.4	66.4	–	1.1	–	8.0	8.7	9.2
Boys	13.6	17.4	5.0	76.1	72.8	80.7	–	2.2	0.8	5.7	7.6	11.8
Ethnic minorities	11.4	9.8	5.0	14.8	8.7	25.2	13.6	21.7	14.3	55.7	58.7	49.6
High attainers	60.2	65.2	37.8	19.3	21.7	38.7	9.1	5.4	6.7	5.7	7.6	16.0
Average attainers	38.6	45.7	23.5	42.0	39.1	59.7	6.8	9.8	5.0	8.0	5.4	10.9
Learning difficulties	22.7	19.6	32.8	17.0	10.9	21.8	44.4	60.9	29.4	11.4	8.7	14.3
Emotional difficulties	6.8	4.3	5.9	19.3	15.2	26.9	40.9	44.6	21.8	27.3	35.9	42.0
	n = 88	n = 92	n = 119	n = 88	n = 92	n = 119	n = 88	n = 92	n = 119	n = 88	n = 92	n = 119

Source: PACE teacher interviews (1993 and 1994), teacher questionnaires (1995)
Sample: Key Stage 1 and 2 teachers in 48 schools, in eight local education authorities
Date: Autumn 1993, Spring 1994, Autumn 1995

dealing, in depth, with all nine curriculum subjects produced some support for the introduction of a limited system of 'supported' subject specialist teaching. Teachers were, however, generally resistant to any increased move towards a secondary model of class teaching, which would cause them to lose close contact with their pupils.

Chapter 7

Teachers and Pedagogy

7.1 INTRODUCTION

In this chapter we consider teachers' views of their practice and how it had changed as a result of the reforms. There was concern in some areas that the introduction of a tightly prescribed national curriculum, combined with a system of externally driven national testing, could limit the ability of both teachers and pupils to be flexible in their approach to learning. Evidence from PACE 1 had shown that there was an increasing tension for teachers in dealing with an overcrowded, subject-orientated curriculum which was regulated through national testing, and a more flexible pedagogical approach. Lack of time could lead teachers to seek to control and structure pupil time and learning behaviour to a greater extent than before, creating what Bernstein (1975) referred to as a 'strong frame' for classroom pedagogy. This allowed less scope for self-directed, independent and flexible activity for both teachers and pupils because issues of the selection, organization, pacing and timing of the ways in which knowledge was presented to the learner needed to be more strictly managed. Bernstein argued that this could both reduce 'the power of the pupil over how he [sic] receives knowledge', on the one hand and, at the same time, reduce the scope of teachers to exercise professional judgement in the selection of appropriate learning tasks for individual children.

These concerns continued to manifest themselves in the data that we collected as we progressed through PACE 2 and PACE 3. We continued to investigate the relationship between policy change and the extent to which classroom activity was being framed by teachers by investigating the timing and contexts in which teaching was taking place, the organization of classroom activities, in terms of the use of both space and resources, and teacher strategies for the grouping of pupils. These data collected through observation and interview were augmented by classroom observation of both teachers and pupils.

7.2 PERCEIVED CHANGES TO CLASSROOM TEACHING

First, we wanted to know from the teachers themselves how they perceived the impact of the recent changes on their current classroom teaching.

Table 7.1 Teacher perceptions of change in teaching approach (percentages)

	Key Stage 1			Key Stage 2	
	1990/1 R/Y1	1992/3 Y1/2	1993/4 Y1/2	1993/4 Y3/4	1995/6 Y4/5/6
None or very little	58.0	49.5	17.0	17.4	45.3
Moderate change	15.9	33.3	15.9	23.9	22.7
Considerable change	22.7	12.9	52.3	46.7	28.9
Not answered newly qualified teachers	3.4	4.3	14.8	12.0	3.1
	$n = 88$	$n = 93$	$n = 88$	$n = 92$	$n = 128$

Source: PACE 1, 2 and 3 teacher interviews
Sample: 48 schools in eight local education authorities
Date: Summer 1990, Summer 1992, Autumn 1993, Spring 1994, Autumn 1995

In 1993 and 1994 both Key Stage 1 and Key Stage 2 teachers were reporting 'considerable change' (52 per cent and 47 per cent, respectively). However, the figure for Key Stage 2 teachers had dropped dramatically to 29 per cent by 1995, with 45 per cent saying there had been 'none or very little' change (Table 7.1). This seems to suggest that changes to pedagogy had been at their height three or four years after the 1988 Education Reform Act had come into effect but that by 1995 these changes had, to some extent, become incorporated into what teachers regarded as their normal practice.

To understand exactly what had changed for teachers we needed to look at their more general comments, which are listed in Table 7.2. Teachers identified the content of the curriculum, the nature of assessment and the need for more systematic, detailed record-keeping as being areas of particular change in practice during the initial years. However, these issues had dropped dramatically in their significance by 1995. Increased involvement with colleagues, though initially important, dropped steadily across the years, whereas an increase in the incidence of curriculum planning

Table 7.2 Teachers' perceptions of change in teaching approach – open-ended comments (percentages)

	Key Stage 1			Key Stage 2	
	1990/1 R/Y1	1992/3 Y1/2	1993/4 Y1/2	1993/4 Y3/4	1995/6 Y4/5/6
Content of curriculum	35.2	51.6	53.4	53.3	9.4
Nature of assessment	29.5	38.7	21.6	18.5	3.9
Nature of record-keeping	26.1	39.8	10.2	10.9	3.1
Increased involvement with colleagues	19.3	14.0	8.0	8.7	6.3
More planning	18.2	30.1	25.0	20.7	16.4
More conscious of own practice	13.6	15.1	20.5	17.4	30.5
Less child-centred methods	13.6	22.6	15.9	12.0	8.6
More structured, subject orientated	–	–	17.0	27.2	15.6
Less opportunity for creative, expressive	–	–	9.1	6.5	3.1
More aware of need for differentiation	–	–	–	–	16.4
More whole-class teaching	–	–	–	–	22.7
Other	29.5	11.8	9.1	17.4	25.8
No comment	20.5	11.8	21.6	17.4	30.5
	n = 88	*n* = 93	*n* = 88	*n* = 92	*n* = 128

Source: PACE 1, 2 and 3 teacher interviews
Sample: 48 schools in eight local education authorities
Date: Summer 1990, Summer 1992, Autumn 1993, Spring 1994, Autumn 1995
Note: Totals do not equal 100 per cent as teachers responded to an open-ended question and identified up to four changes

seems to have peaked in the middle years and dropped back to 16 per cent by 1995. By 1995, Key Stage 2 teachers considered that the major areas of change in practice centred around a more structured, subject-orientated curriculum (16 per cent), the need to allow for differentiation in learning tasks (16 per cent) and the use of more whole-class teaching (23 per cent). Almost a third (31 per cent) of Key Stage 2 teachers in 1995 considered that they were now more conscious of their own practice and were continually reviewing the appropriateness of their own pedagogy.

7.3 TEACHERS' VIEWS ON PUPIL AUTONOMY

In order to establish a baseline prior to the introduction of the National Curriculum it had been necessary to examine some of the research findings of the 1970s and 1980s with regard to teachers' beliefs about children's learning and how those beliefs translated into pedagogy and classroom practice. This has been reported more fully in *Changing English Primary Schools?* (Pollard *et al.*, 1994a). However, in summary, research conducted before the introduction of the National Curriculum had shown that, despite commitments to a child-centred philosophy, most teachers emphasized basic skills and attempted to solve the dilemma of competing ideologies and pressures by drawing upon a mixture of teaching methods.

These competing pressures continued to be a feature of the teachers' pedagogical approach. Many teachers in our study felt that pupils should have some classroom autonomy, within the context of a clear organizational structure, to increase motivation, allow for a more worthwhile learning experience and to enable pupils to become independent learners in the future. However, they also expressed a concern that the pressure of needing to cover the whole of the National Curriculum meant that the actual control that they could allow pupils over their learning was in fact very limited. The following quotations were typical of the way in which teachers expressed this desire to allow pupils some control over what, and how, they learned, together with the frustration which the pressures of a tightly prescribed National Curriculum imposed:

> A lot, definitely. At the end of the day they are going to leave this environment – to spoon-feed a child in education, I feel, is not going to help them when they leave. There are so many decisions that they have to make for themselves that the earlier they learn to make decisions the better, and the earlier they learn to act upon their decision-making and the consequences of their decision-making, the better.   (Year 5/6 teacher, 1995)

and again:

> I think they [the pupils] should have more [autonomy] than they've got. It's been my experience that children have learnt more when they're interested in something. Some of the topics that we are being forced to teach are really not at all interesting for 10- to 11-year-olds. For the time we spend doing them, they don't get enough out of it.
>
> (Year 5/6 teacher, 1995)

Pressure from the demands of an overloaded National Curriculum were creating a situation where teachers found it increasingly necessary to direct pupil activities, creating, in Bernsteinian terms, a 'strong frame' to their teaching approach. Many teachers would allow pupils free choice when they had finished all the set work required of them, but this often took the form of a 'finishing off' period at the end of the week. However, it was also apparent that the teachers in the study continued to be uneasy about this inherent contradiction in their pedagogical approach. The following quotation highlights this tension which many teachers felt between the need to allow pupils choice and the need for teachers to manage pupil learning to ensure adequate coverage of the National Curriculum:

> I've said this before, but having taught fairly formally, then probably I give the children less time to choose than some teachers do. I believe that the teacher should lead from the front, so to speak, and be quite clear and direct regarding what the children are expected to do and the standards expected from them. But yes, I still believe that the children should have choice. They enjoy having choice. I don't think I'd be able to put a sort of percentage to it but there should be some choice.
>
> For example, in The Earth and Beyond, which I think is the title of the science I'm doing at the moment, there will be a section when they're invited to choose a planet and find out about that planet, to choose a star constellation and research that.

Researcher: But they can't choose to cover a completely different subject?

No. There is . . . on Friday afternoon after games, I have a session from 2.00 to 3.15 and I call it 'finishing off', and there is an element of choice there.   (Year 5/6 teacher, 1996)

The extent to which pupils preferred to manage their own learning has been more fully reported in *Policy, Practice and Pupil Experience* (Pollard *et al.*, 2000) but, in summary, it is helpful to make the following observations. As the study progressed, and the children grew older, there was an increasing preference on the part of pupils for their teachers to choose work for them. At Key Stage 1 the reasons which pupils gave for preferring to choose tasks for themselves included having more fun, being able to avoid things they did not like, or found hard, and being able to choose what they liked best. As they got older, evidence suggested that they adopted more instrumental strategies to their learning, which avoided risk and helped to accommodate the progressive challenges that they faced at school. As with other studies (West, Hailes and Sammons, 1997), the data suggested that pupils' preferences for different activities were connected to such issues as interest versus boredom, success versus failure, and the level of difficulty. Pupils in the PACE project appear to have found it increasingly more efficient to be teacher dependent to ensure that the work that they did was appropriate and would lead to 'success', as defined by their teacher. Another important reason for preferring their teacher to choose work for them was the perception of time as a limited commodity and the need not to waste it. This has clear resonances with the teachers themselves, who often justified their need for a tighter pedagogic frame in terms of its being necessary to cover all the work prescribed in the National Curriculum.

7.4 TEACHING METHODS

Most teachers in the study reported that they used a mixture of teaching methods, though they reported an increase in the incidence of whole-class teaching as the study progressed. This could be a response to the pressures of the National Curriculum but it could also have been a function of the increasing age of the pupils in the study.

Teachers were asked to quantify their use of various teaching methods (individual work, collaborative group work and whole-class teaching) as a percentage of their total teaching time. In Figure 7.1 we see that collaborative group work and individual work predominated at Key Stage 1, with 53 per cent of teachers using collaborative group work during more than 50 per cent of the teaching time in 1989–90 and 48 per cent of teachers reporting that they used individual work for more than 50 per cent of the teaching time in 1991–2. However, at Key Stage 2 a more mixed pattern of teaching approaches was reported, though whole-class teaching and individual work were reported by a higher proportion of teachers as being the predominant teaching method as compared with collaborative group work. Teachers reported that lack of resources, pressure of time and the need for differentiation conspired to create a situation where whole-class teaching, often at the beginning of a lesson, followed by individual work was the most common way of working. Some teachers reported that lack of time, together with a lack of space and resources, sometimes meant that some work, such as experimental science, which could be more

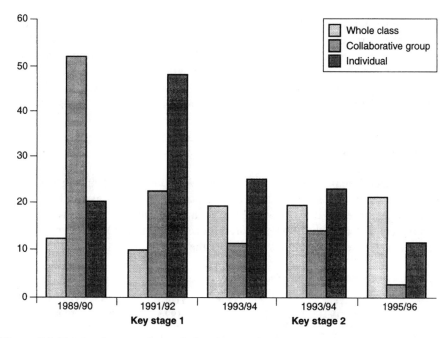

Figure 7.1 Teachers' perceptions of the changes in the predominant methods of teaching (percentages of teachers stating that they use a particular teaching method for more than 50 per cent of class time)

usefully done in groups was compromised.

Evidence was also gathered through systematic classroom observation. Teachers in 54 classrooms in nine schools over the six-year period of the project were observed using the observation schedule shown in Chapter 2. These data, shown in Table 7.3, also confirmed an increase in whole-class interaction, particularly in Year 6, when

Table 7.3 Main teaching contexts (percentage of observed time)

	Key Stage 1		Key Stage 2			
	1990/1 Y1	1991/2 Y2	1992/3 Y3	1993/4 Y4	1994/5 Y5	1995/6 Y6
Whole-class work	34.9	33.3	31.9	27.8	26.0	37.4
Group work	25.6	23.6	11.1	6.6	7.7	9.2
Individual work	31.0	30.9	43.8	45.7	51.9	39.3
Pedagogic mix	8.5	12.2	13.2	19.8	14.2	14.1

Source: PACE 1, 2 and 3 teacher systematic observation
Sample: 54 Year 1–6 classrooms in nine schools in eight local education authorities
Date: Summer 1991 to Summer 1996

preparation for Key Stage 2 national testing was evident. More striking, however, is the marked reduction in group work and the increase in individual work. The evidence from interviews with teachers confirms that although this is partly a function of the increasing age of the target children, it is also to do with the pressure to cover the National Curriculum and the restraints of its testing procedures. However, there is also evidence that a more integrated mix of teaching contexts continues to be used in primary classrooms, particularly at Key Stage 2, where between 13 and 20 per cent of observations recorded a context of 'pedagogic mix'.

7.5 TYPE OF TEACHER ACTIVITY

The type of teacher activity was also recorded every ten seconds during periods of teacher observation. A relatively simple classification system was used which, in particular, highlighted a distinction between task instruction, task direction and disciplinary control (see the Appendix for more details). Table 7.4 reveals some significant developments over the six years of the PACE project.

Table 7.4 Observed teacher activities (percentage of observed time)

	Year 1 1991	Year 2 1992	Year 3 1993	Year 4 1994	Year 5 1995	Year 6 1996	Mean
Instruction	37.2	45.5	46.0	40.0	60.2	63.4	49.6
Direction	35.8	32.5	31.6	38.2	24.2	20.9	30.0
Control	10.4	6.0	6.8	5.9	6.1	5.7	6.7
Assessment	7.2	3.9	5.6	6.9	5.2	5.3	5.7
Encouragement	5.1	6.4	4.3	4.3	2.2	1.1	3.7
Hearing pupils read	4.0	5.4	5.2	3.4	1.2	3.1	3.6
Negative comments	0.2	0.4	0.6	1.2	0.9	0.6	0.7

Source: PACE 1, 2 and 3 teacher systematic observation
Sample: 54 Year 1–6 classrooms in nine schools in eight local education authorities
Date: Summer 1991 to Summer 1996

In particular, the amount of 'task instruction' rose dramatically in Years 5 and 6 to around 60 per cent of teacher activity, compared with approximately 40 per cent in Years 1 to 4. About half of this time replaced 'task direction' activities, perhaps suggesting a lessening need to explain how to carry out tasks with older pupils. Understandably, the time spent hearing pupils read also decreased as the pupils grew older, but so too did teacher activity coded as 'encouragement'. This was always a small percentage, but it gradually fell from 5 per cent in Year 1 to just 1 per cent in Year 6. Overall, teacher activity concerned with disciplinary control was fairly consistent, averaging some 7 per cent.

Teacher activity was also coded during child observation when the teacher interacted directly with 'target' pupils. One-to-one pupil–teacher interaction amounted to just 3.4 per cent over the whole study. However, on such occasions the proportion of 'task instruction' was particularly high at 63 per cent. These data, in line with similar studies (Galton *et al.*, 1999), describe a considerable increase in the proportion of teacher activity spent in active instruction. This suggests that primary classrooms have become more intense places pedagogically, with a higher proportion of time being used for direct teacher instruction.

7.6 CLASSROOM ORGANIZATION AND PUPIL GROUPING

We were also interested to know what strategies teachers used in organizing their classrooms and whether these had changed in any way in response to the introduction of the National Curriculum. Our data, in Table 7.5, show that teachers

Table 7.5 Criteria teachers used for pupil grouping (percentages)

	Key Stage 1			Key Stage 2	
	1990/1 R/Y1	1992/3 Y1/2	1993/4 Y1/2	1993/4 Y3/4	1995/6 Y4/5/6
Attainment groups	79.5	82.8	95.5	94.5	93.7
Mixed ability	59.0	72.0	87.5	81.5	95.3
Friendship groups	62.6	67.8	71.6	84.8	81.3
Gender groups	13.7	9.7	12.6	14.0	32.0
Vertical age groups	20.4	24.8	25.0	24.9	34.4
Homogeneous	44.3	16.2	65.9	56.6	73.5
	n = 88	*n* = 93	*n* = 88	*n* = 92	*n* = 128

Source: PACE 1, 2 and 3 teacher interviews
Sample: 48 schools in eight local education authorities
Date: Summer 1990, Summer 1992, Autumn 1993, Spring 1994, Autumn 1995
Note: Totals do not equal 100 per cent as teachers reported more than one strategy

continued to use a range of strategies for grouping pupils within their classes. Most teachers used a combination of both attainment and mixed ability groups, as well as an increasing use of friendship groups as the children matured. The issue of gender grouping is an interesting one, with a sharp rise reported in 1995 from some top junior teachers, though others continued to use mixed groupings to aid discipline and enhance integration, as the following comment from a Year 5/6 teacher in 1995 illustrates:

> I don't group them ever according to ability. I tend to sit them girl, boy, girl, boy, purely from the discipline point of view, and I think it does them good to work with children of the opposite sex anyway.

When Key Stage 2 teachers were asked in 1995 what factors they took into consideration when grouping children within their classes the four major influences expressed were the ability spread (67%) and the behaviour (64%) of the children in their class, the nature and purpose of the learning task (53%) and the availability of resources (52%). To a lesser extent, considerations such as the shape and size of the classroom (32%), the teacher's own experience (25%) and the number of children in the class (18%) were also taken into account. Very few teachers (5%) considered that recent educational changes had had an influence on their classroom organization;

the main influence by far was the children themselves. This meant that teacher strategies for classroom organization could change from year to year, with similar criteria being applied differentially depending on the characteristics of a particular group of pupils.

7.7 CHANGING RELATIONSHIPS WITH PUPILS

For Key Stage 1 and Key Stage 2 teachers, the years 1992–3 and 1993–4 respectively were when most teachers reported a negative effect on their relationship with the children (Table 7.6). There is some evidence that Key Stage 2 teachers experienced

Table 7.6 Teachers' perceptions of changes in the quality of relationships between teachers and their pupils (percentages)

	Key Stage 1			Key Stage 2	
	1990/1 R/Y1	1992/3 Y1/2	1993/4 Y1/2	1993/4 Y3/4	1995/6 Y4/5/6
Positive	10.2	6.5	17.0	14.1	15.6
Negative	30.7	58.1	29.5	42.4	32.8
Little or no change	45.5	35.5	40.9	32.6	38.3
Mixed/don't know	13.6	–	12.5	10.9	13.3
	n = 88	*n* = 93	*n* = 88	*n* = 92	*n* = 128

Source: PACE 1, 2 and 3 teacher interviews
Sample: 48 schools in eight local education authorities
Date: Summer 1990, Summer 1992, Autumn 1993, Spring 1994, Autumn 1995

the most pressure on relationships with children a year later than their colleagues at Key Stage 1. This is probably a result of the progressive way in which the changes were introduced. However, despite the changes, a group in excess of one-third of teachers reported policy initiatives as having 'little or no change' with regard to their relationship with their pupils. Some teachers regarded recent policy changes as having a positive effect on relationships, a figure which increased over time at both Key Stage 1 and Key Stage 2, perhaps showing a relaxation in the pressure on teachers' time as they adjusted to, and accommodated, the changes.

   The number of teachers commenting that their relationship with pupils was being defended because they considered it to be so important declined dramatically in the later years of the study (Table 7.7). However, Key Stage 2 teachers were more confident than Key Stage 1 teachers that their relationships were not being threatened by the changes. This is probably to do with the differing expectations and ideologies of the two sets of teachers, as an experienced Year 5/6 teacher explained when asked whether recent developments had affected the teacher's relationship with the pupils:

No, I think from the children's point of view, very little has changed. Possibly when teachers are feeling stressed because of the National Curriculum pressures, then that might have an ongoing effect with the children – a knock-on effect, I mean. But generally speaking, very little.

Another experienced Year 5/6 teacher, when asked the same question, responded similarly but showed some concern for younger, more inexperienced teachers:

That's an interesting one – No. But I can see situations where it could, and I think possibly with younger teachers it has been. I think because I've tried to keep a balance of view of the changes, I think the last thing to be affected would be my relationship with the children.

Table 7.7 Additional comments made by teachers (percentages)

	Key Stage 1			Key Stage 2	
	1990/1 R/Y1	1992/3 Y1/2	1993/4 Y1/2	1993/4 Y3/4	1995/6 Y4/5/6
Pressure on teacher time	40.9	60.2	27.3	40.2	19.5
Feelings of stress	31.8	45.2	22.7	17.4	7.8
Defended because of importance	22.7	32.3	11.4	3.3	11.7
Not threatened by changes	9.7	6.5	8.0	14.1	13.3
May be threatened by future changes	13.6	5.4	–	2.2	1.6
By assessment	2.3	8.6	1.1	4.3	0.8
Lack of respect from children to others	–	–	–	–	28.9
	$n = 88$	$n = 93$	$n = 88$	$n = 92$	$n = 128$

Source: PACE 1, 2 and 3 teacher interviews
Sample: 48 schools in eight local education authorities
Date: Summer 1990, Summer 1992, Autumn 1993, Spring 1994, Autumn 1995
Note: Totals do not equal 100 per cent as teachers responded to an open-ended question

Table 7.7 shows that the 'pressure on teachers' time' and their 'feelings of stress' both declined as a reason for damaged relationships between teachers and pupils, and this may have been the result of an accommodation on the part of teachers together with an easing of pressure as a result of the Dearing review. However, many teachers were still referring to feelings of pressure, and arguing that it affected their relationship with the children adversely.

An important new category of concern which emerged in the final round of data collection with Year 6 teachers referred to the lack of respect which pupils showed not only towards their teachers and authority, but also to their peers. Some teachers were concerned that an often fragmented, stressful and uncertain home life, together with a lack of time and space for pupils to interact freely between themselves, was impinging on pupils' ability to come to terms with the positive type of relationships necessary for success at school. As one deputy head pointed out:

Table 7.8 Contrasting aspects of 'competence' and 'performance' models in relation to teachers' pedagogy

	Competence model	Performance model
Teacher pedagogy	'Invisible pedagogies' with weak classification and frame	'Visible pedagogies' with strong classification and frame
Space	Flexible boundaries and use	Explicit regulation
Time	Flexible emphasis on present experiences	Strong structuring, sequencing and pacing
Activity	Emphasis on the realization of inherent learner capabilities through subject-integrated and learner-controlled activities, such as projects	Strong control over selection of knowledge and explicit promotion of specialized subjects and skills
Pupil autonomy	Considerable	Limited
Evaluation	Emphasis on immediate, present qualities using implicit and diffuse criteria	Emphasis on inadequacies of the product using explicit and specific criteria

> Teachers would like to think it [the relationship with children] hasn't [been affected] but teachers are now under more pressure to give evidence and this inevitably means that they put more pressure on the children. They are also overworked and more tired and this affects their relationship with their class.

She went on to say that she had suggested to the headteacher that a playroom/sitting room be created in the school so that class teachers could take groups of their children in and watch and talk to them as they played. This would allow teachers to chat to children about their lives and to help them play with each other, and could be valuable in helping them to learn and to overcome some of the pressures that existed in the classroom.

7.8 CONCLUSION

Overall, these findings suggest that teachers and pupils in the 1990s experienced an increasingly pressured classroom context, where the proportion of instruction and whole-class teaching grew at the expense of a more interactive pedagogy. Taking this together with other studies (Alexander 1991, 1995, 1997; Galton *et al.*, 1999) and expressing it in Bernsteinian terms, it appears clear that the framing of pupil activity through teachers' classroom pedagogy has tightened over the past twenty years, supported and enhanced by changes with the 1988 Education Reform Act. Classroom practice in primary schools is more intense and more teacher controlled. Pupils are less autonomous in their use of space and time and in their choice of activity. Gradually, from Year 1 to Year 6, the extent of teacher control and classroom framing increased as the study progressed. In part, as we have seen, this may be attributed to new curriculum requirements and pressures from the media and government ministers to which teachers felt a need to respond. However, the tightening of pedagogic frame can also be seen as a response to new assessment and inspection requirements which appear to have impacted on the time and space available for teachers to interact in more informal ways with their pupils. These changes can be illustrated by contrasting aspects of a 'competence' model with those of a 'performance' model in relation to teachers, classrooms and their pupils.

A more content-heavy and less 'creative' curriculum, together with more emphasis on individual rather than collaborative ways of working, appear to be changing the emphasis of primary pedagogy. This, in turn, is diminishing the opportunities for teachers to develop and maintain the affective dimension in their pedagogy, which has had consequences for both the job satisfaction of teachers and the learning strategies of pupils.

Chapter 8

Teachers and Assessment

8.1 INTRODUCTION

During the course of the PACE project, the policy discourse of education had begun to shift increasingly towards an emphasis on the use of formal testing and target setting, both to help raise standards and to ensure accountability. As these two extracts from the party manifestos published prior to the 1997 general election show, this emphasis was common to both the main political parties:

> Regular tests and exams are essential if teachers are to discover how much their pupils have learnt ... Rigorous tests show how individual children and schools are performing and expose schools that are not giving children the education they deserve ... We will now go further and require every school to set, and publish, regular targets, and plans for improving their academic results. (Conservative Party, 1997, pp. 21–2)

> Nearly half of 11-year-olds in England and Wales fail to reach expected standards in English and maths ... far too many children are denied the opportunity to succeed. Our task is to raise the standards of every school ... Every school needs baseline assessment of pupils when they enter the school, and a year-on-year target for improvement ... No matter where a school is, Labour will not tolerate under-achievement.
> (Labour Party, 1997, pp. 7–8)

This discourse is uncompromising and, as a result, it can be argued that it was the advent of national testing, with its emphasis on explicit learning targets and overt assessment criteria, which has had, and continues to have, the most profound effect on primary schooling over the past decade. Not since the end of the eleven-plus examination in the 1970s had primary schools in England and Wales been required to put so much emphasis on this element of classroom practice. Primary teachers were required to alter their existing assessment practice in quite radical ways, as this extract from the *Guidance on the Inspection of Nursery and Primary Schools* illustrates:

> Inspectors should evaluate whether assessments are accurate and used to plan future work to help pupils make progress. They need to establish whether teachers' assessments relate accurately to National Curriculum requirements, and external validation arrangements where these apply.   (OFSTED, 1995, p. 78)

This combination of the publication of individual school results, together with teacher accountability through a new form of school inspection carried out by the Office for Standards in Education (OFSTED), had far-reaching effects on the process of assessment within the study schools.

The introduction of more rigorous assessment of subject knowledge, as specified by the National Curriculum, represented a move in the direction of overt and explicit assessment. Following the work of the Task Group on Assessment and Testing (TGAT, 1988) there were to be two forms of assessment: teacher assessment (TA) and Standard Assessment Tasks (SATs). To provide clear sets of assessment criteria, the National Curriculum was expressed with *levels*, *attainment targets* and *statements of attainment* for each subject. In the very early 1990s many teachers hoped to be able to develop TA as formative assessment, and to build it as an integral part of their classroom practice. However, the demand for 'consistency' in comparative assessments (SCAA, 1995a) generated an enormous demand for detailed paperwork as teachers attempted to develop record-keeping systems and 'collective evidence' to support their judgements. As each National Curriculum subject was successively introduced, the scale and complexity of the activity threatened to overwhelm teachers, and Gipps *et al.* (1995) report that teacher assessments in the early days often remained intuitive rather than being evidence based. From 1990, when Key Stage SATs began to be piloted and implemented, their requirements for standardization challenged the values of many teachers. The further requirement on teachers in Years 2 and 6 to aggregate their assessment for each Attainment Target, for each of the three core subjects, for each child into a National Curriculum *level* which was to be reported alongside each child's SAT results was seen as an attack on teacher professionalism.

8.2 TEACHER ASSESSMENT

Teacher Assessment and the findings from PACE 1

The findings of the initial PACE study (Pollard *et al.*, 1994a) reported that the majority of Key Stage 1 teachers, questioned in 1991 and 1992, did not feel that National Curriculum assessment had significantly changed the classroom climate.

achers felt that the constraints of reporting children's achievement
format of the new requirements prevented them from showing a
ual, and hence diagnostic, picture of a child's different achieve-
it classroom prior to the 1988 Education Reform Act the approach
been largely intuitive and continuous, with the central purpose of
providing instructional feedback and encouragement. The requirements of the 1988
Act required teachers to develop their assessment repertoire considerably so that it
included not only diagnostic and formative assessment but also summative and
evaluative assessment activity, which emphasized the explicit categorization of
pupils' achievement.

The initial dislike of this new requirement, particularly in the case of primary
teachers, was not due simply to the increased workload or the need for additional
skills which some did not possess. It had as much to do with the fact that the coercive
power of the law had been used to impose on teachers an obligation to
operationalize a different set of understandings concerning the role of assessment
in helping children to learn and develop. In the first PACE book (Pollard *et al.*,
1994a) we offered a framework for considering a transition in the forms of
assessment that appeared to be occurring (Table 8.1). It characterized teachers'
ideological views on assessment as focused around three main dimensions: *frequency*,
purpose and *mode* (see also Broadfoot, 1996a).

Table 8.1 Mode, purpose and frequency of assessment

	Assessment to support the construction of knowledge	Assessment to monitor the acquisition of established knowledge
Mode	Covert/intuitive	Overt/explicit
Purpose	Encouragement/guidance	Accountability
Frequency	Continuous	Intermittent

Source: Pollard *et al.* (1994a, p. 190)

In 'ideal type' terms, it is possible to identify, at one end of the continuum, a
developmental, 'Plowdenesque' ideology, with a conception of education as the
provision of a curriculum ladder individual to each child. In this model, teacher
intervention is designed to support learners in constructing progressively higher
levels of knowledge and understanding. At the other end of the continuum is a view
of assessment linked to an 'elementary' ideology of primary education with a
conception of education as the initiation of children into a corpus of established
knowledge. This ideology is readily associated with both didactic pedagogy and the
'carrot-and-stick' approach to assessment, with its emphasis on competition and
sanctions. Most teachers' assessment practice will be informed by a mixture of
pragmatism and habit, as well as educational philosophy.

A changing assessment discourse

In the two previous PACE books (Pollard *et al.*, 1994; Croll, 1996) we described the tension being experienced by teachers as they perceived themselves to be under pressure to move from their preferred assessment stance of 'diagnostic discourse' – a constant, intuitive and covert monitoring of individual pupils' activities – to a much more explicit, externalized and even categoric approach to assessment. Typically, teachers felt that such deliberate assessment activity, which also included substantial amounts of recording, produced quantities of 'dead data' (Broadfoot, 1996a) – information which was too general and inaccurate to be of any great use in informing teaching or progression from year to year. This sentiment was clearly echoed in the words of one Key Stage 2 teacher interviewed more recently in 1996:

> we've joked about this … We had at one time, when the National Curriculum first came in, we had observation sheets and you had to sort of write down. We had these sort of running jokes about you'd sit there and you'd be looking at your class closely to see when they grasped the importance of a full stop or something and it would be like a scene from a Hollywood film where the light would come on above their head or something. Then, of course, they would have forgotten five minutes afterwards.

However, as Table 8.2 shows, the general attitude of Key Stage 2 teachers changed as they became both more practised in the new procedures and more skilled in the required assessment processes. Especially in the light of the Dearing review, teachers became increasingly positive about the more structured and formal approach to pupil assessment.

Table 8.2 Key Stage 2 teachers' feelings about the teacher assessment they are required to carry out (percentages)

	1993/4 Y3/4	1995/6 Y4/5/6
Generally positive	15.2	34.4
Neutral	10.9	14.8
Generally negative	44.6	21.1
Mixed: likes and dislikes	29.3	28.9
	$n = 92$	$n = 128$

Source: PACE 2 and 3 teacher interviews
Sample: 92 Year 3 and 4 teachers, 128 Year 4, 5 and 6 teachers in 48 schools in eight local education authorities
Date: Autumn 1993, Autumn 1995

In their general comments, teachers of pupils in Years 4, 5 and 6, interviewed in 1995, demonstrated less antipathy to the amount of writing involved (i.e. recording) than had teachers of Years 3 and 4 in 1993. There was also a corresponding increase in the number of teachers who perceived such assessment to be 'useful' (22 per cent in 1993, 40 per cent in 1995). However, there were some differences in relation to the catchment area of the school and the length of experience of the teachers. Teachers in affluent areas and those with six to ten years' experience were, typically, the most positive, whilst teachers in inner-city schools and those with over twenty years' experience were the most negative. The most often-stated reason for disliking assessment procedures remained the amount of recording required and the consequent loss of teaching time.

In 1993, very few teachers in our sample planned for assessment, but, perhaps as a reflection of the influence of OFSTED, as well as the pressure exerted by the introduction of Key Stage 2 SATs in 1995, this became much more common as the study progressed, as this Year 5 teacher explained:

> I tend to plan to do an assessment at the end of a piece of work – once we've covered all the things we think we need for that assessment, then we'll do it at the end of the piece of work.

Significantly, however, a substantial number of teachers in 1995 (19 per cent) considered that they required further training in assessment procedures and moderation techniques, and there was some evidence that there was confusion among teachers about who was driving assessment policy:

> *Year 5/6 teacher*: There seems to be a lot more emphasis on formal testing and accountability. There seems to be an awful lot of bits of paper in my cupboard for each child with ticks and crosses and filled-in boxes, hanging around in my cupboard.

> *Researcher*: And is all this directly related to the National Curriculum requirements?

> *Year 5/6 teacher*: I'm not quite sure where all this comes from. It's partly the government saying, 'You must have records', and the county saying, 'This is an example of what we think you should do', and the headteacher saying, 'This is what the county have given me, perhaps we could do this.' So I guess that's the route it's taken. Some of it we do and some of it we don't do. Some of it we've done and abandoned because it was just unworkable and time-consuming and not particularly useful.

The provision of training was something that distinguished Key Stage 1 teachers from Key Stage 2 teachers in 1993 and we anticipated at the time that this would inhibit the realization of the full professional potential of teacher assessment.

Teachers' main concern was still the time-consuming nature of assessment, so that they were left with far less time to do other things (20 per cent). Nevertheless, Key Stage 2 teachers in 1995 appeared to recognize that, to a greater or lesser extent, their assessment practice had significantly changed their approach to teaching. It had helped to identify clearer aims for their teaching (60 per cent), whilst at the same time it provided more detailed knowledge of their pupils (24 per cent). These benefits were reflected in the following criterion used by OFSTED inspectors to judge the effectiveness of class teachers:

> Judgements about assessment should focus on how well the day-to-day interventions with pupils, including the marking of work, are used to help them understand what they need to do to improve their work and make progress.   (OFSTED, 1995, p. 71)

and the following quotation is evidence of a comparable change in the assessment discourse of some teachers:

Well, it's to point you where you're going next. We tend to do it to get evidence of what they've done because I have to keep evidence but really it should be to indicate where the difficulties are and what you should do next.

Again:

It forms the basis of your future planning, has to; if you don't know where the children are now, through assessment, you won't know where to take them on to. Teachers have always done it but in a very sort of vague, lackadaisical way.

The concern over accountability and the need to evidence their assessment procedures were also more prominent in teacher discourse as the study progressed, together with a growing acceptance and ability in this area:

I'm more *aware* of it and therefore I've got to make it ... write it down, shall we say, whereas a few years ago I would have kept things in my head. If someone said, 'How's such and such?' and you say, 'Well they were doing well in this, that and the other.' I think I'm more aware that it's got to be written down, that it's not good enough just ... or even to keep it on scraps of paper that are going to get lost. It's got to be kept a more permanent record and it has to be updated. I've got to be aware of when children are actually changing, which took me a while to get used to, I think, to actually realize that children were improving.

Again:

I'm clear about what I'm ... what my aims are first of all, which then helps me to see whether those have been achieved, and also I've got a better understanding of appropriate achievement at each level. You know, I've become more familiar with what to expect for Level 2, Level 3, Level 4, which has helped enormously, because you always feel whether your views are matched by other staff. And also, we've had days to compare each other's work. We've had a recent staff meeting on it which was very useful, especially looking at language work which can be sometimes quite difficult. I'll actually have assessment time now. We'll do it as a lesson in a way. They sit down and I say, 'Right, well, what do you know about this? Can you fill this in and do this?'

Nevertheless, the commitment to a more child-centred, contextualized assessment discourse was still much in evidence with some teachers, as the following quotation from an inner-city teacher illustrates:

Well, obviously it [assessment] has to be there but I think teachers have always done that. This is the argument, isn't it? Possibly you're doing sort of internally ... you have these sort of ... you know each child and you know what they're capable of. This is why, I suppose, if it came to choice I would obviously be in favour of teacher-based assessment rather than external things. External things obviously have a part to play because somebody outside needs to know how the children are getting on, how a school is delivering, but I think the important bit should be the individual teacher. And maybe that's especially in a school like this because, I don't know, but you probably get the feeling that in a way we become almost more involved than most schools with the families, with the backgrounds of the children and therefore there's so many things you have to bear in mind when you judge a child. Sometimes you forget and then you sort of feel guilty afterwards. That's why I think what we know about children is so important.

For most teachers, 'assessment' remained an integral part of the ongoing, minute-by-minute decision-making business of teaching. However, whilst the meaning of assessment for most teachers was still largely intuitive monitoring, there were signs that this aspect of teachers' assessment discourse was giving way to a recognition of the value of those more formal and explicit activities specifically designed to collect external evidence of achievement. There was, for example, a growing emphasis on working with pupils on a one-to-one basis.

Developing procedures for teacher assessment

To help teachers develop more detailed procedures for evidencing pupil progress, the School Curriculum and Assessment Authority (SCAA, 1995b) issued guidelines to help them. The stated wish was not to 'limit teachers' professional discretion' with respect to how they should record their judgements on pupils' progress, nor how they should gather evidence and apply it. This, the documentation suggested, would depend to a large extent on the size and type of school, number of staff and pupils and how the school was organized. However, it did encourage teachers to moderate their decision-making with other teachers in their school as well as with teachers in other schools in the area. This, government documentation maintained, would promote a 'shared understanding' and give teachers more confidence in their decision-making.

As the study progressed, and the influence of OFSTED and SCAA became more pronounced, schools began to produce written assessment policies enabling them to evidence a coherent and consistent approach to the recording of pupil progress through teacher assessment. By 1995 only 1 school in our sample of 48 did not have, and was not currently developing, a whole-school assessment policy, whereas 20 schools said that they already had a whole-school policy in place and 27 said that they were currently developing one. An analysis of the policies which were collected from the study schools revealed the following types of evidence which teachers were being encouraged to collect for each child in their class:

- individual reading record;
- individual maths record;
- child's grouping for maths/English and other subjects, if appropriate;
- child's portfolio containing samples of work;
- teacher assessments plus task or test results; and
- National Curriculum summary record, showing work covered and individual progress.

Much of this evidence would have been collected by teachers prior to the 1988 Education Reform Act. However, there was evidence that these records became more detailed and more directly tied to National Curriculum Attainment Targets as the study progressed. When asked to outline their major assessment procedures, teachers responded as shown in Table 8.3. These responses demonstrated a substantial, and increasing, use of explicit formative approaches such as pupil self-assessment and the use of individual pupil portfolios, which were initiated by teachers with the explicit intention of encouraging both pupils' meta-cognitive skills and their self-esteem. It is the importance of these associated motivational benefits that is described in the following quotation from a Year 4/5/6 teacher in 1995:

> I think things like self-assessment are a good thing because it focuses the children's minds on ... if they have to think of something that's good about a piece of work, they often say 'Oh, I can't do that', 'I can't do that', well they're forced to say, 'Well, what's good about this?' and at least they're thinking that there's something positive in it. And I try with my conferences to ... well, I'm talking about their talks and so most of that will be positive so they can see that even though they're not the best in the class there are things that they can do. And I give certificates for being able to look after the plants or trying at something, even though in the end it's not very good, if there's any kind of improvement.

Table 8.3 Assessment procedures used by teachers (percentages)

	1993/4 Y1/2	1995/6 Y4/5/6
Listening to/observing children	70.5	52.3
Tasks planned specifically	63.6	51.6
Regular spelling tests	33.0	60.9
Pupil self-assessment	23.9	33.6
Selection of work for portfolios	20.5	28.1
Oral questioning	19.3	10.9
Regular maths/tables tests	18.2	43.8
Structured maths scheme	9.1	21.1
Structured reading scheme	10.2	10.9
Hearing reading	–	14.1
Standardized tests	9.1	15.6
Marking work and recording	–	40.6
Other	12.5	4.6
	$n = 88$	$n = 128$

Source: PACE 2 and 3 teacher interviews
Sample: 88 Year 1 and 2 teachers, 128 Year 4, 5 and 6 teachers in 48 schools in eight local education authorities
Date: Spring 1994, Autumn 1995

However, with the increasing age of pupils and pressure of national testing there was also, perhaps predictably, a noticeable decrease in the use of more formative approaches to assessment, such as listening and observing (71 per cent in 1993–4, 52 per cent in 1995–6). These responses may, however, have masked the fact that, whilst these assessment activities still took place, the new discourse of a more active assessment strategy was beginning to take over.

This changed discourse also finds its expression in the higher incidence of a more formal use of assessment, with a marked increase in the percentage of teachers saying that they made use of regular, formal spelling and maths tests, as well as marking work and recording. This supports Harlen and Qualter's (1991) findings on teachers' perceptions of what counts as teacher assessment. They found that this perception that only relatively formal assessment 'counts' had caused teachers to introduce a whole new element into their teaching rather than build upon the implicit assessment which was already a part of their practice.

This inherent conflict in teachers' views over what constituted good teacher assessment was, initially, most keenly felt by Year 2 and Year 6 teachers at the point at which they were required to include a teacher-assessed *level*, for each of the three core subjects, in each of their pupils' end-of-Key Stage reports for parents. An experienced Year 6 teacher in 1995 explained that 'this term, teacher assessment, it used to frighten the life out of me'. The official advice to teachers concerning 'statutory teacher assessment' (SCAA, 1995) was that they were not expected to gather extra information for making end-of-key Stage decisions. Rather, they were expected to make use of evidence gathered during ongoing classroom assessment, using all the knowledge which teachers had built up of a child's work 'over time and across a range of contexts to balance different aspects of a pupil's performance' (p. 4). The document goes on to recognize that this is not a precise science but more a matter of professional judgement, with the teacher determining which *level description* best fits the pupil's performance. However, for the experienced Year 6 teacher referred to above, this translated itself into something more instrumental and categoric, as her continuing statement, in response to a question concerning her assessment practice, shows:

> With their English work as well, sometimes I set a piece of creative writing for a particular purpose. I tell them what I'm going to look for. I say, 'Right, I'm looking for how you plan it, how you lay it out, remember paragraphs.' Not necessarily grammar and punctuation but the purpose and organization. Then the next time it will be grammar. But I tell them before they write the piece that that's what I'm looking for, so that hopefully they can focus a bit as well. Then I give them a mark out of five, which is kind of a level to tally with the SATs. But that's partly for my help, my assessment of where they are. So when the results [of national SAT tests] come back, I can see how they relate.

An analysis of school policy documents also reflected a lack of precise definition, as the following example shows:

> At the end of Key Stages ... a judgement will be made about which level best describes each child. This will be done for each Attainment Target. The process is essentially a little fuzzy, no descriptor will usually completely fit – it's a process of finding the one which fits best. In coming to these judgements, teachers will rely mainly on records of assessments they have made about progress with learning objectives as set out in their planning and the relationship with level descriptors as evidenced by examples of pupils' work.

When Year 6 teachers were asked what evidence they used to assign levels for the three core subjects at the end of Key Stage 2, the answers displayed an underlying uneasiness: 'In terms of teacher assessment, I think you take the broad guidelines and hang it on them somewhere.' 'I ability-group for maths and then, when the class has been broken down into those groups, I look at the work, I look at what they've understood and what they haven't understood and I base my levels on that. It's just knowing the work of the children.' Another teacher emphasized that his decision-making was based on the past work of the children and not what they could do in a single test:

> I'll be able to say, 'Yes, he can do Level 3, Level 4, things on Shape and Space, and work out area using formulae, because he's done it in his book.' The test doesn't necessarily show that he can, but I've seen him do it, so I know he's done it. That would influence me there.

However, another Year 6 teacher was far less confident:

> Well, they work in their books. I suppose I use some reflection sheets that they use, that they do. We use – well, we haven't done, but we're hoping that the evaluation books that they're keeping are going to be of use to us in our reporting to parents and this sort of thing as well. The pupil profile sheets that I have, sort of up to date, they're going to help – they should help!

And then again, another Year 6 teacher was very clear about how he would arrive at his judgement:

> We obviously keep all of their books and I think our marking has become more assessment orientated, so obviously the books themselves are a document. They're a useful means of coming to a decision about the level and the various test results that we've had throughout the school. We also do the mock SATs tests, that we do at the beginning of the summer term, they're quite a useful aid to teacher assessment.

This quotation raises the question of the relationship between the statutory teacher assessment level and that which the pupil gains as a result of taking the Standard Assessment Task/Test. The rhetoric is clear: that the judgements made by teachers at the end of the Key Stage have 'equal status with test results in all forms of public reporting' (SCAA, 1995). However, as far as schools were concerned, a discrepancy between the two presented them with a major problem, as this Year 6 teacher explained:

> What the problem was last year, we were worried there would be confusion between slightly different scores between our assessment and what the children scored in the SATs. As it turned out, most of the numbers were reasonably spot on.

Some schools, in the study, chose to present the two sets of levels to parents without comment, whilst others considered it necessary to draw attention to and explain these differences. Again there was evidence that teachers considered that their professional judgement was being undermined.

The usefulness of teacher assessment records

From our evidence, the issue of the usefulness of other teachers' assessment records in aiding continuity and progression appeared to be a difficult one in practice. There was little evidence of teachers using such records to inform teaching in a constructive way, with only one-quarter of Key Stage 2 teachers in 1995 regarding them as 'very useful'. A Year 5 teacher explains:

Well, when I first started they had the assessment book and I looked in that but I didn't find it helpful at all because it was just stars and, you know, they'd achieved it, and it didn't mean a lot to me at all because basically you want to get in the classroom and find out for yourself.

This approach was supported by evidence of the 'clean slate' view, which maintained that there could be real differences in achievement when pupils change class and teacher. These have been described more fully in the PACE 1 book (Pollard *et al.*, 1994a).

Similarly, the results from Key Stage 1 national testing were also seen to have limited value:

It's got *limited* use for me because they're very *cold* levels and they don't, as they stand, tell me a great deal. I would rather have a detailed piece of writing. I've got the SAT writing, the draft writing, which was useful, but the actual levels are very cold, I like more depth really.

On the other hand, the authenticity of 'real work' and the increasing use of individual pupil portfolios provoked a much more positive reaction from teachers:

Very helpful ... we've just started portfolios where we keep two samples of work from each of the core curriculum areas, I think those will be useful in the future. Two pieces of language, two pieces of maths and two pieces of science which are annotated in great depth, and allocated a level. But we also keep records of achievement, so we keep various examples of work and it might be really good illustration, or a piece of history work, or maybe even best copies of work and that's been useful just to look back and see whether what *you're* getting is what ... it's just really the children's development. And that stems back from, you know, Reception and goes throughout the school ... the files follow them through and so on.

Again,

Especially now that they're being annotated in depth, that's what's really useful. We just started this term; we had, take for example, a piece of writing. They did a draft piece of writing and then you give that a level and then you annotate it according to SAT criteria. Rather than just give it a level, you go through it.

8.3 NATIONAL TESTING

Teachers' experience of Standard Assessment Tasks (SATs)

Alongside the changes which had been taking place in terms of teachers' ongoing classroom assessment practice and in the use of records, there had also been the imposition of 'high stakes' external tests at the end of Key Stage 1 (Year 2) and Key Stage 2 (Year 6). Again this was linked to a specific criterion within the inspection process, as this extract from the documentation shows: 'Inspectors must report, firstly, on how the attainment of pupils at each stage of education compares with national averages in terms of results in key stage tests and assessments' (OFSTED, 1995, p. 55). Evidence from the PACE project suggested that this emphasis on externally set and marked tests for the purposes of public accountability has had a significant effect on both classroom practice and the primary curriculum.

A comparison with Key Stage 1 SAT testing

At the end of PACE 1, when our pupil cohort had taken their Key Stage 1 SATs, we reported on the extent of the manageability of the SATs, the level of standardization achieved and their impact on pupils (Pollard *et al.*, 1994a). Then, as now, the SATs at Key Stage 1 were very different from those at Key Stage 2. They were designed to be similar to normal classroom tasks and hence to be capable of being integrated almost indistinguishably for pupils into normal classroom routine. They were commonly acknowledged to have had, in consequence, a high degree of validity but they also had enormous variations in manageability and standards (Abbott *et al.*, 1994). The PACE team concluded (Pollard *et al.*, 1994a, p. 225) that the SATs did not provide well for any of the purposes originally envisaged for them. These included diagnostic and formative purposes, to enhance teaching and learning; summative purposes, to report on an individual pupil's attainment at a given stage of schooling and evaluative, as aggregated data for comparing school standards. The SATs were neither sufficiently integrated into the curriculum nor timely enough to be capable of being useful to inform teaching, yet neither were they reliable enough to provide for effective communication about individual or institutional achievements. In effect they fulfilled neither the 'curriculum' nor the 'communication' (Broadfoot, 1996b) functions of assessment. Furthermore, they provoked considerable opposition among teachers in terms of teachers' lack of professional control; the categorization of pupils; the inappropriate use of assessment results to inform competition between parents and schools; the undesirable effects of assessment on the curriculum; the unfairness of certain SATs for certain children; the arbitrary procedures of aggregation and moderation; and the lack of genuine formative value as a result of all these impositions.

As the project progressed we had the opportunity to observe and interview teachers and target pupils as they took part in Key Stage 2 SATs in the Spring Term of 1996. These SATs differed from the Key Stage 1 SATs in that they were centrally set paper-and-pencil tests taken by the entire cohort on prescribed days during a particular week in May. Owing to teacher union opposition to the extra workload, the papers were despatched from schools to be marked externally and the results returned to schools in due course. This dislocation of testing and marking gave rise to an increased tension for both teachers and their pupils, and an explicit concern from some pupils that they would 'fail' the tests. The effect of SAT testing on pupils is more fully discussed in *Policy, Practice and Pupil Experience* (Pollard *et al.*, 2000).

Procedural manageability of SAT testing at Key Stage 2

There is no doubt that from an operational point of view, the manageability of the Key Stage 2 tests, based on written papers marked externally, substantially reduced the organizational problems which were evident in our earlier study of the implementation of Key Stage 1 testing in 1992. Key Stage 1 SATs require the tasks to be carried out with small groups of pupils by the class teacher. They were, and continue to be, largely 'performance' based and required a large input of teacher time and effort in organizing and assessing individual outcomes.

In contrast, our data collected during the 1996 Key Stage 2 SATs show that the majority of Year 6 teachers responsible for Key Stage 2 testing considered the organizational process to be either 'very manageable' (29 per cent) or 'fairly manageable' (64 per cent) (Table 8.4). This would appear to be an improvement even on the essentially similar format of 1995 in which a third of teachers studied in an ATL survey (1996) said they were concerned about workload.

Table 8.4 Teacher perceptions of manageability of SATs in terms of demands placed on their time (percentages)

	1992 Key Stage 1 SATs	1996 Key Stage 2 SATs
Very manageable	16.0	29.0
Fairly manageable	73.0	63.8
Not at all manageable	11.0	5.8
Nil response	–	1.9

Source: PACE SAT questionnaires
Sample: 47 Year 2 teachers in 48 schools in eight local education authorities, 51 Year 6 teachers in 48 schools in eight local education authorities
Date: Summer 1992, Summer 1996

However, there was also evidence of concern on the part of some teachers, focused around the increased burden of paperwork involved in the SAT administration:

> The week itself, the testing during the week, went very smoothly. The children didn't seem unduly stressed. They coped with them quite well. I found the administration, the sending off of the material a nightmare. I didn't enjoy that part of it. And I also found organizing the tasks (for lower-attaining pupils) quite a hassle because I just didn't have the time to do them myself and in the end we employed a classroom assistant, albeit a university student who was out of work, to do the tasks.

This begins to raise the question of reliability in the application of the tests. Within the PACE sample of schools there was considerable variation in the way the tests were administered. Some of the larger schools brought the whole age cohort together to complete their written papers, under exam conditions, in the school hall. In smaller, rural schools pupils often completed their tests in their classroom, accompanied by their class teacher. In schools where there were mixed-age classes, difficulties of organization were evident, which some teachers considered to be to the disadvantage of the Year 5 pupils:

> It [SAT testing] really did disrupt the Year 5s ... It meant for at least a whole week while the Year 6s went out, the Year 5s didn't carry on the timetable as usual. We tried to keep it as normal as possible but obviously we couldn't carry on with our topics because the Year 6s weren't there. And that was just for the actual week when the Year 6s were out. We'd had a lot of preparation up to then. (Year 5/6 teacher, 1995)

Content validity and reliability of SAT testing at Key Stage 2

Year 6 teachers in the PACE sample showed a growing accommodation of the SAT content for the 1996 tests, though there were some reservations, particularly relating to the testing of English and science. Teachers were concerned in the case of the Writing SAT that children were asked to produce a piece of creative writing around a given story title and were not able to make use of drafting or editing, as they would in the normal classroom situation. They also considered that Attainment Target 1, 'Speaking and Listening', was not being tested. Again, in the Science SAT they considered that no provision had been made for Attainment Target 1, 'Experimental and Investigative Science', and that in general the test was too knowledge based.

Some teachers also echoed the concerns contained in a recently published report (ATL, 1997) which judged nearly two-thirds of the questions in the English reading test to have been unclear. The report suggested that 'poorly chosen language' meant that many questions were misleading. In addition, the maths tests had been undermined by incorrect use of English. While recognizing that the sample was relatively small (338 test scripts from 143 pupils in ten schools), the report also discovered marking mistakes in every English paper examined, with similar defects emerging in 84 per cent of the science scripts and 54 per cent of the mathematics scripts. This again calls into question the validity of such tests.

A high percentage of respondents in the PACE study had 'no comment' to make on the extension tests (English 61 per cent, mathematics 64 per cent and science 75 per cent). This could be a reflection of the fact that many schools chose, in advance, not to use them as they considered that they were of little value either to the individual child or for the teachers who were about to receive the children in the secondary schools. Teachers also drew attention to the fact that the extension tests were based on areas of the curriculum which they had not had time to cover. The additional disruption to the normal process of teaching and learning was not considered justified.

Not surprisingly, when asked in interview about the effects of SAT testing, 49 per cent of Year 4 teachers and 73 per cent of Year 6 teachers in 1995 considered the tests to have had a 'major effect' on teaching and children's learning by emphasizing the 'categoric' aspect of assessment.

> It's tending to put children into boxes labelled 'levels' and we're ticking boxes and saying that this child is a Level 1 child, this child is a Level 2 child, instead of looking at the child as a whole person. It's taken away a certain element of that feeling that these children are here and they're also learners.

As with studies of the 1995 SATs (e.g. ATL, 1996), there was evidence that the reality of external testing was influencing curriculum content and pedagogic priorities. As we saw in the previous chapter, evidence from systematic teacher observation by PACE researchers, carried out in 54 classrooms over a period of six years, lends weight to the suggestion that whole-class teaching and individual work is increasing at the expense of group work. Similar findings were reported by Galton *et al.* (1999). However, it is difficult to be sure whether this is a permanent shift in classroom practice, and a reflection of the increasing age and independence of the pupils as they move through primary education, or evidence of a change in pedagogy which emphasizes the skills of cognition, tested by SATs, over and above a pedagogy which seeks to develop collaborative, sharing skills. Additional evidence from teacher interviews confirmed the need for teachers to use more individual and whole-class teaching to ensure appropriate coverage of the National Curriculum and adequate preparation for the national tests.

Evidence also suggested that there had been a noticeable increase in the time spent on the core subjects at the expense of others, especially art, music and physical education. Again, evidence gathered from teacher interviews revealed a concern for the lack of opportunity that pupils have to experience some of the more creative elements of the school curriculum:

> They're [SATs] a test of memory. They are certainly going to make teachers teach to a timetable – you've got to cover the work to give the children the best chance, so if you've got to cover that work, you're not going into as much depth as you would have done otherwise, as you've very little time. And I think teachers at the top end of KS2 concentrate on doing those core subjects to the detriment of art.

Again, from another Year 6 teacher:

> It depends what your criterion is for good practice. I think if you put a lot of store on experimental work, practical work, then it probably isn't because it's a paper-and-pencil test. Particularly in science, from the point of view of fair testing and practical work, experimentation, well, there's nothing. Also, in English, something that struck us was the fact that we do encourage the children to first draft, and second draft, and even third draft sometimes. But there they're allowed to plan it and then they write straight away. So I suppose, from that point of view, it doesn't quite tie in.

Issues of equity in SAT testing

There was also evidence that Year 6 teachers, interviewed by the project team in 1996, were concerned that some children were disadvantaged by the format and process of the SAT testing. As this quotation illustrates, there were some children whom they considered could perform badly under test conditions:

> Children who are nervous, who get nervous in a test situation. They certainly penalize poor readers, even though you can ask for help with the science or maths, or even have somebody reading with them, there's still – their answers don't reflect their knowledge, they reflect their language. It penalizes them.

Again:

> I think it's a reasonable guide to their attainment. I think the government are probably right in wanting some kind of yardstick to measure standards by, but there are certain aspects of the test that I think are slightly flawed – in particular, the science test, which is very dependent on knowledge and having a good memory, so children who have a natural kind of scientific bent, but can't remember facts as well, are at a disadvantage.

And again:

> I don't think they give each child an equal advantage because it showed painfully clearly in our tests that one or two children in my class, the less able Year 6s, in my opinion their maths attainment is Level 3, working on a Level 4, who simply because of the wording and their reading skills weren't able to read the maths test. And although I could read various things out to them, I couldn't explain it in any further detail, so they were losing out because of poor reading skills. And it's exactly the same for the science. Scientific language tends to be longer words, more complicated words, more difficult phrases to read. So again, we could read the phrases out to them but couldn't explain any further in detail, for instance what 'evaporation' meant or what 'dissolve' meant. So they were disadvantaged again purely because of their lack of reading skills.

There were even concerns for some children who would normally perform well at school: 'they do have bad days. There are children that really can't cope with the tests. I've got one very bright boy in particular. He's very, very clever but he's so nervous of tests he gets terrible results.' There was also perceived inequity for lower-achieving pupils who were not considered weak enough to get a statement of special educational need from the local education authority:

> I had two statemented children last year in my class and they had support and they had an amanuensis, a person who wrote for them, and the thing was, they did the tasks and they came out ... one of them came out with two Level 3s on the tasks. Now I had children in my class, who had had support but weren't statemented, who got no levels at all because they had no support at all and they were absolutely at sea. So those children with statements and because they'd had all that support, left here with levels and there were those who, because they weren't bad enough or poor enough, got nothing.

In contrast, other children were considered to be advantaged: 'I think children who take things in their stride, who are able to cope with everything without becoming flappable.' This concern for children to function as well as possible in the test situation had prompted teachers to put time aside for revision and mock tests, and to use various strategies for helping children during the tests. This raises issues of standardization and reliability.

> Having the mocks certainly helped – they were aware of the format. Just allowing children to put their hands up so words could be read for them in science and maths, and I did that for all children if they didn't understand a word. I think if they felt worried about a particular subject area, there wasn't really very much I could do about that.

Preparation for Key Stage 2 SAT testing

The study collected increasing evidence of the significance with which teachers regarded both the preparation for SAT testing and the importance of the results for future planning, as this quotation from a Year 5/6 teacher in 1996 shows:

> I probably found the SATs more stressful afterwards when we were analysing the result: the implications for teaching next year ... in the light of last year's results we've had two staff meetings where we've tried to analyse why the children didn't do as well in the English SATs as they should have done and made provision for improving the teaching of English leading up to the 1997 SATs.

Evidence from the study suggested that this change in approach by teachers had been quite dramatic and had taken place over a very short period of time. Teachers from schools with more advantaged intakes were concerned that their pupils should reach the above-average levels expected by their parents. Teachers from schools in less advantaged areas were clear that, although it might not give their pupils the most appropriate curriculum, they needed to 'teach to the tests' because otherwise their pupils would be doubly disadvantaged.

The continuing tension between creating a 'broad, balanced curriculum' and the pressure on teachers to prepare pupils for the SATs is illustrated in this quotation from a Year 6 teacher from a school in a more advantaged area:

> It's very difficult to get the right balance. You can make them thoroughly fed up with it all. On the other hand, you want them to view them [SATs] with a certain level of seriousness. So getting the balance right is very tricky. I think we did it quite well last year. At the moment we are pushing paragraphing and spelling and punctuation and higher reading skills. Whether the children actually connect that with SATs or not I don't know but we are not happy with the lack of Level 5s in English last year.

This quotation also refers to a separation of SAT testing from the learning process and the extent to which pupils recognize the connection between the two. An additional concern arose, particularly from teachers responsible for Year 6 pupils, because they considered that they were bearing an unfair burden for the preparation for SAT testing and that this was restricting their curriculum time:

> They're [pressure of SATs] making me cram everything into two and a half terms. Whereas I should have three in my year for a start. Certainly I have had to rearrange my science to make sure that that gets finished [before the SATs take place]. Consequently, it's caused a big upheaval in my plan and everybody else's because they've all had to change as well to accommodate it. I'm teaching to SATs really – content. That's what those maths sheets are about every day.

SAT utility at Key Stage 2

When asked to what extent SAT testing had enabled teachers to learn anything new about the children's learning and understanding, 41 per cent considered that they had learned 'nothing new'. The following remark is typical:

No. It confirms what you know already, and when children perform badly you can say that it looks as though they've performed badly on the day and I don't think it actually reflects your feeling about how well they can do.

However, occasional benefits were also perceived, mainly by younger teachers who had qualified since the 1988 Act. When one such Year 5/6 teacher was asked which she considered to be more reliable, her assessment of a child or that child's test results, she answered:

A combination of the two, I would say. Blowing my own trumpet, I'm usually right; just every now and then something will go drastically wrong. I might have underestimated a child or completely overestimated them and then I'll have to do work with them to find really where they are.

A survey of teachers' views of SAT utility in 1995, which was conducted by the ATL, found that 54 per cent of teachers thought they were worth while. However, as both HMI (Agambar, 1996) and the evaluation of Key Stage 3 (Radnor, 1996) also found, there is little use made of the scripts and of the data in general for informing teaching and learning.

Teachers in the PACE sample expressed concern over the use of test results for marketing purposes and were sceptical as to their use by secondary schools. However, there appeared to be a growing acceptance of the existence of SATs as a form of externally set and marked assessment. The following quotation illustrates the changing discourse of teachers, which includes both a certain degree of scepticism as to their value, combined with a tacit acceptance of their existence:

Obviously, when they first came on to the scene, it was a bit of a culture shock. But like everything else, you get used to it. I personally think it's a good idea to have national tests, *but* my main reservation at the moment in this particular catchment area is that they are a bolt-on and really not used for any specific purpose. The banding has already been sorted out with the comprehensive school, and so the results are just sent down there – and they say they will look at them, but to what extent they are used is another matter. I doubt whether they're used very much at all ... you can't use them for the particular children and it's too late for the transfer, so all it serves [as] is [as] a yardstick for the government, and something for the parents to see. And that basically is a good idea, but let's make them useful as well.

Although on the surface it appears that teachers have accepted the need for national testing, data from the project suggest that there are serious deficiencies in the process as it stands. As a device for communicating to parents their children's achievements, the indications from teachers are that parents may not understand what the results mean and are interested in quite different information about their child. As a device for comparing school standards in 'league tables', the information is insufficiently valid, reliable and contextualized for these to have much meaning. For teachers, the information would appear to be of some interest but generated too late to be any use in informing practice. For receiving secondary schools, the results come too late to inform class allocations and the quality of the information is too synoptic and broad to be usefully diagnostic.

8.4 CONCLUSION

Whilst curriculum addresses 'content', and pedagogy focuses on 'process', assessment is concerned with the exercise of 'power' in respect of performance. In the liberal-progressive discourse of child-centred constructivism, assessment was conceived for formative purposes, but assessment practices were rarely made explicit. Indeed, at the level of actual practice, teacher perspectives of pupils were formed through intuitive pragmatism, based on the day-to-day experiences of children, but without systematic evidence.

National testing and an emphasis on target setting for both individuals and schools are here to stay, at least for the foreseeable future. Evidence from the PACE project helps to illuminate the strengths and weaknesses of such developments and to raise some interesting questions.

There is much evidence that teachers have developed increased skills and confidence in their assessment practices. Similar findings have been reported by other recent research (Gipps, 1994; Gipps *et al.*, 1995) An increase in the incidence of cooperative planning and Key Stage coordination, together with the processes of inter-school moderation, have been extremely important in exchanging ideas and sharing experiences. However, our data also show that although the national tests may be accommodated by teachers from an operational point of view, the effect of national testing on classroom practice is profound. As well as the more obvious sessions of revision and 'teaching to the test' which were observed in Year 6 classes, there was also increasing evidence of a 'wash-back' effect which reached into year groups that were not immediately involved with the tests.

This is important, because one of the stated purposes for national testing is to provide information to parents so that they can make judgements about the effectiveness of individual schools. With children between the ages of 5 and 11, evidence suggests that parents are seeking more from a school than an improvement in the skills of cognition alone. They also require the schools to help socialize children, develop the ability to work positively with others and maintain children's morale and happiness (Hughes *et al.*, 1990). The pressure from a restricted but overloaded national curriculum, combined with 'high-stakes' national testing, appears to be diminishing the opportunities for teachers to work in a way that enables them to 'develop the whole child' and address the social concerns of the wider society.

Part 4

School Issues

Chapter 9

Case-Studies in Values, Understanding and Power

9.1 INTRODUCTION

The purpose of this chapter is to present three short case-studies drawn from three very different PACE classroom study schools. Each of the cases highlights, through the lives of real teachers and schools, some of the significant issues which have arisen in education since the 1988 Education Reform Act (ERA) and the period of multiple reforms that followed it. All of these illuminate some of the major themes of the book. They illustrate in different ways the extent to which the importance of teachers' values, the understanding they share about their role, and the power and control they have over their working situation are central to an understanding of how educational policy change may be translated into classroom practice. In each case they describe coping strategies developed by schools and teachers as a way of mediating the demands of the National Curriculum and other recent reforms, and trying to come to terms with change.

The case-study of Greenmantle illustrates how a school in a middle-class area, where there was strong pressure for high achievement from parents, reorganized to try to meet these demands. These pressures led the school to reassess the use of ability groups, setting and subject specialist teaching (Alexander *et al.*, 1992). In the process there has been both increased teacher collaboration and the imposition of 'contrived collegiality'. Teachers have experienced a sense of loss in terms of the affective dimension of education and the rupture of the class teacher's traditional relationship with the children he or she teaches, but at the same time, arguably, there have been some observable gains in teaching and learning outcomes. For the children the changes have, in many ways, made the experience of primary education more like that of secondary school. Certainly in Greenmantle there was evidence of a shift from an emphasis on expressive and affective concerns to an emphasis on more cognitive and instrumental outcomes.

The case-study of Orchard demonstrates how a small, rural school with mixed-age classes, also drawing on a predominantly middle-class catchment area, dealt with change. In particular it provides an illustration of the impact of externally imposed and internal change, including the impact of OFSTED inspections and changes of headship on the school and teachers. It traces the experience of these changes by three members of staff, two of them older, more experienced teachers and one a young teacher in her first post. Again it provides some evidence of a shift from the expressive and affective towards cognitive and instrumental concerns.

The third school, St Anne's, provides a case-study of how the reforms impacted differently on a school in a highly disadvantaged area. It illustrates the teachers' strong concerns with the effect on the children of their difficult lives outside school, and about the extent to which the school can compensate for these. The teachers had anxieties that the demands of the National Curriculum do not address the needs of the children they teach. The case of St Anne's also illustrates the dilemma for teachers in finding a balance between relating to children in a differentiated way and demonstrating high expectations of the children, ensuring that they are providing equal entitlement to a full curriculum and range of learning opportunities.

9.2 GREENMANTLE PRIMARY SCHOOL

Greenmantle was a medium-sized primary school located in the centre of a prosperous market town in central southern England, where traditional agricultural occupations coexisted with modern light industry. It was originally founded as a Church of England school in the nineteenth century and was very proud of its history. In more recent times it had expanded and taken on grant-maintained status, which had enabled it to increase its income by drawing its funds directly from the government. However, the school retained its commitment to high academic achievement and firm discipline, set in a strong Christian ethos, seeing the development of the 'whole child' – physical, mental, spiritual, as well as intellectual – as its main purpose.

The original Victorian schoolroom became the school hall where whole-school assemblies took place regularly. They were conducted by the headteacher or the local curate, and were a time to celebrate success, both individual and collective, as well as to reflect on moral issues from a Christian perspective. The pupils sat in rows, by class, on the floor whilst their teachers sat around the edge of the room ensuring orderliness and good behaviour. The assemblies usually started with the playing of classical music and later included the singing of hymns, often accompanied by some of the older pupils. These assemblies were considered to be an important part of the school week.

Not far from the original school hall was a modern one-storey building that housed the staffroom, a library and a suite of offices devoted to the administration of the school. These were occupied by the headteacher, Mr Jones, an experienced educationist in his fifties; a school bursar, occupying a post which was a reflection of the increasing demands on schools caused by devolved budgets through the local management of schools (LMS); and a school secretary. There was a reception area that displayed photographs of significant people, such as the headteacher, the chair of governors and the chair of the Friends of the school, and a glass cabinet containing cups and awards for sporting achievements. Scattered around this administrative hub, within the school playground, were the individual classrooms, which consisted of single-storey semi-permanent buildings, each having their own entrance and lobby for hanging coats and the storage of school bags. They were light and airy with high ceilings and plenty of space for the children to move around. They were well equipped and there was also generous storage space for the teachers to organize their teaching resources. A short distance from the impressive wrought-iron school gates was the town hall and a covered alleyway that led to the busy, narrow high street. From the other side of the school site, miles of rolling countryside were visible.

The school was popular in the district and served both the local community and surrounding villages. Some of its pupils were the children of the indigenous population who worked in agriculture or light industry. Others, however, were the children of prosperous professionals who worked from home or commuted to the cities in the surrounding region. Many of the parents had been successful in their own schooling and were keen to see their successes replicated in their offspring. As a result, they were largely supportive of both the school's ethos and its aims. For the most part the children came from a social environment that was relatively settled and prosperous, with few indicators of poverty. The children's lives were, in general, devoid of many of the acute and chronic social pressures typically found in schools with inner-city locations. The headteacher had an excellent relationship with his governors, who supported him and respected his professional knowledge. He was also diligently supported by an experienced deputy headteacher, Bob Wilkins, who was firmly committed to the aims of the school and considered himself to be a teacher with 'traditional' values, expecting order and application from his pupils. These two experienced educators had worked closely together in developing the school over the previous twenty years.

However, the school, because of its catchment area, had pressures. To some extent it saw itself in competition with the many independent schools in the region. Competition existed both in the direct sense, in that some parents could choose to send their children to independent preparatory schools if the academic results were not considered good enough, as well as indirectly in the sense of appropriate preparation for the next level of schooling. A number of parents had aspirations to send their children to selective, independent secondary schools when they left Greenmantle and so it was necessary for the school to ensure that these children were appropriately prepared for the necessary entrance examinations which they would inevitably face. Many of these pressures were also felt by the local comprehensive school, which was exposed to a similar social and contextual environment. Teaching methods, then, at Greenmantle were fairly formal, with a good deal of positive reinforcement. Given this background, it would have seemed that Greenmantle needed to change little in the face of the 1988 Education Reform Act and that its impact would be minimal. However, if we look more closely at the organization of teaching and learning within the school we begin to see that the pressures were indeed causing changes.

No school can absolutely determine the number of pupils who will come forward at the beginning of each new academic year. This is particularly true of the Reception class, where Greenmantle would make every effort to accommodate all those who wanted a place at the school. This meant that there were often imbalances in the number of children in any one particular year group, and this could lead to inequities, as one of the Key Stage 2 teachers explained:

> We addressed the issue last year when we had a class and a half and the half were with Year 4s and we wanted to make sure that they had equal opportunities basically and the only way that we could do that was by hiring an extra teacher for a couple of mornings a week.

A continuing imbalance at the top end of the school had caused the headteacher and his deputy to consider alternative arrangements for dividing pupils into separate classes. As the deputy head explained, 'for the last two or three years we've had difficult numbers of Year 6s to deal with. This year, for example, we've got 46 Year 6s and they certainly wouldn't all fit into one class.' Early in 1994 the deputy head was asked by the headteacher to prepare a discussion document, in collaboration with his colleagues, that would address some of these growing concerns. The resulting proposal sought to create a 'Cooperative Unit' at the top end of Key Stage 2 which combined all Year 5 and Year 6 pupils in three mixed-ability classes, each with its own class teacher (see Figure 9.1).

It was suggested that the pupils should be set, by 'ability', in English, mathematics and games, but would return to their mixed-ability class groups for all the other subjects on the taught curriculum. The teaching team of three teachers, as well as having a class teacher responsibility for the majority of the curriculum, would also take sole responsibility throughout the year for the teaching of one of the three ability groups in each of the three 'setted' subjects: English, mathematics and games. This innovative organization attempted to use some of the strengths of a quasi-secondary school model of curriculum organization, while at the same time retaining the traditional class teacher model familiar to the majority of English primary schools. In the process, as we shall see, it created a collaborative team of three Key Stage 2 teachers who were also able to address two other major concerns which were beginning to surface as a direct result of the 1988 Act. The first was to do with the need for in-depth subject knowledge in an increasingly prescribed and detailed National Curriculum that had separated the taught curriculum into discrete subject areas. The second, and possibly more pressing, was the perceived need to maximize the forthcoming SAT scores of all their pupils. The government had announced that, from 1995, individual school test results would be published, nationally, in league tables, enabling parents directly to compare the scores at Greenmantle with those of other schools. Greenmantle had taken part in the voluntary Key Stage 2 SATs which

---
Discussion Document

Proposed Cooperative Year 5/6 Unit

Pupil Groupings:

1. Mathematics	– 3 ability groups
2. English	– 3 ability groups (except creative writing)
3. Games	– 3 ability groups
4. 3 mixed ability groups for:	Science
	Technology
	History/geography
	Art
	Music
	Physical education
	Religious education
	Registration

Ability groups could be known by the first initial of the teacher's surname to avoid ranking. Careful splitting would be necessary for mixed-ability groups to split up 'naughties' and ensure a balance of choir members Y5 and Y6, boys and girls.

SUBJECT ORGANIZATION

Mathematics and English (except creative writing) would be taught in ability groups with the same teacher throughout the year.
GROUP 1 – 30 pupils
GROUP 2 – 26 pupils
GROUP 3 – 22 pupils

Mixed-ability groups to rotate each half term for: Science
Technology
History/geography

Teachers to keep the same mixed-ability groups all year for:
Registration
Creative writing
Music
Art
Religious education
Physical education

Spellings and spelling tests would be done in registration groups. This would give an activity during registration (9.00–9.10) and tests could be given at other times allocated for registration groups.

Teachers would take pastoral responsibility for their own registration group. Parents' evenings and reports could be dealt with by registration group with additional notes on mathematics and formal English from the ability group teacher.

Figure 9.1 Discussion document for the proposed 'Cooperative Unit'

had been trialled in 1994 and had been disappointed in the overall attainment of its pupils, particularly in the English SAT.

Initially, pupils were to be allocated to one of three carefully balanced groups, combining a mixture of both Year 5 and Year 6 pupils in each class, with one class teacher. The discussion document (Figure 9.1) underlined the need for balance in these groups by 'split[ting] up "naughties" and ensure[ing] a balance of choir members, Y5 and Y6, boys and girls'. A recently qualified female teacher who formed part of this 'Cooperative Unit' explained further, once the new system had been adopted in the 1994–5 academic year: 'We took great pains when we split the children into classes to make sure that no class was lower in ability than the others.' This then threw up other concerns that led the teachers to focus on another external pressure which was beginning to have an impact on their work, as Jane Kidman, a Year 5/6 teacher, continued:

> Then, while we were doing that, we also looked at ability and decided that the National Curriculum was so specific – differentiation is pushed so heavily – that we decided that we just couldn't teach top juniors at every level adequately. And we thought we'd be able to cover it better if they were in ability groups. So I think it was the intake [imbalance] that started the ball rolling but then we did look at the National Curriculum and saw that the ability span is too wide.

Because of this, the three mixed-ability classes were divided again between the three teachers to ensure comprehensive and differentiated teaching for the 'basics' of English and mathematics, as well as games. The pupils were divided by 'ability' (as determined by test scores and teacher assessment) into three groups: high, average and low. Each of the three top junior teachers would take responsibility for one group for the whole of the year. The pupils would move from class to class at the appropriate time and reassemble themselves into a new class group depending on the timetable. The deputy head, who also formed part of the 'Cooperative Unit', explained how this 'ability' grouping was approached on an ongoing basis:

> We look at the work from the previous year and we test them ... the Y4s will have a test at the end of this year and we look at those results to see where they should go in September. We talk to the class teachers of the Y4s and, obviously, the Y5s; we know them quite well anyway so we know roughly where they should be, and there is a lot of movement even in September, even though we've talked about it quite a bit beforehand.

To address the concerns of teachers with regard to the underachievement of some pupils, a decision was also made to vary the size of these teaching groups to enable more attention to be given to the low attainers. Group 1 contained 30 high attainers, Group 2 contained 26 average attainers and Group 3 contained 22 low attainers. The teachers saw this as a major benefit, as Bob Wilkins explained: 'The lower-ability groups are very small. They get a lot of one-to-one help and they get a lot of encouragement and usually they come on a lot faster than they ever have before.'

However, there was a tension. This type of arrangement, involving as it did the 'setting' of pupils by ability, was increasingly being encouraged by both government and the school inspection service (OFSTED). It nonetheless was in opposition to a more holistic view of primary education, which was unsympathetic to the categorizing and 'labelling' of pupils by test scores. This tension was evident when Bob Wilkins talked about other areas of the curriculum in which mixed-ability teaching was retained:

> I don't group them ever according to ability. I tend to sit them girl, boy, girl, boy, purely from a discipline point of view and I think it does them good to work with children of the opposite sex anyway. In my mixed-ability group I know where all the less able are sitting and I tend to go to them rather than sit them all together and sit with them all the time. I float around. It looks less obvious then.

This concern with the self-esteem of the pupils is also alluded to in the discussion document that suggests that 'ability groups could be known by the first initial of the teacher's surname to avoid ranking'. However, this ideal was difficult to sustain, particularly in relation to science teaching, where the teachers were required to prepare pupils for SAT testing at different levels, as Bob Wilkins went on to explain when pressed on the subject: 'I've said I don't sit them in ability groups but I suppose I do in a way (for science). I make them work in ability groups and yes, they have slightly differentiated activities, but not obviously.' The original discussion document proposed that the National Curriculum subjects of science, technology, history and geography should retain the benefits of mixed-ability teaching but be handled in a slightly different way as compared with the rest of the 'foundation subjects'. The pupils would remain with their 'home' class groups but the teachers would split the work to be covered between them. Each teacher would teach the same topic to all three mixed-ability groups in successive terms. This was seen as a way of helping individual team members to become 'expert' in particular sections of the curriculum and so ease the strain of the need for in-depth knowledge across a ten-subject curriculum by producing a limited degree of specialization. Once this system had been put in place, it gave rise to a great deal of cooperative planning, as Jane Kidman, one of the teachers involved, explained:

> The school week is actually timetabled out at the beginning of the year according to, I think it's the Dearing Report – how much maths we should be doing, how much English, how much science and so on. So we break each subject up and spread it around the week … Then we take the programme of study in, say, science and we share them out between the teachers and that's how we know which science topic we are going to do.

This represented a major change to their previous planning procedures:

> Although we've been doing this way of planning for about three years, it has never been as structured as it is this year. We've never had a timetable written out like this where everybody's doing exactly the same thing at the same time. That's quite hard from the resources point of view.

However, it also contributed to a certain amount of fragmentation of the taught curriculum, and this was worrying to teachers. Not only was the curriculum now divided into ten discrete subject areas but, within these, there were also many separate 'programmes of study'. This represented a major change in the way in which the primary curriculum was constructed. A more traditional view of the primary curriculum considered knowledge to be part of a 'seamless robe' of interconnected ideas. This was reflected in the value placed on teaching through intricately planned topic work which enabled teachers to handle several parts of the curriculum at once by investigating related concepts contained within one area of study. For instance, a teacher might investigate elements of story writing, poetry, mathematics, science, history, geography and religious education under the topic heading of 'the weather'. The following quotation from Jane Kidman gives a flavour of this frustration:

> It's very ... the programmes of study that you're given ... if you could imagine a big bag full of the programmes of study that a Year 5/6 teacher has to teach. It would be difficult to teach them any other way than discrete and fragmented. You could perhaps match a couple together to teach them in an integrated way but there'd always be certain ones that wouldn't fit in with anything, that would be left out at the end.

This complicated patchwork, which involved the movement of pupils between teachers in different classes, had additional drawbacks, as Bob Wilkins, the deputy head, and architect of the new proposal, admitted:

> And of course the usual – the old advantage of the primary school class was that you weren't limited by the end of the lesson and you were always able to carry on and stay with one task all day if you wished. But of course, now we have to stop and they might not look at that book or that subject until the following day or even two days later.

However, on balance he considered the new approach to be more rigorous and to have greater accountability:

> Well, I'm more accountable when I work now and you know, one always feels slightly more on the spot in that one cannot procrastinate in quite the same way! That's one feature of it. But personally, having always been a very formal teacher, I prefer the system that we're using now to the whole-class system whereby I was teaching ten different subjects to the same group all the time. I prefer a subject-orientated timetable. I know a lot of teachers regret the demise of the umbrella topic in Year 5 and Year 6 but it doesn't bother me at all.

The new system also brought perceived benefits in the terms of planning and collaborative working, as he explained:

> Well yes, ten years ago I worked basically on my own, did my own planning. So planning cooperatively is new for me, though teachers may have worked cooperatively before that ... I can't think of any particular example of where I've enjoyed working with a colleague but I do enjoy the system whereby we can plan together and share out the various bits of the curriculum and use each other's strengths and lean on each other with regard to our weaknesses ... there's far more cooperative teaching now, cooperative working together, planning, etc. And I suppose any clashes of personality would be highlighted in that situation. On the other hand, it may have forged new, very pleasant relationships. I think both of those situations have occurred in my experience.

However, another of the teachers involved, Marion Hughes, was less sure of the benefits with regard to the whole school:

> Well, I think we're far more fragmented now. Although I work very closely with two other colleagues, we have very little to do with the lower juniors and even less to do with the infants. Maybe once or twice a year ... two classes from different departments would get together and do a small project. I've worked many times with Mrs T with an infant

class. There was far more opportunity to just swap classes and I could go into a lower junior class and teach something that I wanted to teach, perhaps IT or something. It's very difficult to do that now because we're so timetabled.

Again:

It's got pros and cons. There are some things I really like. I think it's good that we sit down and plan together. I just wish that we could have more of an opportunity to plan as a whole school. I don't like really being fragmented into three departments within the school (infant, lower junior, upper junior). I think that's a shame but I do like the new cooperation between the top juniors. I think that's good.

Perhaps the most controversial aspect of the new arrangements was the weakening of the long-established link between a single class teacher and his or her class. This relationship has constituted a fundamental building-block in the ideological make-up of the majority of primary teachers, as other researchers have shown (Nias, 1989). It provides that nurturing dimension to teaching that enables practitioners to define their role in terms of looking after the well-being and development of the 'whole' child. It is also regarded as a necessary prerequisite for the creation of an appropriate learning environment for each individual child and an important element in the intuitive understanding and formative assessment of each pupil. This complicated movement of pupils between teachers meant that this close relationship was being fractured, as Jane Kidman explained:

It means that we don't have as much pastoral care with our own class. I don't see certain children very often in my class. I personally don't like that but I'm not sure how it's affecting the children. There doesn't seem to be any more bullying or anything like that but I don't feel as if I can have the same relationship with a child that I don't see very often.

Bob Wilkins, while recognizing that there may be clear benefits to the pupils in terms of a growing maturity and independence, coupled with the need for them to take more responsibility for organizing their own learning, also had reservations:

I don't like not seeing my children so often but I think that's a personal view and I think academically, socially and personally that they're coping very well with it. It remains to be seen whether it does work or not. I think we've only really been doing it to this extent for a year. It's very difficult to say whether it's worked or not. Give it a couple more years.

This change in relationship between teachers and their pupils was also evident in more subtle ways. The initial proposal (see Figure 9.1) allowed for a period at the beginning of each day when each class teacher would register his or her own class. This period was now limited in time to ten minutes because of the strict timetabling of the rest of the day. It was also suggested that 'Spellings and spelling tests would be done in registration groups' so that maximum use could be made of this time. Prior to this new system, however, the beginning of each school day would have been a time when teachers could address the pastoral needs of their pupils in a more relaxed way. Now the day was to start with what could be a threatening situation for some children, colouring their view of themselves as learners as they moved on to other areas of the curriculum. Their initial contact with their class teacher would also be viewed in categoric terms, perhaps one in which they 'passed' or 'failed'.

The initial proposal also foresaw a potential problem with regard to the reporting of pupils' progress to parents. If one teacher was no longer responsible for all the learning of each individual pupil in their class, how were they to report effectively and accurately to parents? This would need more cooperative work between the team of teachers, with each teacher contributing an assessment of that bit of the child's learning for which he or she had personal responsibility. This shows a significant move towards a secondary school model of reporting which could remove a holistic overview of each pupil's progress.

This physical movement of pupils around the school was also a concern with regard to wasted teaching time and security, together with the fragmented learning experience of the pupils. For one teacher, at least, time seemed to have been constrained: 'Then they all come back to class about two minutes before home time. If they're not already in the class, they come back. Then they're dismissed.'

In proposing this new organizational system, the deputy headteacher had already anticipated some of these tensions, and he accompanied his discussion document with a list of advantages and disadvantages as he saw them (see Figure 9.2).

Advantages:
1. Children benefit from the skills and expertise of three or four teachers
2. Avoids a few Year 6 children being left out of a Year 6 class
3. Avoids a few Year 5 children being left out of a mainly Year 5 class
4. Enables all Year 5 and Year 6 children to be seen to be treated equally
5. Teachers become 'expert' in the areas they cover three times
6. Smaller teaching groups
7. By necessity, more liaison and shared responsibility in the Upper Junior Dept.
8. Three or four teachers gain experience with Year 6 children, rather than being left in the hands of one teacher.

Disadvantages:
1. Diminishing of Y6 kudos
2. Need for Y6 pupils to be extracted for: health education talks, cycling proficiency, transition to secondary school work, SATs, Year 6 camp
3. Administration of SATs?
4. Lack of security with no specific class teacher, only registration groups
5. Responsibility for pastoral care?
6. Parents' evenings?
7. Report writing – who does general sections?
8. Filling in general sections of new pupil files?
9. RE needs to be approached on a Y5 and Y6 basis
10. Hall times for drama and PE might cause a problem
11. Might be accused of being too secondary orientated
12. Loss of group integration, less chance of interrelated themes
13. Greater restriction imposed by a more rigid timetable

Figure 9.2 Advantages and disadvantages of the 'Cooperative Unit'

In discussion he recognized that once the new system had been put in place for the 1994–5 academic year there were some criticisms from both teachers and parents:

> We have had criticisms from time to time regarding the Year 5/6 unit and the fact that perhaps the Year 6s have lost a little bit of their identity. There isn't a single class or a single unit of Year 6s that feel that they're top of the school and have the kudos that goes with that – they're rather watered down across the three classes. And also that there's too much movement from one group to another and that some time is lost in the process. And also there has been a feeling that perhaps it's a bit more difficult to keep tabs on individual children, monitoring their lulls and their peaks. It's much easier to do that if you've got one class all the time.

But despite these reservations, he recognized that the new system had positive benefits for both teachers and pupils and gave them the flexibility to deal with problems in a way that had not been possible before:

> Mr Jones [the headteacher] said to me just this lunchtime that one of the advantages of the Year 5/6 unit is that at the moment in Year 4 we have a group of particularly difficult boys – about seven of them – and if they were all going to the same class as a Year 5 or Year 6 then they would be hard to handle. As it is, we'll be able to split them up three ways.

Greenmantle, then, had responded in a creative, positive and pragmatic way to the tensions that had introduced themselves to the organization of teaching and learning within primary schools since the introduction of the 1988 Education Reform Act (ERA). The changes had enabled the school to maintain its ongoing aspirations to provide parents with an educational process that emphasized academic attainment, whilst at the same time supporting teachers in a context of increased workload. However, as we have seen, tensions had occurred because of the teachers' efforts to maintain a comprehensive pastoral organization and affective experience for the pupils. Moreover, difficulties with recording and reporting each individual pupil's overall experience, especially in science, technology, history and geography, had been a problem, as was the development of a comprehensive view of the child's social and emotional development. There was also an impact on how the teachers interpreted and carried out their role in their work with the children and with each other. Furthermore, the children's experience at Greenmantle had gone some way to imitate the experience that would await them when they entered secondary education, where the beginning and end of patterns of work would be controlled by bells and strict timetabling. Teachers were enabled to build up some degree of specialist knowledge within subjects, and had their burden of work eased through the introduction of ability setting in English and mathematics. This was accompanied, although masked, by a change in the school's approach to the identification and categorization of what they perceive to be individual pupils' learning ability. This may have had adverse effects on the ability of pupils who were struggling with their work to build up a positive learner identity, which, as other research has shown, can be crucial to academic success (Pollard and Filer, 1999).

Overall, there have been costs as well as benefits, as this final comment from Bob Wilkins, the experienced deputy headteacher who devised the new organizational system, explains:

I think a lot of the spontaneity has gone out of teaching. It was a job in which one could use one's imagination and flair and personal interest in certain specific areas. That's gone now. We feel compelled to find out information, from whatever source, in order to deliver the National Curriculum and sometimes that can be a bit tedious.

Footnote: It proved too difficult for the class teachers to cover 'creative writing' in their mixed-ability class groups and it had to be approached through the main English curriculum. However, Greenmantle was very encouraged by the increased English SAT scores which their pupils gained in the 1996 SAT testing.

9.3 ORCHARD PRIMARY SCHOOL

Orchard Primary was a small rural school with three mixed-age classes located in an attractive village in the south of England. Most of the children came from professional and business families, although there were also children from local farms. The school had acquired a good reputation with parents, who had high expectations for their children, and children attended from several surrounding villages as well as from within the village itself. Some were transported by school bus; others were driven there daily by parents. The school was located in pleasant modern buildings and surrounded by green playing-fields and trees. Most of the classes were relatively small (around 20–25 children). The teachers knew most of the families fairly well, so that the relationship between home and school was relatively close.

At the time the study began, the headteacher, Mrs Maynard, who had moved from being a deputy head in the private sector, was relatively newly appointed. She had come into the school with a great deal of enthusiasm and a determination to 'provide a stimulating and colourful educational environment where the children are happy and bubbling and enjoy coming to school'. It was particularly important to her to build up relationships with parents and ensure that they were contributors to the school community, and to create opportunities for music and art activities. So far as the National Curriculum was concerned, she felt that she would not allow it to be a straitjacket and that 'there were plenty of exciting opportunities for children's learning within the curriculum requirements'. She was not a great supporter of the record-keeping requirements of the National Curriculum and was critical of the profiling scheme adopted by the cluster of schools of which Orchard was one:

The profiles are pages longer than everyone else's. Far too detailed and they take ages to fill in. They tell us what the children have done but not what they know. I'm not happy with them. The old-style reporting was more valuable. They [the profiles] can lead to preconceived ideas about children, putting children into slots, labelling them right through secondary school.

This reaction was characteristic of her attitude towards many of the ERA record-keeping and paperwork requirements, and was a source of friction with at least one of the other members of staff who worried that the school was not fulfilling requirements. Mrs Maynard's priorities were primarily to provide a rich and stimulating educational environment where each child has something to offer and where individual gifts can be developed. Children have limitless potential. I want to open gates for them, capitalize on any opportunity. That includes having book weeks, visiting speakers, and developing educational activities outside the school.

During the time that Mrs Maynard was head, she was very successful in building up the school's reputation still further and attracting an increased number of children. As a consequence of this and of her connections in the community, she was able to have an attractive extension built to the school which provided a library and additional facilities where small groups could work. The school was very successful in putting on concerts and music events which attracted parents and also contributed to its reputation in the community. Mrs Maynard was a teaching head with responsibility for the mixed Year 5/6 class, but the success of the school enabled her to reduce her teaching time considerably and share the class with another part-time teacher, May Edwards.

After several years in post, Mrs Maynard moved to become head of a larger school on the outskirts of the neighbouring university town. She was replaced by Mr Firestone, who had also moved from the deputy headship of a neighbouring school. This was something of a watershed for the school and the teachers within it, since Mr Firestone's approach was very different. He was more management oriented, had done a master's degree in management and enjoyed the challenge of headship, strategic planning and budgeting. In discussing his leadership style he argued:

> It is fundamentally important to have clarity of purpose, direction and clear principles – to aim for quality and excellence. The children's learning is fundamental. My greatest challenge is how best to use staff skills and support in their own professional development. I'm a team player. There are many instances where I will consult and share. However, sometimes the staff will need me to say what should happen and make decisions.

Mr Firestone's role as he saw it had changed from that of class teacher to one mainly concerned with management, PR and team building. He saw himself as having less time to make decisions and having to be ruthless in prioritizing and in time management. Many of his decisions showed his concern with developing the potential of his staff. He was well liked by all the staff and pupils, and, as we shall see, for one member of staff in particular his arrival meant a revitalizing of her view of her own career and potential.

Very shortly after his arrival at the school, Mr Firestone received the notification of a forthcoming OFSTED inspection. He came into the staffroom at break with the letter in his hand saying that he felt 'shell-shocked'. Since his arrival the school had already had a mini-inspection from local education authority (LEA) OFSTED-trained advisers as a training session for them, so the news of yet another, far more major and significant inspection so soon after a change of headship was not welcome.

The inspection had major implications for staffing in the school, and for one teacher in particular resulted in considerable stress and an eventual unhappy conclusion to her career. May Edwards was the teacher of the top primary class, of mixed Year 4, 5 and 6 children, a responsibility she shared with Mr Firestone, who taught the class one day a week. She was in her fifties, had been secondary rather than primary trained and had taught in a grammar school prior to leaving teaching to have a family. As a mature woman returner she had originally joined the school as a supply teacher, later becoming part-time, and eventually, in her own words, she 'just drifted into a permanent four-fifths job'.

She found it very hard to fit in everything she needed in the four days of shared time she had with the class, time which was also broken up by games, swimming lessons and activities such as workshops with visiting artists. The stress she experienced was exacerbated by a fairly difficult group of children in Year 6, and a classroom which, although relatively large, was very crowded, and full of tables, chairs and children. Access to the room was either directly from the school hall or through two other adjacent classrooms and the library which opened off it. The result was a slight feeling of claustrophobia which May experienced often, commenting that she felt rather hemmed in and sometimes had to go outside to eat her sandwiches to avoid claustrophobia.

The difficulties of working in this way are illustrated in the following field note made by the PACE researcher working in the class, and by the teacher's own comments.

> This week has been very fragmented and 'bitty' for the teacher, making it difficult to keep to any class schedule. In some ways the children's experience also seems bitty and fragmented. They are taught by two different teachers and the lines between them seem blurred and indistinct. They don't cover distinct areas of the curriculum (as the children will experience in secondary school). Both do similar things with the children, but the head often has other calls on his time and has to change arrangements, so there is not a great deal of continuity. This week the children have also had a visit from the rector (for RE) and today, an all-day workshop on batik with a visiting artist. They also had swimming, games and a library visit. So although they have been doing many exciting and significant activities, there has not been time for any sense of continuity in the ordinary work they are doing. Their teacher feels this too, but feels powerless to do anything about it. According to her this is fairly typical of the class experience most weeks.

May Edwards commented that she had never really felt in control as a teacher since she had returned to teaching after having a family. She had always had to share a class with other teachers and had to fit herself around their planning. Since she now was responsible for the class four days a week she felt that the situation should be different, but somehow she still did not feel in control because the teacher she shared with was the head. She did not feel totally confident in all areas of the work she was doing with the class and felt the need for more training in primary methods. However, because of all the demands on her time, she argued, she did not feel able to take the time away from the class to go to courses, even though the head had urged her to do so.

One event in the class illustrated this feeling of lack of control and constituted what Woods (1995) would call a 'critical incident'. A visiting artist came into the classroom for a whole-day art workshop on batik. This had not been arranged by the teacher and she had been given very little information on what was likely to happen. It was a difficult day, one on which she felt totally responsible for the class, but all the events were actually controlled by the artist. There were a number of gaps in the activities, for example whilst the class were waiting for the wax to get to the right temperature, when the children were left with nothing to do. At one point a boy accidentally knocked over a pot of boiling wax and one of the girls in the class was badly scalded. Her skin was blistered, her parents had to be summoned and she was rushed to hospital.

The teacher blamed herself for this and spent the rest of the day in a state of anxiety about what she should have done to prevent it. Events became very chaotic in the classroom and she stayed all day and after school in the classroom without a break for tea or lunch because the artist wanted to work on and so did the children. She did not feel she could leave them without a teacher in charge and by the end of the day she was very stressed. The classroom was full of spilt wax which she spent time after school until six o'clock trying to clean up. Later she commented that she had felt 'out of control and lacking in confidence', definitely not 'on top of events'.

The incident illustrated the difficulties of being given a professional responsibility that seems endless and infinite, and yet with no real control. It is arguable that another teacher would perhaps have taken charge in a different way, but it is also evident that teachers in other countries such as France would have felt that their responsibility ended when a visiting expert entered the class to run a workshop and would not have felt to blame if anything had gone wrong.

More generally, so far as the requirements of the ERA and all the policy changes that followed were concerned, May described being a bit tense and feeling under pressure to get everything done:

> Well, I keep looking ahead and hoping that things are going to be better. Try to keep yourself calm really and do as much as you can. It's never going to be enough. But then teaching itself is a bit like that. But you do get in a bit of a panic sometimes, and then you can't think straight and then ... erghh! Once you begin to panic you really are in the soup, aren't you?

She described going for a walk with her husband on a Bank Holiday Monday, a relatively rare event, and deciding deliberately not to feel guilty because she wasn't preparing for school the next day:

> We went for a walk on the Monday afternoon and we were really enjoying it and Don said to me, 'Are you worried because you're not ... Are you thinking of school and you ought to be at home doing school ...?' I said, 'Well no, I'm not for once. I decided before I came out that I should be able to go for a walk on a Bank Holiday Monday and so I went and I was determined I was not going to worry about school.'

For May the stresses continued. The batik incident had shaken her own confidence still further. When the OFSTED inspection took place, although the school as a whole emerged as 'satisfactory' the teaching of Year 5 and 6 in English and mathematics was described as 'unsatisfactory'. As a result, May took long-term sick leave as a result of stress and went on to retire early owing to sickness.

For the other teachers in the school the inspection results had been more positive and had confirmed for them that their teaching was of high quality. However, an enormous workload had been generated in terms of preparation for OFSTED and also in terms of implementing the action plan that resulted from the inspection.

Plans which were made to reorganize the teaching of the school all had to be changed because Kate Gill, who was going to take over the Year 4/5/6 class, had to have a term's sick leave for an operation. Another teacher who had been appointed also went sick, or 'walked out', as the other teachers described it. A general sense of trauma following the inspection was exacerbated still further by all these events that followed.

For all the teachers in the school the OFSTED inspection and its consequences had been a traumatizing event. Change of headship is also a significant event in the life of a school and can have considerable influence on how the staff respond to externally imposed change. For one of the other teachers, Kate Gill, changes in the headship of the school had a significant impact on the way in which her professional identity and sense of self as a teacher developed. At the beginning of the study, Kate had been in the school for seven years but had been a teacher for nearly twenty years with a gap following the birth of her son. She knew most of the children's families and a considerable amount about their personal lives. She described herself as 'middle-aged and middle-class' with a 'firm but fair' approach towards the children. She felt that most of the parents, like herself with her own son, had high expectations and that she had to be fairly tough with children about producing a good finished product within a certain time period. These high expectations were evident in the way she responded to the demands of the National Curriculum. She planned and prepared meticulously to cover National Curriculum attainment targets in a thematic way, and was particularly imaginative and enthusiastic about the science work she introduced to the class.

Tensions existed for Kate in her relationship with the then recently appointed headteacher, Mrs Maynard, whose approach seemed in some ways diametrically opposed to her own. Kate had enjoyed a good relationship with the previous head and had felt highly valued as a teacher. During his headship it had been a priority to establish good record-keeping and curriculum planning, and a strong school development plan. In contrast, Kate saw Mrs Maynard as not particularly concerned about the National Curriculum or assessment. She worried that requirements such as careful planning and developing curriculum coordination responsibilities were being ignored, and that all the school's hard previous work was being jettisoned. She also saw her own contribution as undervalued by the new head.

Mrs Maynard was 'creative, bubbly and spontaneous', concerned to make the school an exciting place, but at the same time she was seen as something of a maverick by Kate and by other heads in the area for her lack of emphasis on National Curriculum requirements. In Kate's view, Mrs Maynard's 'private school' whole-class teaching methods were not working with her own class. Certainly, in terms of staff development opportunities Kate was not receiving the encouragement and support she had had from the previous head.

A major change came for Kate with the arrival of the new headteacher, Mr Firestone. Her careful planning and organization, assessment and meticulous work with the children were highly valued by the new head, and she took on a number of senior management responsibilities, more or less acting as deputy head, although she could not have the official title in a school that size. Over the eight years of the

PACE study Kate had moved from a period of reassessment (Huberman, 1993) as a result of the introduction of the National Curriculum and assessment, during which she was initially very optimistic and creative in her response, to a phase of self-doubt and undoubted exhaustion. During this middle period she no longer derived the fulfilment she had originally obtained from teaching. She felt that her enjoyment had slumped over the five years since the introduction of the National Curriculum. However, the opportunity to move into more management responsibilities after the arrival of the new head meant that she felt revalued and more positive about the future. In spite of all the constraints of the reforms and a feeling she had expressed earlier in the study of stress and burn-out, by the end of PACE in 1996 she was feeling slightly more fulfilled and valued than she had been two years earlier.

> There are more constraints on teachers than in the past. Expectations are higher. Everything has to be recorded. It's become more bureaucratic. There is more shuffling of papers. The time pressure element is greater. You are never free as a teacher even when shopping on Saturday morning. You are always thinking about it. But my own position has changed. I have more leadership responsibilities now. I work closely with colleagues as a coordinator and as a cluster coordinator, which I like. I don't enjoy teaching as much but I do enjoy the leadership roles. Also, I feel more fulfilled working with the new head. I derive more satisfaction from being valued as a teacher and as a person.

More details of Kate's experience of teaching in a time of change are given in the second book of the PACE study (Osborn, 1996a). Kate's case illustrates the impact a change of headteacher, together with a move to new responsibilities in a time of externally imposed change, can have on a teacher's sense of professional self and identity, even where that teacher is older and relatively experienced.

In contrast, the third teacher of junior age children at Orchard in 1996, Rebecca Dalton, was a newly qualified teacher in her first temporary post. She had responsibility for the Year 4, 5, 6 class previously taught by May Edwards and which would have been taken by Kate Gill if she had not been recovering from an operation.

Comparing what primary school was like now in contrast with her own experience as a pupil, Rebecca identified the pressure to succeed which she felt children were now under and a change in the affective relationship that had existed between teacher and pupil in the past:

> Well, just from the SATs, the children seem to feel they're under a lot more pressure at primary school. When I think of my days at primary school, it was really, really happy days. There was no pressure ... It was a time when you really enjoyed school, which is important because hopefully you can instil the right attitude about learning and education so that they keep those and then go on to apply them.
>
> In terms of relationships, I was always quite close to my primary school teachers. I can remember even sitting on their laps in assembly, whereas you would not have that at school today. But having said that, I feel it is still important to get the right balance. I try to always maintain a distance, if you like, between myself and the children. I don't like them asking personal questions. The other day, Jack turned round and said – I told him off because he'd done something wrong – 'I'm not your friend any more,' and I said to him, 'Jack, I'm not here to be your friend. I'm your teacher.'

> Sure, if we can get along even better and make it a nice atmosphere, fine, but at the end of the day, you're here to learn. I do try to have a little bit of laughter and a joke. We do some activities as well as quite hard work and quite often I'll say at the end of the day if they've worked really hard and been really good, I'll say, 'Let's pack up early, and finish with a story and go.'

Rebecca's emphasis on school as a place where first of all children are there to learn and on the need to maintain a distance between teacher and pupil is more evocative of the priorities expressed by teachers in France than those expressed by teachers before the National Curriculum was implemented. She found the time constraints of teaching enormous, and it was particularly difficult to encompass not only teaching to the requirements of the National Curriculum and assessment but also continuing to fulfil all the emotional demands of being a primary teacher in England.

> Well, I think teachers have always been expected to do a lot more than just teach. Certainly, with having such a challenging class as I've got I find that quite often you feel almost at the end of the day as though you are a social worker as well ... I'm having to talk to the educational psychologist every term about teaching children who were previously very difficult. That makes it very difficult because you're not only having to teach but you're dealing with emotional problems as well, which makes it very, very difficult.

The behavioural difficulties of some of the 35 children in this mixed-age class posed problems for Rebecca even outside normal classroom hours, and as a result of that and all the other demands on her time she rarely had a break or much time to discuss or get support in the staffroom.

Because of all the recent staffing difficulties the school had experienced there was very little time for any of the more experienced staff to give support to a newly qualified teacher. It was largely a case, as Rebecca, said of 'sink or swim'. She felt particularly anxious about her forthcoming class assembly, the first one she had been responsible for as a class teacher. She had not felt able to ask more experienced teachers for help because of the extra pressure everyone was under. She was having to prepare for this in a context where the children had recently returned from school camp and a Bank Holiday weekend. This was followed by a week preparing for a maypole dancing display to parents. The children had then taken their Key Stage 2 SATs. Naturally the children were generally in an excitable frame of mind and one not particularly conducive to concentration. Just as Rebecca thought she was through the worst, she had to prepare them in a very short time for presenting an assembly to parents, a considerable amount of stress for a new teacher to cope with, especially as she had moved house the same week:

> I've been worried about doing this assembly because I know when I first came here as a newly qualified teacher one of the stipulations was that I didn't have to do assemblies and now of course I am. I don't mind. I think it's a good thing for the children to show their parents what they did when they were [on school camp]. But it's a case of you've been left to get on with it! I just hope I am doing the right thing really ... It's only now that I feel I've got to know the other staff that I could go and say to them that I'm a bit unsure about something. I must admit, generally speaking, I've just got on with it on my own.

They're all under so much pressure and they've got so much work to do themselves that I just feel I don't want to add to it.

Rebecca's case illustrates the point made by Darling-Hammond (1990) that the support required by new teachers is most unlikely to be forthcoming in conditions of high staff turnover and multiple change, ironically just when such support is most needed. It also suggests that as new teachers come into schools there may be an added impetus for a shift from expressive to more cognitive and instrumental concerns as they experience the enormous difficulty of taking on the new cognitive demands without losing any of the expressive and affective dimension.

Orchard, then, had experienced multiple change which had a profound impact on a small school. Quite apart from all the changes imposed by the ERA itself, there had been two changes of headship, numerous staff changes and an OFSTED inspection which, in itself, had a profound impact on the staff and their relationships. The three teachers discussed here had experienced the impact on their professional identity very differently. One teacher had ended her career as a result of the stress resulting from OFSTED; another, very experienced teacher had undergone stress and come close to burn-out as a result of multiple change, but had come through this to a sense of feeling revalued through a change of headship and a movement to leadership responsibilities. The third, a newly qualified teacher, was experiencing a struggle as a result of a redefinition of the cognitive and instrumental aspects of teachers' role without any lessening of the affective and emotional demands of the job. At the same time, she was having to solve these problems with very little support from more experienced teachers because of the other staffing stresses this small school was undergoing.

The school came through these difficulties, although at considerable personal cost to some of the staff, and in 1999 received a second OFSTED inspection in which it was praised for its 'high standards in all areas of the National Curriculum, particularly in core subjects English, maths and science'. Teaching standards were seen as 'good or better' in 83 per cent of lessons.

9.4 ST ANNE'S PRIMARY SCHOOL

St Anne's was in a very different position socio-economically and geographically from Orchard and Greenmantle. A large Catholic primary school situated in an urban council estate on the outskirts of a northern city, the school took its intake of children from some of the city's most disadvantaged families, many of them under a great deal of stress. The majority of parents were unemployed and there was a very high take-up of free school meals. Some of the children were living with extended family members – grandparents, relatives or friends – rather than their own parents, and a number were being closely supported by social services.

However, the school had a very caring, close-knit family ethos, deriving in part from its Catholic philosophy, and, in the early years of the study, this was reflected a good part of the time in the children's behaviour and the way they related to each other and to adults. Most children were responsive and affectionate towards their teacher and towards visiting adults. As the children grew older, however, behavioural difficulties increased amongst a minority, including several of the target children, such as Philip, whose career in school is described in some detail in the companion volume to this (Pollard *et al.*, 2000).

Although the school was in a highly disadvantaged area its surroundings were not unpleasant. The main building was constructed in the 1950s and had a new wing which was attached to the Catholic church next door. It was surrounded by a concrete playground, but behind this were large green playing-fields and trees which belonged to the Catholic comprehensive that many of the children would eventually attend. In the early years of the study, the priest from the adjacent church maintained a strong presence in the school and was to be seen in the staffroom several times a week. He taught the children religious education (RE) and would visit the parents if there were problems with the children or with their attendance. When he retired he was replaced by a new young priest who seemed to visit the school less often, although he was still involved in preparing the children for their first communion.

Mr Ravenscroft, the headteacher, had grown up in the city himself. He had strong beliefs about the importance of providing structure for children whose lives outside school were 'often very chaotic and unstructured'. Most of the teachers in the school shared an emphasis on a highly structured and relatively formal pedagogy in which there was strong teacher direction and relatively little child choice. Children were taught in groups for some of the time, but there was a fairly heavy emphasis on whole-class teaching in the latter years of the PACE study. The school had adopted a different approach for maths teaching in which children were set into different levels for maths, regardless of age, and were taught in these levels by the same teacher throughout the year. Several times a week they moved to a different classroom for maths teaching and were taught by the teacher who had responsibility for that level, who was not necessarily their class teacher. Throughout the school as a whole there was an emphasis on motivating the children extrinsically through the use of team competitions and house points. Rewards were a regular feature at school assemblies, at which commendations for individuals were read out and the winning team in terms of house points was applauded.

One of the teachers of our target children was Peter Matthews, who taught the children in Year 2 and moved with some of them the following year into Year 3. Both the social context in which he worked and his own family background seemed to be crucial in the formation of Peter's values in relation to teaching. He had a very firm set of beliefs about teaching, and a highly distinctive teaching style that derived from his own experience as a child in a large Catholic family and as a pupil in a tough area of the same northern city where, as he put it, you had to either be 'fast on your feet or be able to talk your way out of a situation' in order to survive. He believed strongly in providing a firm structure and guidelines for the children, something which he felt was largely lacking in their home lives:

> I think that especially for children from round here, school is probably the only time in their lives that they do get some sort of structure, some sort of reliability. They know that it's Tuesday, so they're going to do PE. It's Monday, so they're going to do singing,

Wednesday so they're going to watch a TV programme. Because you get the feeling from between the lines, or even from direct observation, that they go home, they don't know if they're going to be let in, if they're going to be outside, if they're going to be fed tonight, or if they've got to go over to Gran's.

At the same time, he wanted to make school enjoyable and aimed to keep the children's attention as much as possible through turning many lessons and even the SATs into games and competitions in which the children competed either in teams or as individuals for house points which eventually might earn them small prizes or commendations read out at assemblies.

This meant a high concentration on whole-class teaching and a very individual teaching style which appeared to be successful in keeping the children's attention and in achieving results. In terms of David Hargreaves's typology of teaching styles, Peter could be described as an 'entertainer' who ran lively, game-like teaching sessions rather in the style of a television quiz-master or a circus ring-master. Peter saw the National Curriculum as a 'very middle-class, Southern sort of curriculum', 'assuming a lot of cultural background which the children don't have' and 'making use of inappropriate reading texts and materials in science which were not easily available in the children's homes'. Although he did not use these words, his argument was that the National Curriculum, although intended to ensure equal entitlement for all children, nevertheless required a certain amount of 'cultural capital' which was not available in the majority of families of the children in his class (Bourdieu and Passeron, 1970, 1977). He was very clearly aware of the National Curriculum's emphasis on equal entitlement in a situation where he felt that nevertheless there was a need to find a starting-point which was relevant for the children. He was therefore concerned to build bridges between the children's experience and the demands of the National Curriculum, and to mediate some of its 'middle-class' effects.

The initial effect of the National Curriculum, he felt, had been to make a typical day in his classroom 'far more loaded and more structured and rigid'. Nevertheless, he felt that he had been able to protect his relationship with the children through making a game out of learning and even out of the Key Stage 1 SATs. As he described it, 'You dress it up with stories and a bit of a joke and make fun and a game out of it' so that 'half the time they don't realize that they're working'.

In terms of the teacher strategies outlined in Chapter 3, Peter was clearly a 'creative mediator' who was filtering the demands of the National Curriculum through his own values (which in turn were influenced by his own personal biography and the school context in which he worked) to produce a particular style that he saw as protective of the children. Yet he nevertheless aimed to give them entitlement to a wider set of experiences that they would otherwise not have had access to. It was particularly important to him to build up children's self-esteem and confidence, and, at the same time, to introduce them to an experience of literature and to, as he put it, 'bring some poetry into their lives'.

More of Peter's story is presented in the book reporting the second phase of the pace project (Osborn, 1996a). In Peter's career it was evident that his personal and his professional 'self' were closely fused so that there was a heavy investment of self in his work as a teacher (Pollard, 1985; Nias, 1989). In order to maintain this integrity between his beliefs and his professional identity, he had worked very hard, but had also isolated himself in his classroom, sacrificing the informal collaboration with colleagues which might have helped to sustain or to reinforce or 'renew' him (Woods, 1995). Towards the end of the PACE study he was beginning to feel close to burn-out and doubted that he would be going on with teaching for many more years.

Many of the other teachers in the school expressed strong concern about the future of some of the children, arguing that the children had difficult and chaotic lives outside school. Like Peter, they expressed some doubt as to whether the demands of the National Curriculum were well suited to the children's needs. Most felt committed to providing some structure in the children's school lives, which they felt was missing outside. They faced a dilemma in finding a balance between relating to the children's needs in a differentiated way and yet continuing to ensure entitlement to the whole curriculum and range of learning opportunities. Another Year 3 teacher perceived many changes in the children he had taught over the years. He felt that the children he now taught had more health problems and a poorer diet than in the past, and far more came from split families:

> Many more children have broken homes, far more than in the past. Their parents can often rely on grandparents to help out. These children will not be able to do that when they become parents. Their parents won't be available to play a grandparent role. It's worrying for the future. There are more children with difficulties now than when I first started teaching. At home they are often ignored and told to go out to play. They are deprived of a carefree childhood. They live like 'East-Enders'. Their lives are dramas at home and they have less respect for authority. Some of the children are so close to the edge. We need to win children's respect for adults. They don't see a work ethic at home.

Mike Rowlings took most of the PACE children in Year 4. He was younger than Peter and had taught for five years. He was enthusiastic and energetic, and managed the children and class activities with verve. No doubt his physical presence (he was tall and of a large build) helped here. Although he shouted a lot in the class, he never exercised rigid control. There was often some latitude given to children where appropriate, to enable them to finish something or to develop something they were engrossed in. He was able to control conflicts between some of the boys quite easily and had some 'fun' ways of sanctioning. For example, he used a water pistol in a humorous way as a negative sanction and lollipops as a positive reward. On one occasion he was observed actually using the water pistol to get the children to sit down quickly after a technology lesson. Most children seemed to enjoy his class and responded to him better than they did with the other teachers to whom they went for maths and English sets.

Mike felt that although he had come into teaching with the National Curriculum in place, there had been changes in teachers' relationship with the children. To start with there had been a feeling that all freedom had been lost, but more recently there was a slightly more relaxed feeling in the school:

> It is not as bad now but there was definitely a time when every second of every day felt as if it had to be accounted for and it had to be educationally viable. Now there's a feeling that it can be balanced more over a longer period, which is much better ... Although it

has slackened off a bit now, there was so much content to do, you couldn't concentrate on making sure that a process was done well. You just had to get over information or complete a certain activity. Now that pressure seems to have dropped off a bit. We're actually dropping history and geography topics. The National Curriculum says we don't have to do as much, which is nice.

Recently this place has seen a lot more freedom, but over the three years before that there was a lot of constraint, a lot of pressure to be doing this, that and the other at this, that and the other time. If you were down to do geography at ten past nine, you should have been doing geography at ten past nine. Now there's a lot more freedom in the idea that it can be balanced over a year.

He had some fears, however, that the OFSTED inspection due in two years' time might result in more panic and tightening up as it approached.

Unlike Peter, Mike worked extensively with other teachers. He participated in regular meetings with the other teachers in the junior department. In particular, because he had a large number of special needs children in his class, he worked with the special needs coordinator. As assessment coordinator himself, he had been working closely with the headteacher over the past year to put together the school assessment policy. He liked the system of curriculum coordination which had been introduced since the National Curriculum, and felt that it worked well in an informal way in the school. However, he was concerned that there needed to be more clarity about the curriculum coordinator role:

I don't think that people know what they expect of the coordinators themselves. I don't think the coordinators know what's expected of themselves. When words like 'schemes of work', 'forecasts of work', 'curriculum policies', 'curriculum statements' are all bandied around and nobody really understands which one is which ... Most of them are exactly the same thing, but you find yourselves arguing amongst yourselves about what each one means without actually being able to get down and do them.

Although he was a very competent teacher and a science and technology specialist, like most of the teachers we interviewed Mike did not feel totally confident about teaching every National Curriculum subject. In particular, he did not feel happy having to teach music and some aspects of art:

Some of the levels of art I'm not so keen on at all. Some things that they ask you to do in art are just totally pointless. One of my main aims during art is for Philip to be able to use a paintbrush without stuffing it in somebody's ear, not whether he's appreciating something at a particular level!

In spite of the difficulties of teaching every subject at the level required for Key Stage 2 he did not feel happy about the idea of more subject specialist teaching than already took place because of the difficulties that would occur if he was out of his class even more:

There has been a powerful suggestion that we should do more specialist teaching and that has been rebuffed at the moment, but I think it is still lurking. I think it's lurking to see what officially [OFSTED etc.] ... whether they suggest it should be done more. We *do* specialist teaching in maths really because each teacher takes a specific level so you become a specialist in that level. I've already said that I don't have my class enough, so I would hate to be out for even longer.

A number of the children in Mike's class had severe family difficulties which reflected on their life in school. Chapter 11 of the companion book to this volume (Pollard *et al.*, 2000) describes some of these children in more detail. One child about whom Mike was particularly concerned, Susie, was on an at-risk register and her family was known by, and extensively involved with, social services. She suffered at school with stigmatization from the other children because of hygiene problems at home. She was also frequently absent from school, and this had been a problem from her earliest years in the school. One of her earliest school reports read:

> *Teacher's comments*: Susie is a bright child and very well behaved. She could be a lot more advanced if she could come to school regularly.

> *Headteacher's comments*: Susie has plenty of potential. Please get her to school more regularly so we can help her. A very cheerful girl.

Her infant teacher described her social circumstances in the following way:

> Mum at home, Dad on job creation scheme. They are entitled to free dinners but she goes home. She often comes in with no breakfast. Her mother doesn't get her up in the morning, she gets herself up. Family home apparently is strewn with dirty clothes and pets. She's left to fend for herself. She's the youngest of four children who all have the same problem. Their clothes and their hair and their general appearance and smell which affects other children's reactions to her. We are at the moment trying to sort something out with the family.

Mike was well aware of the social stigma attached to Susie and did what he could to encourage those children who were prepared to help her or at least tolerate her some of the time.

> It's terrible, terrible. They won't sit next to her. They won't stand next to her. A lot of it can't be blamed on them because she does smell a lot of the time. When she was younger ... her brother's just left here. So many emotional problems he had over it because he was exactly the same. He was treated like a pariah too. When she was younger – she still does – she would chase the children around because they didn't want to be touched by her. They would say, 'Oh, Susie touched me', and she liked the attention. She still does like the attention of that. She'll still play up to it, but it isn't a healthy interaction, shall we say. She doesn't have any friends really. There are a group of girls who will help her but if they were actually found to be Susie's friend, they would have seen a lot of stick.

Yet he was able to describe a time when Susie had a learning breakthrough and had achieved something unexpected for her, both in her writing and in mathematics:

> For me to say a learning breakthrough indicates that she knows it now and she'll know it for ever. I wouldn't like to say that but it struck me at the time that she did it, which was last week and ... I can't quite remember what it was now ... when we were doing the bridges the other day ... her level of understanding of some of the structural things we were talking about – bridges – and the week before we'd done this suspension bridge and we were saying what the nearest equivalent of the suspension bridge was. I'd said that the nearest equivalent was the bicycle wheel because it was actually hanging from the spokes that were above it rather than resting on the spokes that were below it. To which there was a classroom of blank faces, except for Susie, who – you could almost see it ticking over in her mind – was grasping it.

She came up with some good questions which I praised there and then. She responds very well to praise, and she was let loose then, and she was coming up with not just good answers but excellent answers ... She was thinking creatively around the problem. I think she's actually caught a glimpse of the fact that she ... as I say, she was praised straight away and I think she caught a glimpse that she did understand, she could do it. Whether it was for the second or not, she was doing it. She responded to that. She shone for five or ten minutes.

Mike had come into teaching just as the National Curriculum was in place, whereas the teacher to whom many of the PACE children moved on in Years 5 and 6, Bill Bridges, was a new teacher in his second year of teaching. His perspective differed from that of Mike, but was not dissimilar, and in all three of the teachers and their beliefs about pedagogy it was possible to discern the same threads of argument that had been put by the head and which were evident in the school ethos. These include a concern with equal entitlement and a structure that built bridges between the children's experience and the curriculum, and a readiness to motivate the children in any way which seemed to work, whether it was with humour and entertaining lessons or with extrinsic rewards such as lollipops.

As a new teacher, Bill was very much enjoying having his own class where he could begin to take control and establish his own relationships with the children. Because he felt closer to the children and had got to know them better than he ever had been able to on teaching practice, he had gained in confidence considerably: 'I feel a lot closer to the children, able to motivate them more, able to put down my own levels of discipline and so on, purely because of spending more time with them and getting to know them.' He had not lost a sense of enjoyment in teaching, in spite of having to cope with the difficulties of some of the children in the class, which made it hard to get on with what he felt was the real job of teaching:

I am enjoying teaching. I do enjoy it and I hope I continue to enjoy it but at the moment a lot of the time at this school I'm feeling, especially with this class, I'm being more of a disciplinarian rather than a teacher, and a lot of my time or too much of my time is spent trying to just get a situation where teaching can actually be done. So I've been spending a lot of time in a lesson, a lot of teaching time, just getting the children calmed down, settled down, able to work and then, because of that I've been missing out on this ... because as you know, there's the statemented children and so on in my class, and they've been missing out on, say, 20 minutes of valuable time, whilst I've been making, say, Danielle sit down or Steven stop fighting and so on.

Bill gained considerable support from other teachers and felt that he was gaining a lot from them. As a new teacher he enjoyed learning from others' experience and felt that a sharing of the workload could only be beneficial to everyone. Because of the high number of special needs children in his class, he worked particularly closely with the special needs coordinator and with an adviser from the Learning Support Centre who came in twice a week to work with the special needs children. He also planned and worked closely with the other Year 6 teacher in order to sort out the SATs which were due to take place in the summer term and to share games teaching with her. Since they both had Year 6 children in their classes they did a number of things collaboratively. Mike Rowlings had helped considerably with science and technology, an area where Bill felt less confident. Mike had made many suggestions about experiments that could be done in the class, such as the tin can rolling experiment observed during the one of the PACE classroom study weeks which was designed to teach measurement.

> I'm not too confident about science and technology and music. However, music has become slightly easier because of the BBC tapes where the National Curriculum requirements are being met by somebody on a tape, so the only bits I do are the pause bits ... Science and technology, again I've been working with Mike quite a bit, asking for his help as he's the coordinator for those subjects and I think I've been getting quite a lot more out of them as regards that as well. We did a lot of work on Friction and they've all got the concept of friction sorted. We did a bit of work on Storing Energy and because of the experiment it was something they could see, touch and feel and so on. They seemed to have grasped that concept well as well ... I still feel I've an awful lot to learn in science. I actually applied to go on a few courses for science but they were undersubscribed so they got cancelled.

Bill's experience of support from other teachers contrasted with that of Rebecca at Orchard, who, as a new teacher, mainly had to find her own way through, largely because of the pressure on other staff in a small school and because of the crisis conditions prevailing in the school during her first year of teaching.

Like that of the other two St Anne's teachers we have described above, Bill's pedagogy was highly structured and teacher directed. As he himself described it:

> The vast majority of things that go on in my class are teacher led. However, things like technology, art and so on, they have a certain free rein in that. They have a loose instruction from which they can interpret their own meaning ... There isn't – or there's very little, should I say – children-led stuff. There's not a lot of time for it.

He described some activities involving the more able children which had led to their initiating an idea and being given some responsibility for following it through, whilst the activities were carefully structured by the teacher. For example, a group did a survey throughout the school on children's attitude to school meals, and this had enabled Bill to get them to analyse the information, make bar charts and pie charts and to write a report on their results. On another occasion the same group of able children had asked to do extra work on their topic of study, the ancient Greeks, and had been provided with extra resources and material by Bill to enable them to carry it through. This work had been displayed on the walls.

However, he did query how much children *ought* to be in control of their learning:

> I think it's fine to have those opportunities but, as I said, I'm not too sure how often they ought to be given those opportunities. I think there's a place for them because it's a different learning skill which can't – I wouldn't have thought anyway – harm a child's educational development, but I'm not sure exactly how much they should be in control.

He described his pedagogy as mainly whole-class teaching, but with a considerable amount of individual work and paired work. He felt unable to do as much group work as he would have liked because of the nature of the children in the class:

> They don't interact very well together, as a whole. There are fractious elements – whichever grouping you have, there tends to be some kind of an argument, so that

renders the activity pointless almost. You end up having to sort out one group from fighting, arguing or whatever. Then you don't get to keep as tight a hold on the other groups as I would like.

Perhaps because of this pressure to keep hold over the class as a whole, when he heard children read he often listened to two readers at a time, while doing something else at his desk. The only opportunity the children in his class had to read to an adult one-to-one was done outside the classroom with volunteers.

The teachers of the PACE children at St Anne's had responded to trying to make the needs of the National Curriculum meet their children's needs by emphasizing structure and teacher-led whole-class activities. Sometimes this was done as a deliberate strategy based on a strong belief that this was the best way to ensure that all children received their entitlement to a full range of experiences, as in the case of Peter; sometimes it was a response to the conditions in the class and the need of a younger, more inexperienced teacher to maintain classroom control and still get through all the targets he was expected to meet, as in the case of Bill.

9.5 CONCLUSION

These case-studies give a brief flavour of the complexity of the issues surrounding teachers' response to externally imposed change. The stance teachers take and the coping strategies they adopt are immensely varied and may be influenced by many factors including personal biography, beliefs and values, gender, the social background of the children they teach, the type of school and the conditions of stability or turbulence, support or crisis that exist at the time, the headteacher's style and the school ethos. All the case-studies show the extent to which teachers mediate government directives and external requirements to produce their own personal blend of teaching style and approach to coping with change.

There has been a tendency in much of the recent research on teachers to focus on school experience and to ignore other important aspects of teachers' lives, to present teachers as having neither a past nor a future, as being without life beyond the classroom (Lightfoot, 1983; Acker, 1995). Whilst there are many aspects of these teachers' stories which we lack space to present here, this chapter has attempted to portray some of the complexities and contingencies in the lives of teachers in three different schools and to illuminate some of the influences that have affected their values and beliefs about teaching and their identities as professionals.

Part 5

A Changing Culture

Chapter 10

The Changing Role of Headteachers

10.1 INTRODUCTION

The 1988 Education Reform Act (ERA) spearheaded what Wallace (1991) has referred to as 'multiple innovation' which was system-wide and included a major shift from local authority control to the local management of schools (LMS). This, in turn, heralded devolved budgets, new school inspection requirements, a teacher appraisal system and revised school accountability structures, including new patterns of school governance. These changes were also accompanied by the introduction of a market philosophy with respect to education policy-making (Menter *et al.*, 1997), through such mechanisms as open enrolment, opting out and the publication of league tables of pupil assessment performance. Not only did headteachers find themselves in the position of taking overall responsibility for the successful implementation and management of these changes, but they had to do so in an evolving management framework that had given them little preparation, support or training.

The government intentions behind the reforms were to push for transformational change: change in the headteacher's role itself and, more widely, radical alteration to both the processes and the product of education in an effort in 'raise standards'. Headteachers were identified by government as key 'change agents' at school organizational level, who would be both the recipients and the initiators and managers of this change. Hence, these structural and system changes have affected not only the context of operation for headteachers but also the content of their role (Pollard *et al.*, 1994a). Before the 1980s the main function, as their title implied, was considered to be that of 'leading professional'. Unlike school principals in the USA, headteachers in Britain were seen primarily as teachers, responsible for curriculum matters and the motivation and support of staff, rather than as administrators and managers. They were essentially autonomous and assumed a strong moral and ethical component to their leadership (Grace, 1995, p. 142).

The time line (Figure 10.1) illustrates the scale of the changes, which not only have been unprecedented in both their volume and rate of occurrence, but were also introduced in a climate of low teacher morale, teacher industrial action, restructured salary levels, falling pupil rolls and teacher unemployment. These would have been difficult circumstances for any group of managers, whether in education or elsewhere.

Although the main focus of the PACE study was on those changes that had directly affected teachers and pupils, the main sample of nine case-study schools was set within a larger sample of 48 schools to enable the research team to gather information on the effects of more system-wide changes. Data were collected, at regular intervals over the six-year period, by way of questionnaire and semi-structured interview from the headteachers of this larger sample of schools. As with any longitudinal study, there were changes of staff, with some older headteachers taking early retirement and some younger teachers moving into headship posts, bringing with them different expectations of the role. Caution has therefore been employed in the interpretation of data collected from a constant, though changing, sample. The way in which individual headteachers reacted to the pressure of these changes was also affected by individual differences such as past experience, length of service, training and gender, as well as issues to do with school size, catchment area and its relationship with the local education authority (LEA). The sample, though representative, was small and so care needs to be taken in interpreting these additional influences. However, where they were considered to be of particular importance, attention has been drawn to them in the data analysis.

Three dimensions of change were distilled from the PACE 1 data and these continue to provide a useful analytic framework with which to draw out the major themes that became apparent over the six-year study. Three interrelated dimensions of 'autonomy/constraint', 'collegiality/managerialism' and 'resistance/compliance' were modelled in the form of a cube (see Figure 10.2), and this forms the basis for the following analysis.

10.2 CONTEXT OF OPERATION

Over the six-year period, headteachers' main focus of professional accountability and concern was consistently on their own personal and moral responsibility towards their own consciences as well as to those immediately under their personal leadership, notably pupils and staff (Table 10.1). This reflects an earlier model in

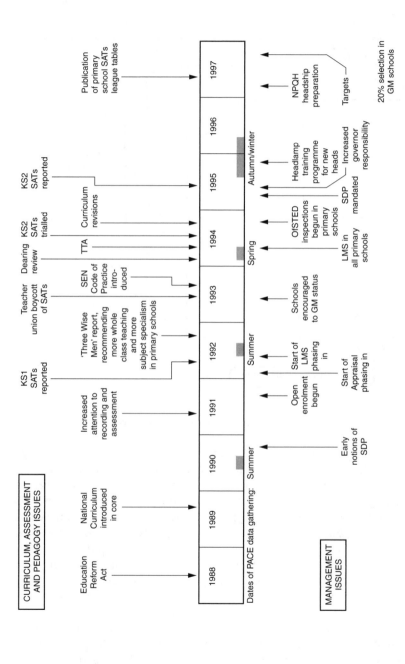

Figure 10.1 Time line of government policy reforms in relation to PACE data collection.

KS = Key Stage; SAT = Standard Assessment Task; SEN = special educational needs; TTA = Teacher Training Agency; SDP = School Development Plan; LMS = local management of schools; GM = grant-maintained; OFSTED = Office for Standards in Education; NPQH = National Professional Qualification for Headship

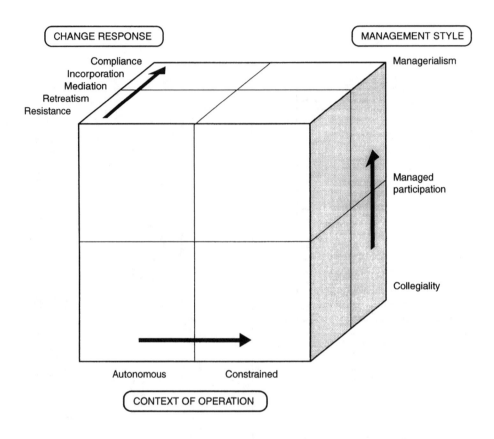

Figure 10.2 Dimensions of headteacher responses to externally imposed change

which headteachers were seen as senior teachers, sharing the professional ideology and aspirations of their colleagues. When we interviewed headteachers in more depth, however, there appeared to be a reduction over time in the number of headteachers feeling 'very accountable' to their own consciences (93 per cent in 1990 to 85 per cent in 1995). This seemed to reflect the difficulty that some headteachers were experiencing in reconciling the requirements of their role with their personal educational values. For some this resulted in a more instrumental approach to their work as they felt more and more driven by pressures for external accountability and could no longer feel free to act according to their own consciences.

As the study progressed, there was clear evidence that headteachers' feelings of accountability, overall, were increasing. They considered themselves to be 'very accountable' to a wider range of stakeholders, including outside agencies, which resulted in some distancing of their relationship with their staff. The new school governance structure, with its statutory responsibility for delivering the National Curriculum and its associated assessment procedures, managing school budgets, and hiring and firing staff, had brought heads into a much closer working relationship

Table 10.1 To whom did headteachers consider themselves to be 'very accountable' (percentages)?

	1990	1992	1994	1995
Yourself/own conscience	92.8	78.4	90.0	85.4
Pupils	88.1	64.9	76.7	68.7
Parents	57.1	62.2	60.0	64.5
Governors	35.7	32.4	50.0	56.2
Colleagues	66.6	54.1	60.0	50.0
Employers	9.5	2.7	16.7	22.9
Society in general	9.5	10.8	13.3	22.9
Inspectors/advisers	*question not asked*		10.0	16.7
Government	2.4	2.8	6.6	8.3
	n = 42	*n* = 37	*n* = 30	*n* = 48

Source: PACE 1, 2 and 3 headteacher questionnaires
Date: Summer 1990, Summer 1992, Spring 1994, Autumn 1995
Sample: 48 headteachers

with their school governors. In 1995, for the first time, a greater number of headteachers felt 'very accountable' to their governors (56 per cent) than to their colleagues (50 per cent). An increasing proportion of headteachers felt 'very accountable' to both parents and inspectors/advisers as the study progressed. Employers and 'society in general' also steadily rose in importance (from 10 per cent to 30 per cent in both cases) in headteachers' feelings of accountability. These findings indicate an increased awareness, and responsiveness, towards meeting government demands for higher educational outcomes that were both economically and socially instrumental.

However, there were also some examples of headteachers who offered some resistance to government pressure with regard to achievement of attainment targets. This can be illustrated by one head, who commented in interview:

> Perhaps I have an inbuilt resistance to targets as such. But we *have* developed in terms of what and how we deliver. The more sterile the exercise ... it stifles useful motivating initiative if the move is expressed as a sequential target for achieving change ... you get resistance.

Headteachers were also asked to rate the importance of various educational objectives. An analysis of these showed a noticeable shift of emphasis away from the purposes of serving the individual developmental needs of children, the hallmark of the 'progressive' tradition, towards more 'instrumental' or 'traditional' aims. Although 'basic skills' had always been a high academic priority, with between 81 per cent and 83 per cent rating it as 'essential', for the first time in 1995 it was ranked slightly higher than the general aim of 'developing the child's full potential'. More affective objectives for the children such as their 'being happy and well-balanced' and 'enjoying school' fell significantly, whereas economic and social objectives such as 'equipping the child to take his/her place in society', 'developing respect for others' property', promoting 'obedience to authority' and enhancing 'moral and social development' all rose in importance.

A contradictory picture was emerging. On the one hand, headteachers appeared to have become more compliant in aligning themselves and their professional thinking with government policy. On the other hand, their enduring notions of their professional responsibility towards pupils and teachers appeared to sit uneasily with their lowered levels of accountability to them and signal a dilemma for headteachers. Their professional relationships with pupils and colleagues had been the main source of job satisfaction and fulfilment in the past, a finding confirmed by other research (Nias, 1989). By PACE 3 the loss of contact with children was still a cause of sorrow, although it was mentioned less frequently. It was not, as might have been predicted, felt only by older headteachers or female headteachers, a finding confirmed by Hill (1994). For example, a new male headteacher feeling the loss commented, 'I want to get back in class, know the kids, get closer'. Taken together with the other interview evidence, the ratings on accountability to 'yourself/your own conscience', to pupils and to colleagues indicated a separation of the 'self' of headteachers from their role: it was becoming more a job than a vocation. Recent research by Jeffrey and Woods (1996) also found a movement away from teachers' former vocational commitment towards an 'instrumental' attitude to their role, as a result of the pressure of OFSTED.

In this chapter we will look more closely at what the interview data tell us about the way in which headteachers have experienced these changes along the dimensions of *autonomy/constraint*, *collegiality/managerialism* and *resistance/compliance* before illustrating these issues with case-studies.

10.3 AUTONOMY/CONSTRAINT DIMENSION

During interview, headteachers were asked, 'With regard to your freedom of action as a headteacher in different areas of your work, how free do you feel to act as you think best?' The responses were then coded and an analysis of their perceptions of freedom was made (Table 10.2).

There was a marked increase in feelings of constraint in 1992 and 1994, when two-thirds of headteachers felt either 'very' or 'fairly' constrained. This coincided with a period of major change for primary schools which directly affected headteachers, namely the introduction of LMS and the first Key Stage 1 SAT reporting to parents in 1992; and the introduction of new special educational needs (SEN) procedures and full LMS in all schools in 1994. By 1995 the pattern of responses much more closely resembled that of 1990, with approximately half of the headteachers feeling either 'completely' or 'fairly' free. The evidence suggested that a normalization process had occurred in which headteachers became acclimatized to operating within their new management frameworks. However, compared with 1990, there was some evidence in 1995 of a greater polarization of opinion, with heavier weighting at both ends of the spectrum of responses, 'very constrained' and 'completely free'.

In 1995 all the headteachers who felt 'completely free' were male and those feeling 'fairly free' were also more likely to be male. This raised the question of whether the new management framework, a rational, 'masculine' model, was more readily adopted by male headteachers. Handy (1994) notes that such systems pay great

Table 10.2 Headteachers' perceptions of freedom of action in different areas of their work (percentages)

	1990	1992	1994	1995
Completely free	4.2	2.1	2.1	8.3
Fairly free	50.0	31.3	27.1	43.8
Undecided	8.3	2.1	6.3	10.4
Fairly constrained	29.2	33.3	31.3	20.8
Very much constrained	8.3	31.3	33.3	16.7
	n = 48	n = 48	n = 48	n = 48

Source: PACE 1, 2 and 3 headteacher interviews
Date: Summer 1990, Summer 1992, Spring 1994, Autumn 1995
Sample: 48 headteachers

attention to the 'harder', more 'masculine' aspects of organization but go against the grain of 'softer', more 'feminine' management approaches, typical of a collegiate headship role with the emphasis on people and relationships. Those headteachers who said that they felt 'free' to act as they thought best were also more likely to say that they felt only 'partially influenced' by the availability of financial resources. Not surprisingly, therefore, a correlation was also found between the socio-economic status of the school and the freedom/constraint dimension. Headteachers of 'disadvantaged' schools were more likely to feel 'very much constrained' by financial concerns, which continued to be a major issue affecting headteachers' feeling of autonomy. There was a tendency for new headteachers, of less than four years, or long-serving headteachers, of more than twenty years' service, to feel 'free'. This suggested that initial enthusiasm and the lack of previous conceptions of the role, as well as long-term experience, played a part in headteachers' perceptions of their freedom.

Table 10.3 Perceived changes to the amount of freedom headteachers had to act as they think (percentages)

	1990	1992	1994	1995
Much more freedom	0.0	0.0	4.2	8.3
Slightly more freedom	2.1	4.2	18.8	14.6
No noticeable change	29.2	16.7	6.3	33.3
Slightly less freedom	50.0	25.0	22.9	20.8
Very much less freedom	16.7	52.1	41.7	18.8
Not stated	2.1	2.1	6.3	4.2
	n = 48	n = 48	n = 48	n = 48

Source: PACE 1, 2 and 3 headteacher interviews
Date: Summer 1990, Summer 1992, Spring 1994, Autumn 1995
Sample: 48 headteachers

Table 10.3 shows headteacher responses to the follow-up question concerned with the extent to which they considered that their freedom to act had been changing. It can be seen that there was a gradual reduction in the number of headteachers who perceived an increase in constraint, the proportion having fallen from 67 per cent in 1990 to 40 per cent in 1995, with a peak in 1992 of 77 per cent. Again, the years of the greatest volume of change in 1992 and 1994 produced the lowest percentage of headteachers who considered that there was 'no noticeable change' in their amount of freedom to act. The substantial minority who continued to feel 'slightly' or 'very much' less free by 1995 were predominantly from urban LEAs and those reporting 'more freedom' in the same year were more likely to be male and from 'advantaged' rural schools.

Further detail about the substance of the demands on headteachers was provided in answers to a question concerning the ways in which their freedom to act had been changing (Table 10.4). Again there is a noticeable difference in the responses in 1992,

Table 10.4 Nature of the changes in freedom/constraint – open responses (percentages)

	1990	1992	1994	1995
More financial planning	31.3	50.0	87.5	64.6
More record-keeping/paperwork	52.1	0.0	22.9	45.8
More time spent curriculum planning	39.6	0.0	47.9	45.8
Pressure to justify (inc. OFSTED)	18.8	0.0	47.9	54.2
More emphasis on governors' meetings	25.0	0.0	29.2	31.3
Less free time	27.1	0.0	12.5	22.9
Less curriculum choice	0.0	62.5	47.9	20.8
Less contact with pupils	27.1	0.0	8.3	16.7
NC as tool for change	25.0	0.0	20.8	14.6
Constraint of central government	0.0	50.0	0.0	0.0
Assessment constraints	0.0	22.9	0.0	0.0
	$n = 48$	$n = 48$	$n = 48$	$n = 48$

Source: PACE 1, 2 and 3 headteacher interviews
Date: Summer 1990, Summer 1992, Spring 1994, Autumn 1995
Sample: 48 headteachers

when pressures appear to have been at their height and spontaneous responses were concentrated on the general constraint of central government legislation, the increasing pressure of ensuring the delivery of a tightly prescribed National Curriculum, and the introduction of SAT testing and LMS. The focus of concerns uppermost in headteachers' minds had changed over the six-year period of the research, showing a sequential attention to different issues as they were mandated.

Curriculum and assessment

PACE 1 and 2 data showed that the new demands on headteachers' use of time meant that they had become increasingly distanced from day-to-day involvement in curriculum matters. Responsibility for the detail was left to the deputy headteachers or the curriculum coordinators. These findings are supported by Webb (1993), who also noted that headteachers were increasingly unable to play a full part in curriculum development, planning and teaching. Many of the responses of the PACE 3 sample of headteachers showed that their personal involvement had further decreased, to the extent that they no longer felt competent to comment on the detail of changes. However, these responses were, for the most part, expressed not as regret but as a fact of life.

In 1992 there was almost exclusive concern, on the part of the headteachers, over perceived constraints associated with the introduction of the National Curriculum and its assessment requirements. The constraint of central government policy was mentioned specifically during the introduction of reporting requirements of Key Stage 1 SAT test results to parents. Subsequently, the proportion of those reporting concern over the loss of freedom over curriculum choice diminished from 63 per cent in 1992 to 21 per cent in 1995, indicating that, over time, the initial major curriculum changes became largely taken for granted. As the study progressed, the view that the National Curriculum was both overcrowded and too prescriptive began to hold sway and a review was commissioned under the leadership of Sir Ron Dearing, which reported its findings in the spring of 1994. There was a subsequent pruning of the curriculum, and tightly defined *attainment targets* were replaced with more general *statements of attainment*. There was also a notional 20 per cent of curriculum time that was left to the discretion of the school to use as it saw fit. These changes had just begun to take effect by the time of the 1995 round of data collection, and headteachers' responses began to reflect this new situation (Table 10.5).

Table 10.5 Headteacher perceptions of change in manageability of the National Curriculum (percentages)

	1995
Manageable	18.8
Almost/by combining	39.6
Manageable/superficial	20.8
Too crowded	20.8
	$n = 48$

Source: PACE 3 headteacher interviews
Date: Autumn 1995
Sample: 48 headteachers

However, concern still remained about the manageability of the National Curriculum. When asked about the impact of the 20 per cent of discretionary time, headteachers were clear in their responses: 'no difference' (54 per cent), a 'small difference' (42 per cent). Only two headteachers in the sample considered that it had made a 'marked difference'. When asked what use they had made of this extra freedom, almost a third of the sample said that the time had been used to 'justify existing practice'. This had enabled them to continue with activities such as school plays, concerts and sports days – activities that had been under threat because of the pressure of limited time. A quarter of headteachers said that it had given them the opportunity to create a more structured personal and social education programme, which they considered an important element of the primary curriculum. Another 23 per cent said that the time had been used to cover additional work on core subjects (English/reading, maths) or to give extra depth to other National Curriculum subjects. The concerns of headteachers reflected both the individual headteacher's values and the relative importance he or she placed on different aspects of the National Curriculum in the context of the school and its pupils. Thus, 25 per cent considered that the 'basics' (reading, writing, arithmetic) were being neglected, but others felt that the 'core' curriculum was occupying too much of the timetable to the detriment of the expressive arts (15 per cent). Others mentioned the emphasis on 'knowledge' at the expense of 'key skills', such as the ability to choose an appropriate method or materials for an activity, or gathering information independently. This was in contrast to those headteachers who were positive about the National Curriculum because they considered that it was skills based: 17 per cent mentioned an improvement in process and investigative skills.

By the time of the 1995 interviews, schools had already experienced four years of formal reported assessment at Key Stage 1 and the first year of Key Stage 2 reporting. The requirement for teacher assessment to be formalized appeared to have become an accepted part of practice by the majority of headteachers. The Dearing review had addressed concerns about the manageability of Key Stage testing (SATs), and calls by the headteachers for a reduction in the time-consuming process had noticeably decreased, from 56 per cent in 1994 to 8 per cent in 1995. A new concern was reliability and consistency in determining the attainment level achieved in Key Stage 2 SATs and their comparability across schools. Headteachers perceived a danger of some schools 'cheating' by giving more help to their pupils in the test situation. Others considered that more flexibility in the procedures for the administration of the SATs could enable more help to be given to children with special educational needs so that they could demonstrate more easily what they 'know, understand and can do'. Concerns about the reliability of SAT scores were, in part, a reflection of headteachers' nervousness about the publication of the results in 'league tables' which ranked their school in order against the performance of similar schools in the area. One-quarter of the headteachers interviewed in 1995 made reference to this concern.

Over one-third of headteachers in 1995 considered that SATs were stressful for children, just under a half continued to try to keep assessment 'low key' and two-thirds had a policy of stressing other positive achievements of their pupils. However, in the same period, there was a significant increase in the number of headteachers adopting a different strategy. Rather than playing down assessment and keeping both teacher assessment and national testing low key, schools were increasingly routinizing assessment procedures through the regular use of tests (up from 2 per cent in 1994 to 29 per cent in 1995). Increasing emphasis was also placed on acclimatizing pupils to the demands of external testing, with 42 per cent of headteachers in 1995 reporting a strategy of 'teaching to the tests'. This, they recognized, resulted in an overall reduction in teaching time, the superficial coverage of some topics and the marginalization of some subjects, such as art and music.

However, slightly more than one-third of headteachers interviewed in 1995 considered that the current assessment arrangements supported children's learning.

By 1995 it was apparent that there had been a shift in the attitude of headteachers. Whilst half of the headteachers would have liked to see more emphasis placed on teacher assessment, and 20 per cent expressed a view that it should completely replace national testing, the majority of their responses to open-ended questions relating to assessment were to do with fine-tuning the detail, rather than a return to previous practice.

Accountability and OFSTED

The data in Table 10.4 also show headteachers' increased attention to demonstrating accountability, with an increasing emphasis being given to governors' meetings (from 25 per cent in 1990 to 31 per cent in 1995) and an even greater perceived pressure from OFSTED inspection (from 19 per cent in 1990 to 54 per cent in 1995). By September 1994 the new structure for primary school inspection had been put in place by the Office for Standards in Education (OFSTED), which was to have a major influence on schools. By the time of the headteacher interviews in 1995, a quarter of the sample schools had already had an inspection, another 29 per cent had been informed that their inspection would occur within the next year and the remainder had yet to be notified of a date. Some headteachers (40 per cent) saw this as positive and spoke of using the inspection process, or the post-OFSTED report, as a focus for getting things done and a potential lever for change. The following remarks come from two headteachers who were preparing for an inspection: 'I'm trying to make teachers aware of learning objectives – skills, concepts, knowledge – asking, "Can you justify this? Is it effective"' and 'we are finding a common language for talking about curriculum issues which we didn't necessarily have before'.

Although headteachers from all categories were represented in this 40 per cent figure, these views were significantly more likely to come from heads in post between one and four years, followed by heads in post for five to ten years. Twenty-seven per cent of headteachers also spoke of using the inspection process as a focus for classroom issues: 'The staff are more aware of how they teach, they're analysing more ... the quality of learning is looked at through the *evidence* of books.' However, a further 15 per cent recognized inspection as a potential threat and saw it as another area of increased accountability that impacted on their relationship with their staff:

> I'm the herald of change ... they expect it of me with a 1996–7 OFSTED planned. I know the weaknesses of the school, but we need to analyse everything, how the provision of resources is translated into quality education ... it permeates everything ... I'm not the ogre.

It also created a gulf that may not have been there before: 'It's less easy to empathize with teachers because I'm dragged away from classrooms ... I don't want to be critical from on high, I want to be supportive.' Or similarly,

We've always worked and planned as a whole school ... as a team for the past eight or nine years. Therefore we were able to take on board the changes. [Then notification of the inspection date arrived.] Suddenly, everyone was trying to do their own bit, getting schemes of work and documents ready ... it was frantic despite the school development plan ... the poor secretary!

All categories of headteachers were represented in this range of responses. However, the greatest stress associated with inspection was amongst headteachers who had not been notified of their inspection date. In a school where the notification had been cancelled and an unspecified date given for the next academic year, the head said, 'It's horrendous. We promised we wouldn't use the OFSTED word for a term! It would be all right if you could take away the anxiety, but it's impossible.'

These findings indicate an increasing focus on the effectiveness of the delivery of the curriculum, together with other school improvement issues. The pressure of external requirements began to take their toll and a third of headteachers spoke of protecting their staff by deliberately taking a slow, steady approach to impending inspection. For example:

We shall try to have the requirements in place ... the policies in *practice*. It's supposed to be stressful and I don't relish it but it's part of life in education now and so we make the best of it. I'm determined it won't be demoralizing. I hope we'll be aware of areas of weakness and strengths. I hope there'll be no surprises.

A third of headteachers also spoke of developing an action plan to tackle areas of weakness, identified before or after an inspection, of tightening up on planning and sharing together. Most headteachers attempted to make changes through the mechanism of the School Development Plan. In order to do this, many headteachers had taken on a detached, 'instrumental' or pragmatic leadership role, distancing themselves from more interpersonal, close collegiate relationships and moving towards a more directive management style in order to drive through changes. As one headteacher put it, 'It's my responsibility to pace what OFSTED is looking for and see that it ties in with the development plan and the budget and the timescale.' There was increasing evidence that change was being managed through more formal procedures, rather than developing in an evolutionary or organic fashion. The need for strong leadership and the capacity to deal with the consequences of a poor OFSTED inspection were also becoming crucial. One newly appointed headteacher in a disadvantaged inner-city area explained:

I'm trying to be supportive and a good listener to staff, parents and children: a confidence-building exercise. However, since OFSTED, 10 per cent of the pupils have left and there is a steady trickle out, which will have a knock-on effect on the budget – loss of teachers and therefore larger classes – the worst thing that could happen.

Paperwork and increased workload

Some issues of constraint faded in importance, only to re-emerge in 1995. Two such issues were the lack of free time and the loss of time spent with pupils (23 per cent and 17 per cent, respectively, in 1995). Another issue was the amount of paperwork and record-keeping, which was mentioned by half the headteachers in 1990, by only 23 per cent in 1994, but by 46 per cent in 1995. These items are probably interrelated, and appeared to re-emerge as long-term issues. High levels of work activity, which were expected to be a response to short-term demands, have instead become a regular feature of the job. This frustration was expressed by one headteacher who was interviewed early in the morning, before the start of the school day, having worked a fourteen-hour day the previous day: starting at 8 a.m. in school until 3 p.m., then on a course until 6 p.m. and then straight to a meeting until 10 p.m.: 'There is an increasing expectation by the LEA (local education authority] on heads to get you to take on more and more – the ability to say "No" is key.'

Local Management of Schools (LMS) and devolved budgets

However, the main focus of concern in 1995 was finance. Levels of concern about the time spent on financial planning rose in tandem with its phased introduction, peaking in 1994 (88 per cent) when LMS was fully introduced into all primary schools. It remained a concern in 1995 with more than double the mentions of 1990. Three-quarters of headteachers said that school planning was 'greatly influenced' by the financial resources available. This figure included the majority of headteachers from urban or inner-city/estate schools with disadvantaged catchment areas, as well as all the headteachers in two particular local authorities, suggesting that these constraints differed with specific circumstances. Rural schools in advantaged areas were least likely to be affected. Initially, a quarter of headteachers in the sample welcomed the devolved budget but the proportion had declined to 15 per cent by 1995. The original promise of greater flexibility through LMS was replaced by the reality of small margins of manoeuvrability for most headteachers with limited financial resources. Their budgets could be managed only through strict priority-setting and by postponing all but the most essential expenditure. The appointment of younger, less experienced teaching staff on lower salaries was also mentioned as a means of managing limited budgets. Overall, most headteachers felt constrained by a real reduction in income as they met the increasing costs of teachers' salaries. For many, this meant an added pressure to raise extra funds from parents and other entrepreneurial enterprises.

However, there were exceptions. In one LEA, headteachers of primary schools that had been formed from the recent amalgamations of infant and junior schools found that they had more money available for classroom resources and refurbishment of the buildings. European 'City Challenge' money enabled a major playground development for another inner-city school in the sample. Table 10.6 gives a flavour of what budget constraints meant for headteachers and their staff in practical terms. These data paint a picture of headteachers managing schools with fewer teachers, who were themselves managing with less support, less preparation time and fewer resources. Few schools in the sample had taken advantage of the possibility of becoming grant-maintained and so receiving a higher level of funding directly from central government.

Table 10.6 Open-ended responses to the perceived effects of the Local Management of Schools (percentages)

	1995
Fewer classroom resources	33.3
Less non-contact time for teachers	27.1
Teaching staff reductions	20.8
Support staff reductions	12.5
School maintenance reductions	8.3
Increased reliance on parental fund raising	8.3
Increased funds through grant-maintained status	6.3
	n = 48

Source: PACE 3 headteacher interviews
Date: Autumn 1995
Sample: 48 headteachers
Note: Totals do not equal 100 per cent as some answers were coded more than once

Influence of school–parent relations

With school funding linked closely to pupil numbers, some headteachers were concerned about the impact on enrolment from competition by neighbouring schools. In trying to make their school attractive to parents, headteachers emphasized the importance of developing good relationships with parents, rather than relying solely on good SAT results. However, the evidence from longitudinal data (Table 10.7) was that the nature of headteachers' relationships with parents had

Table 10.7 Percentage of change in parent–school relations (percentages)

	1990	1992	1994	1995
Great/noticeable change	8.3	31.3	20.8	29.2
Moderate change	43.8	31.3	25.0	31.3
Little or no change	47.9	37.5	54.2	39.6
		n = 48	*n* = 48	*n* = 48

Source: PACE 1, 2 and 3 headteacher interviews
Date: Summer 1990, Spring 1994, Autumn 1995
Sample: 48 headteachers

altered with the introduction of the Parents' Charter (in 1991), which enshrined parents' rights as consumers. By 1995 nearly one-third of headteachers considered that there had been a 'great' or 'noticeable' change to their relationship with parents. This compared with only four headteachers considering this to be the case in 1990. A further third considered that there had been 'moderate' changes, and this represents a significant shift. The general trend discernible from PACE 1 and 2 data suggested a move away from the various informal links which schools had with parents to a more formal contact, partly as a consequence of the new reporting procedures.

Table 10.8 Headteacher open-ended comments regarding parent–school relations (percentages)

	1990	1992	1994	1995
Require information/explanation about NC	0.0	60.4	43.8	73.0
More demanding/anxious	20.8	12.5	25.0	50.0
Concerned/supportive	33.3	10.4	52.1	50.0
Relaxed/passive	10.4	18.8	41.7	35.4
Difficult to involve	18.8	37.5	0.0	0.0
	$n = 48$	$n = 48$	$n = 48$	$n = 48$

Source: PACE 1, 2 and 3 headteacher interviews
Date: Summer 1990, Spring 1994, Autumn 1995
Sample: 48 headteachers
Note: Totals do not equal 100 per cent as some headteachers' answers were coded more than once. NC = National Curriculum

As Table 10.8 shows, this initial trend was confirmed by PACE 3 data that continued to show an increase in the need for information expressed by parents, and a concomitant increase in the 'demanding/anxious' nature of this parental involvement as perceived by headteachers (mentioned by one-fifth of headteachers in 1990 but half of headteachers in 1995). One headteacher in 1995 expressed this tension as follows:

> There's less parental involvement in organizing things. Parents are more for their rights, what they read in the newspapers. But there's better involvement in their own child's progress – that's up if anything ... but if there's an argument with the child's teacher, they go straight to the education officer, not the headteacher first.

This could be interpreted as an indication of the increasing pressure on parents with regard to their free time. However, it could also be an indication that they became alienated from a more casual relationship with their schools because of the new discourse of SATs, Attainment Targets, continuity and progression, which may not have come easily to them.

Nevertheless, half of the headteachers in each of the last two rounds of interviews felt that most parents were still supportive, even if the support was passive support. Overall, these data suggest the beginning of a change in the approach of parents, away from a 'partnership' or 'covenant' relationship based on trust, towards a more market-orientated, 'supplier–consumer' relationship. Although there is evidence that communications between parents and schools had increased, comments from the headteachers suggested that this was more to do with the school fulfilling its legal contractual obligations than with parents and schools developing equal and productive partnerships. Newer headteachers (of less than four years' experience) appeared to be more sensitive to parents as consumers and were more likely to mention 'taking into account the wishes of parents' in their approach to leadership than were longer-serving headteachers.

10.4 APPROACH TO LEADERSHIP

Managerialism → Managed Participation → Collegiality

A second dimension that was used to analyse the data concerned the approach which individual headteachers had with regard to their leadership role and their management style. The most obvious effect of government reforms was the move in focus of the work of the headteacher from the classroom to the office. This reduced headteachers' day-to-day contact with pupils, removing them from their area of greatest competence – teaching – to one in which they had little preparation or experience, and required of them a steep learning curve. In the early years of the reforms the most common initial response was for headteachers to try to comply with the new requirements by incorporating them into existing ways of working. One headteacher expressed this as seeking to 'deliver the primary curriculum *through* the National Curriculum'. The most significant influence on headteachers' practice was not the formal apparatus of external obligations but the personal sense of professional obligation. Headteachers, like teachers, filtered the changes through their existing personal and professional experience and adapted them to meet the practicalities of the local situation. The result was, in some cases, to alter or modify the effect of the reforms in relation to the government's intended outcomes. This distortion was usually not the result of intentional sabotage, as claimed by some (Lawlor, 1993), but often a recognition that the 'delivery' of the educational process necessarily involves the exercise of judgement and decision-making. For some headteachers these pressures had resulted in demoralization and early retirement: in 1994 the National Association of Headteachers (NAHT) spoke of a 'dramatic increase' in the levels of premature retirement. For others, they heralded a change of approach to managing their schools, from the more widespread individualist model of school organization, as described by Handy and Aitken (1986), to a new managerialism.

In seeking to understand and explain these changes, the project used the following typologies to analyse the data collected, in questionnaire and interview, from the 48 headteachers involved:

- *Managerialism* was defined as a top-down management strategy where decisions were imposed through formal hierarchical structures, and the final responsibility of the headteacher for decision-making was emphasized.
- *Managed participation* emphasized consultation in decision-making processes but recognized that this was circumscribed by the headteacher's need to guarantee effective change.
- *Collegiality* was defined as emphasizing collective approaches to whole-school development within a culture of collaboration, under the leadership of the headteacher.

However, in interpreting the data, the difficulty of operationalizing these terms and of interpreting different headteacher's notions of management practices was recognized. For example, reference to collaborative ways of working may be related to the requirement for formal planning meetings, in what Hargreaves (1994) has referred to 'contrived collegiality', rather than to a more organic, informal way of working. To help bridge the gap between what could be clearly recognized as a managerialist approach on the one hand and a truly collective or collegial approach on the other, the term 'managed participation' was used. This described an approach which sought to include staff members in the decision-making process but recognized that the headteacher must have the final decision-making responsibility.

When asked to describe their leadership style, headteachers made the following responses to the open-ended question, 'Would you say that you currently have a particular approach to your leadership role in the school?' These responses were then analysed and coded as shown in Table 10.9.

Table 10.9 Headteachers' approach to the leadership role (percentages)

	1990	1992	1994	1995
Democratic	81.3	77.1	81.3	79.2
Take final responsibility	27.1	31.3	37.5	64.6
Senior management team	31.3	25.0	20.8	31.3
Delegate through clear management structure	0.0	0.0	0.0	22.9
Discussion with governors	18.8	29.2	18.8	10.4
Try to be proactive	16.7	14.6	8.3	14.6
Wishes of parents	10.4	2.1	6.3	8.3
Wishes of LEA/governors	8.2	2.1	2.1	0.0

Source: PACE 1, 2 and 3 headteacher interviews
Date: Summer 1990, Spring 1994, Autumn 1995
Sample: 48 headteachers
Note: Totals do not equal 100 per cent as some headteachers' answers were coded more than once

Over the six-year period of the study, the majority of headteachers consistently reported a 'democratic' approach to their leadership style. This confirmed what other researchers have referred to as the democratic nature of some primary school cultures before the changes took place (Nias *et al.*, 1989, 1992). However, Table 10.9 also shows a remarkable shift in the number of headteachers reporting the related need to 'take final responsibility' for decision-making; from 27 per cent in 1990 to 65 per cent in 1995. These figures indicate that headteachers had a heightened awareness that they carried the final responsibility for implementing the legal requirements and were seeking to achieve this through a more deliberate exercise of their leadership role. This tension had been resolved, to some extent, by the existence of a senior management team in between one-fifth and one-third of schools. In addition to this, a new category of delegation 'through clear management structure' was reported by 23 per cent of headteachers in 1995. These developments were not, however, always seen as positive and were not necessarily an indication of collegial decision-making, as one headteacher explained: 'We are becoming more managerial. The Senior Management Team is set apart from colleagues. It's inevitable really as the SMT have overall responsibility for the quality of teaching.'

Although, at an operational level, teachers could be considered to be working in a collegiate way, which the headteachers had labelled 'democratic', this appeared to be set within a tighter framework of top-down managerialism which enabled the headteachers to respond effectively to external pressures. The need to discuss management decisions with school governors was also important, with nearly one-third of headteachers mentioning this in 1992 when, it could be argued, the changes had their greatest impact. Consultation with the local education authority and, to a lesser extent, parents became less significant as the study progressed – though a slight increase in the significance of the wishes of parents in 1995, to 8 per cent, may have been an indication of the pressures from both SAT reporting and OFSTED requirements to keep parents informed.

When headteachers were asked specifically about their strategies for managing curriculum development a similar picture began to appear (Table 10.10). Over the

Table 10.10 Headteacher strategies for curriculum development within the school (percentages)

	1990	1992	1994	1995
Collegiate/whole school	79.2	70.8	81.3	79.2
Top-down/LEA strategy	9.2	16.6	12.4	20.8
No strategy/lack of awareness	2.1	6.3	4.2	0.0
Other	9.5	6.3	2.1	0.0

Source: PACE 1, 2 and 3 headteacher interviews
Date: Summer 1990, Spring 1994, Autumn 1995
Sample: 48 headteachers

six-year period of the research, the majority of headteachers consistently said that they used approaches categorized as 'collegiate', with an emphasis on staff involvement and consultation. There was very little variation over the six years in the percentage of headteachers who preferred this strategy (from 79 per cent in 1990 through 71 per cent and 81 per cent back to 79 per cent in 1995). The dip was in the difficult year of 1992, when the highest figure of 17 per cent for the opposite, 'top-down' driven strategy was reported. However, managerialism does not appear to be directly and inversely related to collegiality but to have increased separately, according to the 1994 and 1995 interviews. Collegiality existed amongst the staff through their formal planning meetings, alongside increased direction from the head within a tighter top-down driven policy framework. Again, this approximates more to a 'managed participation' model, as opposed to the more informal, organic, consensual decision-making of true collegiality. Comments from headteachers confirmed that there had been a greater distancing from their colleagues, which was experienced as a loss by many. This resonates with the comments made by their staff reported in Chapter 5 about increasing distance between themselves and their headteachers, and the growth in managed participation. An increasing proportion of headteachers also reported that their approach to leadership had become more authoritarian – from 8 per cent in 1990 to 25 per cent in 1992 and 1994, to 17 per cent in 1995, when new patterns of authority may have become well established. Interestingly, no rural or small schools were included amongst those with a top-down strategy. This suggests that informal collegiality might be more easily maintained as a viable option where numbers are small (Webb *et al.*, 1997).

Relationships with staff

Headteachers' perceptions of the changes in their relationships with staff were also used as a barometer to give some indication of how well the change processes had been managed. Table 10.11 again mirrors the pressure points of the waves of legislation, with 1992 being a particularly stressful year.

Table 10.11 Perceptions of change in headteacher–staff relations (percentages)

	1990	1992	1994	1995
Improving	22.9	14.6	25.0	22.9
Mixed or neutral change	27.1	20.8	20.8	20.9
Deteriorating	12.5	35.4	27.1	10.4
No change	37.5	28.4	27.1	45.8
	$n = 48$	$n = 48$	$n = 48$	$n = 48$

Source: PACE 1, 2 and 3 headteacher interviews
Date: Summer 1990, Summer 1992, Spring 1994, Autumn 1995
Sample: 48 headteachers

There is evidence of both positive and negative responses to the changes in reciprocal role relationships between heads and their staff and the movement towards a greater formality in management style. The most negative period was in 1992, with over one-third of headteachers reporting a deterioration in relationships. However, 'little or no change' and 'mixed and neutral change' constituted the majority of responses from headteachers in all phases of the PACE research. By PACE 3 nearly a quarter of headteachers saw relationships as improving to some degree. Perhaps this reflects staff acceptance of changes as the new arrangements became more familiar. It may also indicate that in a situation of continuing change and uncertainty, teachers liked the firmer direction of some headteachers' management style. This could help to reduce the tension of uncertainty. Nevertheless, the strains for headteachers were evident. The tension between being supportive and encouraging to staff, on the one hand, and being responsible to the various stakeholders for pushing forward change, on the other, took their toll. This was particularly evident in spontaneously offered additional comments that headteachers made in interview in relation to the changing pattern of headteacher–staff relationships, which were later coded by the research team in Table 10.12.

Detailed analysis showed that the group of headteachers who reported a 'democratic' approach to their leadership were also significantly more likely to mention 'exercising a protective role' towards their staff, whereas those headteachers who mentioned an 'activating role' with regard to their colleagues were more likely to mention becoming more 'authoritarian' and to say that their relations with staff

Table 10.12 Perceptions of influences on the changing pattern of staff relationships (percentages)

	1990	1992	1994	1995
Activating role to staff	22.9	37.5	33.3	47.9
Protective role to staff	29.2	25.0	27.1	43.8
Relations more strained	12.5	18.8	27.1	18.8
NC tool for welcome change	31.3	33.3	12.5	18.8
Less time for staff	25.0	33.3	16.7	14.6

Source: PACE 1, 2 and 3 headteacher interviews
Date: Summer 1990, Spring 1994, Autumn 1995
Sample: 48 headteachers
Note: Totals do not equal 100 per cent as some headteachers' answers were coded more than once

were becoming 'more strained'. It was not possible to find any clear relationship between these variables and the location or socio-economic status of the catchment area of a school.

10.5 RESPONSE TO CHANGE

Resistance → Retreatism → Incorporation → Mediation → Compliance

The third and final dimension that has been used to analyse the data from headteachers is that of their response to change. Fullan (1991) has suggested that the imposition of new policies and practices on a group of workers can give rise to various coping strategies ranging from resistance to compliance as outlined above and in Chapter 4. Our data show that many headteachers in the sample used a combination of these various coping strategies, depending on the situation. However, there were some clear trends that could be identified.

During the six-year period of the research, headteachers' overall adaptive response appears to have shifted in the direction of compliance. In the initial stages of the research, as the weight of change made itself known, we found instances of both 'resistance' and 'retreatism'. An increased workload, coupled with a feeling of helplessness, left many headteachers demoralized. Early retirement was being sought by a few. Between PACE 1 and 2, however, there was some movement through a strategy of 'incorporation' to one of 'mediation'. This reflects headteachers' growing confidence in their ability to deal with centrally imposed change by creatively mediating it so that it fitted more closely with their basic ideological perspective. The variations in responses to open-ended questions concerning change strategy help to illustrate this. In 1990 and 1992 between a half and two-thirds of headteachers said that they were 'building on present practice'. This proportion dropped to one-third in 1994, which possibly indicated a major dislocation. However, by 1995 half of the headteachers interviewed felt they were again building on present practice. They were more likely to be from rural schools and to report that relationships with staff were becoming more relaxed. They were less likely to be from inner-city schools and to report that relationships with staff were becoming more strained. Overall, though, the increase since 1994 could be an indication of the gradual institutionalization of the new management structures and procedures as headteachers became acclimatized to operating within them. It may also indicate an increase in compliance and that the new imposed policies were being accepted and integrated into headteachers' management philosophy and approach.

By 1995 there was more evidence of 'compliance' in that the attitudes and values of those headteachers who remained in post appeared to have moved towards a genuine acceptance of government policy, particularly with regard to curriculum, assessment and pedagogy. Fewer headteachers said that they felt constrained by the external requirements or felt that constraints had been increasing – despite the fact that, by an objective assessment, the degree of regulation had increased. Thus their expressed attitude to OFSTED inspection was predominantly one of acceptance and of the need for schools to demonstrate and justify practice. The evidence indicates that there has been a cultural transformation in some schools, supporting the Chief Inspector of Schools' Annual Report for 1997, reporting that 'there is evidence of a more positive culture' in schools' responses 'to measures designed to raise standards'. Whilst compliance involving a change of values may best describe some headteachers' responses to selected reforms and aspects of their changed role, a more appropriate description for other aspects would be one of an outward conformance to requirements. Thus some headteachers spoke the rhetoric of accountability and the demonstration of quality, whilst at the same time deploring some of the effects of the systemic changes. Coping with these paradoxes had resulted, for some, in a more detached 'instrumental' attitude to their role. It represents a pragmatic limitation to their personal commitment to their role, which is now regarded as a 'job' rather than a 'vocation'.

Headteachers as managers of change

Applying Young's (1991) model of change types, the PACE data indicate that the experience of many headteachers involved a movement from crisis management, through transformation, to building incremental change in the longer term. Managing these changes has involved them in redefining their role as headteacher, as well as their more personal 'self'. Some have found personal qualities and skills more suited to one type of change management than another. Some have had to radically alter their previous style of management and role relationships, and this could depend on their individual school circumstances. Some have found their school culture more responsive to the demands of the external policy environment than others. Some school communities that previously operated in informal, collegiate ways with the headteacher as a team member, have required stronger management steering. For other schools, where staff had previously operated in relative isolation, it has meant the start of more formal staff involvement in devising whole-school policies.

By 1995 there continued to be some headteachers who were still operating in crisis management mode as they faced the pressures of falling school rolls and budget constraint. Their staff preferred to deal with the uncertainty and strain of changing demands and external accountability by 'being told' what to do, rather than invest time and energy in devising policies that previous experience suggested would not be of any lasting value. In these circumstances, headteachers adopted a more managerial approach.

However, the imposed change has not simply been about getting schools to adopt better management systems to achieve their aims effectively, efficiently and economically. Most significantly, it has also involved ideological questions about the purposes of education and who should control it. For some headteachers, change has meant a redefinition of their aims, as well as an examination of their methods. Headteachers, as managers of change in conjunction with governors, have had to take difficult decisions constrained by tight budgets. In some cases this has been achieved by operating through more formal, hierarchical management structures and has led to a further distancing of headteachers from their previous involvement in collegiate relationships with staff. This has involved an assault on their shared values and culture, often resulting in dislocation. For some it has entailed the loss of a sense of 'direction', of 'continuity', of a 'connection' with a particular community.

Reacting to the immediate demands of government legislation involved intense workloads for headteachers and was often accompanied by a feeling that their response was inadequate. The experience produced short-term stress which developed, in some cases, into long-term overload as new requirements, and revisions to previous ones, meant that headteachers were operating in crisis mode for extended periods, gradually eroding their energy and morale. For some this was a factor in early retirement on the grounds of ill-health.

Headteachers' perspectives of the future

In response to these dilemmas, some headteachers have moved out of the role altogether. By 1995 half of the original sample had left their schools and yet more were planning early retirement at the end of the academic year. Many headteachers continued to express feelings of a loss of job satisfaction and fulfilment. Nearly 50 per cent considered that life as a headteacher was worse than it had been – 25 per cent 'noticeably' so. Table 10.13 shows that, in response to a direct question, only half of the sample would still have chosen to be a headteacher; six headteachers would have become teachers but not have chosen to take on the additional responsibilities of a headteacher; six headteachers were undecided and one-fifth of the sample were so disillusioned that they would choose neither to be a teacher nor a headteacher.

In interview, the headteachers were asked, at regular intervals, what their expectations were for primary education during the next five to ten years. The responses were coded under four broad headings: optimistic, mixed, pessimistic and unsure (Table 10.14). The number of headteachers in the sample who have had an optimistic outlook was always less than one-fifth of the sample. This number has waxed and waned as continuing waves of legislation have moved forward, reaching a low in 1992 with only one teacher expressing an optimistic view. The number of

Table 10.13 Headteacher perceptions: would you still choose to be a teacher/headteacher? (percentages)

	1990	1992	1994	1995
Yes: teacher and headteacher	41.6	58.4	47.9	50.0
Yes: teacher but not h'teacher	16.7	8.3	22.9	12.5
Yes: h'teacher but not teacher	0.0	0.0	0.0	4.2
No: neither	16.7	20.8	12.5	20.8
Undecided	25.0	12.5	16.7	12.5
	$n = 48$	$n = 48$	$n = 48$	$n = 48$

Source: PACE 1, 2 and 3 headteacher interviews
Date: Summer 1990, Summer 1992, Spring 1994, Autumn 1995
Sample: 48 headteachers

Table 10.14 Expectations for primary education in the next five to ten years (percentages)

	1990	1992	1994	1995
Optimistic	14.6	2.1	18.8	8.3
Mixed	37.5	14.6	33.3	37.5
Pessimistic	45.8	68.8	22.9	25.0
Unsure	2.1	14.6	25.0	29.2
	$n = 48$	$n = 48$	$n = 48$	$n = 48$

Source: PACE 1, 2 and 3 headteacher interviews
Date: Summer 1990, Summer 1992, Spring 1994, Autumn 1995
Sample: 48 headteachers

headteachers expressing uncertainty about the future has steadily increased (from 1 to 14) over the six years. However, there does seem to be a lessening of pessimism because after a low in 1992, when 69 per cent were pessimistic, only one-quarter of headteachers continued to have a pessimistic outlook.

From their additional comments, shown in Table 10.15, despite a belief that the pace of change would slow, their main anxieties were the emphasis on organization and evaluation and a concern that the introduction of market forces and the 'opting out' of local authority control would cause gaps between schools. Two issues to arise spontaneously in the 1995 data collection included concerns over a deterioration in funding and staffing (35.4 per cent) and the increased use of setting and streaming (20.8 per cent) at primary level.

10.6 CASE-STUDIES

To demonstrate in more individual and personal terms how these tensions have been played out in the lives of headteachers, we have looked at two particular headteachers in more depth. We have chosen two male headteachers who were in post in their schools for the full six years of the study. We fully recognize that some

Table 10.15 Expectations for primary education in the next five to ten years: additional comments (percentage of sample)

	1990	1992	1994	1995
Pace of change will slow	31.3	14.6	50.0	33.3
Emphasis on organization/evaluation	14.6	18.8	6.3	27.1
Anxiety/gaps between schools	20.8	22.9	20.9	14.6
More standardization/continuity	10.4	14.6	10.4	4.2
Becoming more formal	0.0	0.0	10.4	4.2
Deterioration in funding/staffing	0.0	0.0	0.0	35.4
More setting/streaming	0.0	0.0	0.0	20.8
	$n = 48$	$n = 48$	$n = 48$	$n = 48$

Source: PACE 1, 2 and 3 headteacher interviews
Date: Summer 1990, Summer 1992, Spring 1994, Autumn 1995
Sample: 48 headteachers
Note: Totals do not equal 100 per cent as some headteachers' answers were coded more than once. NC = National Curriculum

female heads may well have a distinctive management style and response to change (Hall, 1996), and had there been a female headteacher who stayed in one of the case study schools throughout the research, we would have included her in these case studies. We have focused on Mr Stokes and Mr Saunders because they shared a number of characteristics and yet adopted a different response to change. Both were of a similar age (45-plus) and both had approximately ten years' experience as headteachers of their present schools. Both worked in primary schools within the same LEA, in the Midlands, and therefore had the same level of support. However, as well as their similarities, they were also chosen because of the difference in size, location and socio-economic status of their schools, factors that were found to be of some significance in many of the findings of the study.

Mr Stokes's school was larger, with a roll of approximately 265 pupils, plus a nursery containing approximately 40. It had an inner-city location and served a community with many social and economic disadvantages. Mr Saunders, on the other hand, was the headteacher of a small rural school with approximately 184 pupils and 23 children in the nursery. It was a popular school that served a community with relatively few social or economic disadvantages. At the beginning of the study, the small original wooden building built in 1931 was surrounded by a collection of temporary classrooms. However, as the study progressed the roll went from 129 in 1990 to 184 in 1995, and a new, purpose-built school was being erected on an adjacent field.

Mr Stokes

In PACE 2 Mr Stokes had spoken of increased pressure of work, particularly administration and paperwork, taking work home and consequent tiredness. What Black (1996) had referred to as 'the burden of overload and its deleterious effect on both [headteachers'] working lives and on their private lives' was a theme revisited by Mr Stokes in his PACE 3 interview in 1995. Overload resulted in his feeling 'split in four different pieces' and meant that he felt he could do nothing as well as he should. In fact, by 1995 he had reached the point of urgently seeking early retirement in an effort to ensure that other things of value, including his family and his church activities, would remain. Speaking of colleagues, he bemoaned the fact that there were 'so many breakdowns'. He had reached a point in his life of 'disengagement' from his career (Huberman, 1993). What he personally valued most in his teaching and early headship career had largely been eroded: 'We can't give a child time. Gone are the days when you could walk round and talk with children.'

He also highlighted the consequences for his former role as lead teacher, which had been compromised because he now had no time to spend in classrooms with teachers needing support, or just to gain greater awareness of what was happening at classroom level. The trends he identified amounted to a loss of enjoyment and fulfilment in his role as he lost touch with his teaching 'competencies'. When he was asked if he would choose to be a headteacher again, his response indicated a dilemma:

> Don't get me wrong, I've enjoyed a lot of it, but seeing the way it's going, with more, you know, on the business side, managing a school rather than teaching, I don't know whether I would. I'd prefer to be with children. That is what a headteacher was. That's why we all came into education in the first place, to teach.

Whilst he acknowledged that younger headteachers might enjoy management, he said that he knew a number of older headteachers (50-plus) who did not and who were seeking retirement or alternative employment.

Autonomy/constraint

Financial management

Initially Mr Stokes had welcomed the autonomy of LMS, which had allowed greater discretion in spending and had enabled the refurbishment of the library. However, by PACE 3 he recognized that financial limitations had left him, together with the governors' finance committee, with little room for manoeuvre and had compromised the school's long-term planning. He was grateful for good LEA support and for efficient clerical assistance with the day-to-day management of the budget, but the consequent lack of flexibility was seen as an increasing problem and a cause for pessimism about the future. In particular, the newly introduced voucher scheme for nursery school places was implicitly short term as it operated on a termly basis. The extent of the take-up of the scheme could have far-reaching implications for Reception class staffing in his school but this would be difficult to plan for. Thus the operation of the market in determining educational provision, together with the limited opportunity in practice for financial autonomy, had brought increasing constraints. His response could be seen as 'retreatism' and an acceptance of the inevitable.

Curriculum and assessment

Mr Stokes regarded the National Curriculum as constraining 'railway lines' that did not allow for diversion from what had been planned: 'often the source of a lot of the best teaching in the past'. But he also accepted that there were positive aspects to it as well: 'I like the idea of a national curriculum because it does mean wherever children go they can move between school and authorities.' Likewise, he recognized positive aspects to the compulsory assessment arrangements: 'It makes you do it.' But the negative aspects included the interruptions to children's learning, the panic induced in some children and inappropriately devised tests: 'I don't like testing children. Children mature at their own stage. It's like the eleven-plus.' In effect he was distinguishing between the benefits of formative assessment by teachers for diagnostic purposes and what he considered to be the less appropriate external, summative assessment use for accountability and comparative purposes. There was evidence of compliance in his stance towards some aspects of imposed change. This is supported by his acknowledgement that Key Stage 1 teachers had now become familiar and comfortable with the process of teacher assessment. However, there was also evidence of passive acceptance of negative aspects, indicating retreatism. Overall, the tenor of his interviews was one of weariness with change and an identification with his staff, who were also suffering increased demands on their time:

> There've been so many changes. A lot of staff would say, 'I just wish the authority, or I wish somebody, would just say, "This is what you've got to do", and all do it.' We seem to have been bombarded with things over the last few years.

Leadership and management style

Evidence suggests that Mr Stokes was moving towards greater managerialism in his role as headteacher, despite his stated preference for a collegial approach and the delegation of curriculum coordination to teachers. The shift can be explained partly in terms of a reciprocal realignment of roles in deference to staff preferences and partly as a coping strategy (Pollard *et al.*, 1994a):

> I'm not authoritarian. Maybe some people would think I should be a little more. I like to work alongside, cooperative, make decisions together. Sometimes you work one method. Sometimes you give them information – you are directive. We're changing slightly to more directive. Staff want to be told, with all the pressure on them now. Staff say, 'I'd rather be told.' It makes it easier, in a way, for the one doing the leading.

This view, taken together with his earlier remarks about the loss of time for spontaneously going into classrooms to work with and alongside teachers, confirmed his regret at losing a previous informal collegiality. This was underlined by a reference, in 1994, to an increasing formality in staff meetings to aid cooperative curriculum planning. However, further evidence from his 1995 interview suggested that a systematic approach to cooperative planning and review had not yet become totally embedded in staff practice, despite an implicit acknowledgement that this needed to happen:

> It's awful to say but I probably haven't got an overall strategy [for curriculum development]. We look at the whole and see where we possibly need work doing, and we do it. We look at how it's planned. If there's a weakness, hopefully either somebody will tell us there's a weakness, or we'll find a weakness and work on it.

> *Researcher*: Who manages the review process?

> It's got to be the head and the deputy a lot of the time. I mean, we've been looking at planning folders. We looked at the infants' earlier in the week and we're getting the junior folders in tomorrow. And we will look and see where the weaknesses possibly are in the planning. Curriculum coordinators *will* be planning for the summer with all the teachers throughout the school. Do the planning together, timetable as a staff to allocate time to subjects.

Further probing elicited a continuing concern with the linking of curriculum policy documents, as and when they were produced, with actual classroom practice: 'What is difficult is how do you know it is actually happening?'

There was no evidence of ownership by the staff of the notion of quality planning, including systematic monitoring and reviewing processes. Overall, the evidence pointed to a lack of clarity in the development of a strategy to manage change and a despondency on the part of Mr Stokes.

Mr Saunders

The PACE 2 data showed Mr Saunders to have made a successful transition to his new management role; he found his work 'satisfying, challenging and very stimulating'. He did not resent being removed from the classroom and the immediate demands of the children. He claimed that he was not by nature a proactive innovator but had been driven to make changes by external needs. These changes were personal, as well as school focused. On a personal level he felt propelled from a comfortable, 'in a rut' position into a new challenge, supported by the opportunities for reflection and further study afforded through LEA financial support. He had taken a B.Phil. in Education, followed by a period of secondment to complete a management course, and felt that these opportunities had revitalized him. 'In one sense the National Curriculum came at the right time in career terms for me' – although he saw the National Curriculum as only one contributing factor. These sentiments were confirmed in his 1995 interview, although there had been substantial changes to his role. In part these were driven by external demands. They were also occasioned by the relocation of the school to new buildings and its planned expansion from a three- to an eight-teacher school.

Autonomy/constraint

Financial management

Whilst the school had been an initial 'gainer' through LMS, the limitations of this independence were now being felt through budgetary constraints. A positive relationship had been built in the past with the governing body:

> They have a very high degree of confidence in my professional abilities and take the stand in the first instance that I am the professional lead person in the school and so there has been a lot of freedom and a lot of independence.

However, government intervention and clarification of the governors' financial responsibility had led to some reduction in Mr Saunders's financial autonomy. Nevertheless, his responses indicated that he still felt very much in control, within these limits, and able to act and justify his decisions. For example, he felt justified in putting money into enhancing staffing support in infant classes. In strictly 'value for money/efficiency' terms, judged by an indicator of higher SAT levels achieved by the children, this could be construed as overstaffing with no tangible benefit. He had anticipated criticism from the impending OFSTED inspection, but countered, 'I won't be worried by it. I'm prepared to take whatever criticism is levelled against me, because I actually believe I am managing the change that's necessary appropriately.' Mr Saunders's response to the externally imposed constraints of financial management appeared to have been one of mediation, by developing a creative response and actively taking control.

There was also evidence of mediation in his approach to managing curriculum priorities in tandem with non-academic priorities. He had appointed new young staff, whose training had specifically equipped them with the competencies to deliver the National Curriculum yet who shared the philosophy of maintaining 'child contentment at the top of a list of priorities'. This articulated well with his concept of a partnership between parents, teacher and child in the education process, and feedback from parents already in the system indicated that 'Parents were overjoyed with the working relationship that class teacher and children had got – the way in which there was a feeling of pleasure and enjoyment with children coming to school.'

Curriculum and assessment constraints

Mr Saunders's school demonstrates that where there is some correspondence between imposed change and the predominant school philosophy, compliance, or even creative mediation, is more likely to take place. This was exemplified by the school's response to Key Stage 1 SAT testing. In part this became possible because of changes to the nature and administration of Key Stage 1 SATs recommended by the Dearing review in 1994. In addition, Mr Saunders considered that a culture was developing within the school which was beginning to identify opportunities for assessment at the curriculum planning stage and that this would be useful in informing future planning. This suggests that an adjustment has been made over time which had altered Mr Saunders's professional ideology so that it could accommodate and even mediate new, imposed practices.

> I think that what I am recognizing is that, as teachers, we don't always have at hand the *evidence* to support attitudes ... I'm viewing it as a means of more objective evidence. Evidence [on pupil attainment] is available in alternative ways, but it takes more time.

Mr Saunders was not so happy with Key Stage 2 testing and felt 'uncomfortable with competition and ordering'. There was evidence of incorporation as a response to this externally imposed market mechanism, as he regretfully acknowledged that assessment would inevitably drive some adaptations. He was publicly accountable through the published SAT statistics, and results had not been as good as expected. This had, he felt, been due to a combination of a quarter of the small Year 6 group in 1994 having statements of special educational need, coupled with the disruption caused by the change of school buildings. Despite this, Mr Saunders considered that the poor results had been a deciding factor in turning an otherwise enthusiastic parent away from choosing the school for her child. He therefore acknowledged that

> SATs were perceived as the yardstick by which satisfaction was judged ... We haven't allowed assessment processes to affect the way we teach at all so far, but we'll have to ... Next year we will be better prepared ... the children need to realize that they are being made to jump through hoops and they need to learn how to do it.

This was despite the perception that

> The SATs for Key Stage 2 were inappropriately established and imposed for my school. We have a school here which does not and never has operated on a formal testing structure. Last year's results do not do justice to children's ability and the philosophy of the school. I feel badly about that.

There was also evidence of the incorporation of central recommendations in that there had been a recent increase in separate subject teaching, rather than a more integrated, topic approach to learning. There had also been an increase in whole-class teaching. This was in order to get through the volume of material required by the schemes of work, and was in spite of the difficulty of having some mixed-age classes.

Leadership and management style

What were the implications of these shifts in responses to externally imposed changes for Mr Saunders's management and leadership style and for his relationship with his staff? Whilst he acknowledged that the requirement for him to monitor the National Curriculum had caused one or two strains in the past in his relationships with staff, he felt that there had now been an improvement:

> because we are finding a common language for talking about curriculum issues which we didn't necessarily have before, and there is also the added benefit that in talking about the National Curriculum we are talking about things which impact on us from outside and

we are both on the same side in learning to cope with them. It's not an initiative of mine which is being introduced and there isn't the same level of potential conflict or resistance.

Nevertheless, despite the suggestion that cohesiveness had resulted from a common stance against an external threat, Mr Saunders felt that he had moved away from being 'one of the team'. He now considered that he was 'more of a team leader and slightly more remote and proactive in determining targets for staff'. He found he had to take on more responsibility for 'sorting out hiccups' and for boosting staff morale. He admitted that 'there have been breakdowns in communication, although not intent'.

The legal requirements for formal job descriptions, clear line management structures and accountability procedures had all been factors in altering his relationship with his staff. Even so, he felt that the way forward was to establish more, not less, formal procedures for management, for communication and for decision-making. Despite a stated aim to promote consultation and collaboration in decision-making amongst the teachers, in practice Mr Saunders's management style had become less collaborative. This had given rise to some problems. Teachers in the school felt unhappy that their curriculum coordination role was being developed as an 'expert' role. In order to resolve this, Mr Saunders had attempted to build teams within which the subject coordination role could be seen in terms of a team leader. However, these tensions were compounded by the need for Mr Saunders to take a wider brief with regard to his responsibilities for school organization. Increasing size meant that he had to consider wider staff issues and that he was no longer simply a headteacher. Some teachers found it difficult to accept that the usual staff meetings had been renamed 'teacher meetings' as a reflection of the wider concerns and additional non-teaching staff with which their headteacher had to deal.

Whilst Mr Saunders was attempting to positively maintain and develop collegial approaches to planning and decision-making, he was at the same time realistic about their limitations within a new operating and management context. He had developed a pragmatic approach. He also felt that it was inevitable that external constraints on schools would increase. In the recent past they had driven unwelcome changes in pedagogic practice and in the future they might lead to streaming, coaching and even selection. Although he regretted this, it did not mean the abandonment of his commitment to valuing individual children, who 'in this school will always be very special'. Whilst there were also negative implications for his relationship with the teaching staff, he appeared to be able to hold the paradoxes in tension and to continue to enjoy and gain satisfaction from the challenges of his new role.

Two different responses to change

These case-studies illustrate the complexity of factors that are involved in individual reactions to change. Responses to change, and strategies for managing them, vary according to both the individual issues being dealt with and individual circumstances. Simple generalizations do not do justice to this complexity and range. Mr Stokes and Mr Saunders varied in their approach to change: one was a proactive partner in change management, the other a reactive receiver of imposed change. Their differing attitudes to their changed role were bound up with their self-identity and personal and professional development, which in turn impacted differentially on job satisfaction and fulfilment. Mr Saunders drew energy from the challenge of the changes. The personal development which he derived from his courses was not just the acquisition of a further set of instrumental skills to be applied to the job but also the source of a new definition of his professional self. His job enlargement became a positive source of satisfaction, providing a sense of achievement, recognition and responsibility, which he was equipped to meet, and the opportunity for personal growth and advancement. By contrast, Mr Stokes valued his relationships with pupils, which he saw in the context of a lead-teacher role. This had effectively been removed from him. He appears to have been reacting to a sequence of imposed changes which he experienced as a loss of control over both the content and pacing of his work. These took their toll on him in terms of motivation, energy and commitment to the job. In an interview in 1994 he had spoken of the need to 'plug another battery in, you've got to keep smiling, you can't let anybody see how you feel'.

Individual headteacher responses, therefore, depend on a complexity of factors including personal values, career aspirations and contextual circumstances. All of these need to be borne in mind by policy-makers when planning support and training for wholesale system change.

10.7 CONCLUSION

The PACE evidence suggests that many headteachers were inadequately equipped to deal with the major changes to their role. They experienced the changes as piecemeal initiatives, and their reaction was one of crisis management or the sequential attention to different goals. There was little evidence in this period of multiple innovations that headteachers were able to understand fully how the jigsaw pieces of reform might fit together. This meant that it was difficult for them to create a management framework that would help them to integrate these changes comprehensively. In those cases where an overview began to emerge, it had been developed independently through management courses or through the political perspectives of their professional associations. LEA support, which focused on the implementation of specific initiatives such as financial training to aid the introduction of LMS, was less good at helping to show the whole picture. Although headteachers relied on this type of training and were mostly appreciative of it, the quality varied. More comprehensive management training schemes, such as the Headlamp Training Programme and the Management Charter Initiative, were introduced some time into the reforms. The competency-based modular National Professional Qualification for Headship (NPQH), now a prerequisite for new headteachers, was not introduced until 1997, after the completion of the study.

In response to these tensions some headteachers assumed a more detached stance from their role, often as a coping strategy because of their low morale and feelings of pessimism. This may have created a greater physical and emotional distance between headteachers and their staff and pupils. The extent to which this detachment could hamper long-term improvement in schools – by their being fashioned into learning organizations, a process requiring active engagement – needs to be investigated. According to Young (1991), 'hands-on' knowledge is the basis for leading the incremental change that is necessary for long-term building. It requires the 'capacity to tolerate steady state environments and to gain satisfaction from small-scale, relatively low-profile actions, and the willingness to blend one's identity with the whole organisation'. In the case of primary schools, this would imply the need for headteachers to be the leading professional as well as the manager, emotionally committed to the organization and identifying closely with its success. Signs that some headteachers are distancing themselves emotionally from their schools may be cause for concern.

There are also concerns in relation to the training that is currently available to headteachers. Shipman (1990) notes that initiatives to raise attainment come primarily from teachers and their concern with learning. If these initiatives are to continue, he suggests that they require a management style that encourages teachers to be enterprising. A concentration on administration in the training and support for headteachers could be construed as a straying away from giving priority to learning. In other areas of work, Peters (1989) recommends management by 'walking about', to keep vitally in touch with issues at an operational level. This ability could be compromised if headteachers become too removed from day-to-day contact with staff and pupils and no longer have their finger on the teaching and learning pulse.

The research also demonstrated that headteachers in disadvantaged inner-city/ estate areas experienced higher levels of strain than did headteachers in rural schools or those with more advantaged catchments. This suggests that there were other factors at work besides the competence of the individual headteacher to manage change. This raises questions about the appropriateness of the tools and techniques of reform with which the headteachers were provided. Satisfactory results cannot be achieved where the resources within the system are lacking, whether these are tangible resources, such as adequate school budgets or headship training, or less quantifiable factors, such as supportive parents. Pressure to produce results exerted through exhortation and the fear of failure will produce only demoralization and distortion within the system. Such pressure needs to be accompanied by positive support in the form of both tangible resources and training.

Chapter 11

Conclusion

> Teachers are people too. They have interests; they have lives; they have selves.
>
> (Hargreaves, 1991, cited by Helsby and McCulloch, 1997)

> The feelings associated with teaching seem always to be contradictory. Successful teachers learn to keep them in balance, but even they swing, sometimes by the minute, between love and rage, elation and despair. To 'be' a teacher is to be relaxed and in control, yet tired and under stress: to feel whole while being pulled apart; to be in love with one's work, but daily to talk of leaving it. It is to learn to live with unresolved uncertainties, contradictions and dilemmas; to accept that the very nature of teaching is paradoxical.
>
> (Nias, 1989, p. 191–2)

> The heart of the educational project is gouged out and left empty.   (Ball, 1999, p. 1)

11.1 INTRODUCTION

We open this concluding chapter with three powerful quotations which, together, evoke the themes of the book and the territory of this final part of our analysis. These epigraphs underline the importance of situating the findings that have been presented in this book in terms of time and space; the importance of asking how far the perspectives and practices that we have described are the products of particular policy initiatives embedded within a specific professional context in the late twentieth century and how far they represent some of the enduring features of what it means to be a teacher of young children. Thus in what follows we attempt to tease out some of these core distinctions in seeking to throw light on the central themes of the PACE project, namely to describe and analyse the responses of pupils, teachers and headteachers to the introduction of the National Curriculum and assessment procedures in English primary schools.

This book has focused particularly on the impact of these initiatives in relation to teachers and our goal of monitoring changes in teachers' practices in terms of curriculum, pedagogy and assessment. The research questions that informed this part of our study have centred on the consequences of national policies for teachers, and the mediating effects of teacher perspectives, cultures and behaviour as these are embedded within prevailing notions of professionalism. We have been concerned to document how teachers *perceived* the effects of these changes on their work. We have also been concerned to document changes in their classroom practice in terms of curriculum, pedagogy and assessment – the three 'message systems' which, Bernstein (1975, 1990a, 1996) argues, convey the 'education codes' of a particular society. This focus has necessarily required a rather broader effort to contextualize the *reasons* for the changes which we have observed to be taking place, and their potential significance. Our attempt to understand the causes and effects of these developments has necessarily involved some consideration of developments at the level of the school as a whole, such as the impact of OFSTED inspections, and in terms of the more general national policy context with its growing emphasis on raising standards and competition between schools. It has also required us to see these developments as in their turn part of more general international currents within which our small island is inevitably caught up.

Our detailed findings concerning the impact of these developments on pupils are reported in this book's companion volume (Pollard *et al.*, 2000). However, in seeking to understand the significance of recent developments for both teachers and pupils, we have found a remarkably close match between the two. As we discuss in subsequent sections of this chapter, we have come to realize that the issues with which we have been concerned in the PACE studies go right to the heart of the relationship between systems and individuals. They concern the way in which external requirements are mediated by the perceptions, understandings, motivation and capacity of individuals and groups to produce particular practices and actions. They evoke the core PACE themes of 'values', 'power' and 'understanding' which we introduced in the book that reported the first stage of our study (Pollard *et al.*, 1994a). These themes have remained central to our attempts to explain the emerging changes and tensions that the policy developments impacting upon English primary schools since 1988 have produced. However, they are now overlain by a series of more specific dimensions which together describe the principal features of the changes we have documented in this book.

In this chapter we re-present this argument, which has been progressively distilled over some eight years of empirical study. We use it here to give a more synoptic answer to the core PACE research questions concerning the impact of the advent of a national curriculum and national assessment on teachers. These were:

- What have been the changes in primary teachers' perceptions and definitions of their work and professional responsibilities?

- What changes have characterized their practices concerning curriculum, pedagogy and assessment?
- How have national policies for teachers and headteachers been mediated by teachers' perspectives, cultures and behaviour and, in particular, their perceptions of their professional responsibility?

Thus the first part of this final overview chapter presents a résumé of the empirical findings reported in the various chapters in this book that address these questions. The second part of the chapter builds on the picture of both change and continuity among English primary teachers that our research has revealed in order to offer some more theoretical explanation concerning these developments and the lessons to be learned from our analysis of them.

11.2 WHAT WERE OUR KEY FINDINGS CONCERNING TEACHERS?

Throughout the PACE study of teachers' responses to recent policy initiatives, we have been concerned to document both their *perceptions* of change, which we have explored by means of interviews and questionnaires, and the *reality* of change, which we have documented by means of observational data gathered in classrooms. The results show some interesting differences which underline the importance of using such a combined methodology for this purpose. But they also provide some important 'triangulation' that reinforces the credibility of the core findings to emerge from our study. In broad terms these findings may be expressed in terms of a number of key 'dimensions': control, conflict, collegiality, context, confidence, compliance, creativity, classification and commitment. These dimensions recur again and again in the different aspects of our study in terms of both teachers' perceptions and their classroom practice. In summarizing our results below, we have clustered these dimensions into three broad groups which represent different facets of the contemporary culture of teaching. The first of these relates to the broad theme of the balance between professional autonomy and external coercion, and encompasses the first two of the dimensions listed above.

Control and conflict

In Part 2 of the book we described how teachers had experienced the progressive policy initiatives of the late 1980s and the 1990s. We documented their experience of feeling increasingly accountable to outsiders, especially parents, whilst losing none of their deeply held sense of moral accountability to their pupils. We described the experience of increasing stress that was the reality for many teachers as a result of a growing proliferation of bureaucratic requirements which they perceived as leaving them less and less space for their own professional discretion. For many, the effects of this increase in control were exacerbated by their belief that what they were being asked to do was not educationally desirable or in the best interest of some or all of their children. The increasingly high-profile and externally controlled national assessments provided one of the most widespread causes of such conflict. However, for some teachers, particularly those working with pupils from deprived back-grounds, the National Curriculum itself caused stress and frustration since teachers did not perceive it to be meeting these children's particular needs.

In Part 2 we also described the changes that have characterized teachers' work, values and culture. We reported the growing instrumentalism that characterized many teachers as they found themselves increasingly constrained in terms of what and how to teach and the underpinning logic of these instructions, which was rooted in a 'delivery' model of education. We described the conflict they experienced between the more affective side of teaching – the sense of vocation and an investment of self – and a growing pressure to become expert technicians in inculcating in their pupils predefined knowledge and skills. The shift from professional autonomy to contractual responsibility as the basis for accountability was associated for many teachers with increased stress and reduced job satisfaction. Because of the additional burden of bureaucratic requirements and the experience of an increasingly managerialist culture, many teachers experienced value conflict.

The growing unease of many teachers concerning the changes they were experiencing in their professional role evokes, once again, our key themes of values, power and understanding. In relation to values, many teachers experienced a tension between the emotional commitment, the investment of self which is at the heart of being a teacher as both the PACE project and our other, related international studies of teachers have revealed (Broadfoot *et al.*, 1993), and the growing emphasis on contractual responsibilities and cognitive, rather than affective, transactions in the classroom. The developing policy emphasis on education as a 'commodity' to be delivered and measured was at odds with many teachers' views of education as fundamentally about personal development. This tension manifested itself in the classroom, where many of our teachers felt under pressure to be more of a 'technician' with a contractual responsibility within a state bureaucracy, rather than a professional with a covenant based on a moral commitment to service. For a good number of the teachers in our study, as for many of the pupils, the result was an unwillingness to take risks; a growing instrumentalism, increasing stress and anxiety levels, and a lowering of commitment.

Another facet of the contemporary professional culture amongst primary school teachers concerns the role and significance of intra-professional relations. This facet embraces the three themes of the following sub-section.

Collegiality, context and confidence

For a considerable number of teachers the worst effects of these changes were mediated by a significant growth in collegiality. Teachers increasingly found the need to work together, partly because many of the policy initiatives required it but also because they found such collaboration helpful in coping with the effects of change. Thus curriculum planning and coordination, preparation for inspection and external communication, as well as teaching itself, were increasingly likely to be characterized by teachers pooling their different knowledge and skills in complementary ways. At their best, these developments were highly creative and empowering, resulting in some or all teachers in the school feeling a new sense of professional empowerment.

Examples of such developments have also been documented by other, related studies such as that of Richards (1988), who refers to the 'confident domestication of the National Curriculum' in small rural primary schools because of their necessarily pragmatic approach to implementing policy directives in the light of their own particular circumstances (p. 330). Nixon *et al.* (1997) also refer to such developments in terms of the emergence of the 'new professional' whose values and practices are a composite of the creative incorporation of new requirements into core professional values.

Such positive developments may now in turn be under threat, however, as a result of the government's proposals for a more individualistic approach to defining teaching quality through the implementation of a performance-related approach to teachers' pay which is set out in the government recent paper, *A Fast Track for Teachers* (DfEE, 1999). We return to the implications of these more recent policy developments in the concluding section of this chapter.

Other factors too were found to inhibit the development of the positive effects of collegiality and the 'confident domestication' of the National Curriculum. Our data document teachers whose experience was much more one of 'contrived collegiality' and a contractual, rather than a professional, engagement. Where the individual teacher or the school as a whole lacked the confidence to engage in the 'creative mediation' of external policy directives, or where individual or personal circumstances made this difficult, the picture was likely to be one of conflict, stress and disillusion.

As many other contemporary studies have documented (e.g. Halsey and Heath, 1980), recent policy initiatives appear to be creating an ever-widening gulf between 'the successful' and 'the unsuccessful'. For individual teachers this has manifested itself in terms of a distinction between those who are able to generate a creative response to change and those who, often for reasons to do with their personal biography or with the school climate, were defeated and disheartened by it. As we have shown, these tended to be older, more experienced teachers who found it more difficult to change the well-established link between their professional values and particular educational practices.

More idiosyncratic factors rooted in personality and family background were also found to be relevant. A key variable in the capacity to cope with change was found to be *confidence* – in terms of both the individual teacher's professional skills and knowledge and more generally as a person. This finding mirrors the parallel finding that is reported in our study of pupils, which documents a growing divide between those pupils who are intellectually and socially confident and those who for various reasons – academic or personal – are not. Interestingly, it also mirrors the evidence documenting a growing divide between schools in more or less favourable circumstances. We suggest that this evidence concerning the widening gulf between individual pupils, teachers and schools in terms of their perceived capacity to succeed in the current climate relates to the pervasive presence of externally defined, standardized and pervasive performance indicators in relation to which teachers, pupils and schools must compete if they are to be judged successful. These performance indicators are in most cases 'criterion-referenced' rather than 'norm-referenced' in that they require a judgement to be made against a defined standard rather than in relation to other individuals or institutions. Nevertheless, in defining an explicit and common standard to be reached, they inevitably imply a more difficult journey for those less well equipped by circumstances.

Thus it is important to stress once again that our story is one that documents many different responses to the common policy initiatives which were imposed on every school. As the case studies that we present in Chapter 9 illustrate, schools varied considerably in the way in which they were willing and able to mediate external directives, just as individual heads and teachers did. Some of the reasons for these differences have been illuminated by in-depth studies of teachers' working lives, as Woods (1990) documents, in which the relationship between self and subjectivities on the one hand and structure on the other is brought to the fore. Such *different* responses underline a further key conceptual element in our analysis: the relationship between structure and agency, to which we return later in this chapter.

Creativity, classification and compliance in the classroom

Although we found considerable variation in the nature and scale of teachers' *feelings* about the changes they were experiencing, and in their ways of working, there was by contrast relatively little variation in the impact of these changes on their classroom practice. The powerful combination of National Curriculum directives and public rhetoric on the one hand and national assessment and OFSTED inspection requirements on the other left little room for individual teachers or schools to redefine what was to be learned, when and to what standard. Discretion concerning time and space and control over the content of learning was increasingly denied to both teachers and pupils. Indeed, the progressive reduction of both teacher and learner autonomy is arguably the most pervasive and significant result of the policy agenda that was launched by the 1988 Education Reform Act. Moreover, the initial stages of the introduction of a mandatory national curriculum and national assessment have been successively reinforced by the introduction of a high-profile inspection system based on a standardized national framework, a national system of target-setting and most recently, the prescribed pedagogy of the national literacy and numeracy hours.

However, even before these most recent developments, the findings we report in Part 3 document a clear shift away from 'constructivist' models of learning to one that emphasizes the delivery of an established body of knowledge. Chapters 6, 7 and 8 document in some detail the changes that have taken place in terms of the three key 'message systems' of curriculum, pedagogy and assessment in the classrooms which our core sample of pupils experienced in the nine schools we studied throughout the project. It is a situation in which, as Part 3 makes clear, the curriculum is increasingly strongly 'classified' in the Bernsteinian sense of an explicit division between subjects. It is also increasingly strongly 'framed' in that teachers' discretion over how it is to be taught is progressively being reduced.

The potential effects of the trend towards whole-class teaching, teacher instruction, subject timetabling and ability grouping are being reinforced by an assessment system that increasingly commodifies achievement, shifting the educational balance to recognize intellectual ability, rather than the feelings that encourage or inhibit learning; emphasizing product, rather than process. The result, as Part 3 makes clear, is an increasingly pressured classroom life in which a reduction in interactive pedagogy has been replaced by a highly instrumental focus on performance in which it is the *quantity* of pupils' learning experiences, rather than their *quality*, that has become the prime focus. The implications of this changing classroom focus for pupils' learning and motivation are the subject of the companion volume to this one (Pollard *et al.*, 2000).

It would be wrong, however, to assume from the above that the picture of change has essentially been one of teachers accommodating to the requirements placed upon them. Since the early 1990s it has been recognized that policy initiatives are not translated wholesale into school and classroom practice but rather are subject to a series of mediations that are the product of successive interpretations and reinterpretations of them by actors at various levels of the system. As Woods and Wenham (1995) point out, the implementation of policy initiatives may be seen as a 'career' during which their usages and meanings undergo often considerable change. The way in which different interest groups 'interpret policy initiatives and use different discourses to imbue sense to them, rather than taking sense from them' (p. 119) underpins the now familiar distinction between 'readerly' and 'writerly' approaches to policy initiatives made by Bowe *et al.* (1992). In the book that reports the second phase of the PACE study (Croll, 1996) we highlight the way in which teachers had become 'policy-makers in practice', striving in particular to protect their pupils from what they perceived to be the worst effects of recent policy changes. We returned to this theme in Chapter 4 of this book in describing the various manifestations of 'creative mediation' that we observed as an increasingly confident teaching body reasserted its professional interpretation of nationally generated requirements.

In this, teachers may have been assisted by the changing political climate in which the reforms were embedded. One of the major principles underpinning the 1988 Education Reform Act was that of entitlement – that a national curriculum should ensure access for every child to a broad and balanced curriculum. Thus, when it was first introduced, the National Curriculum specified virtually every aspect of the subjects to be taught, and, hence, the allocation of teaching time. But, starting with the Dearing review of the National Curriculum in 1994, which was concerned to address issues of manageability, this commitment to a broad and balanced curriculum was steadily eroded to a point where almost the opposite became the case. The primacy given to literacy and numeracy hour requirements at the end of this decade of change and the impact of national testing in only these two subjects plus science combined to threaten the time available for the full range of National Curriculum subjects. Moreover, as Woods and Wenham (1995) suggest, policy initiatives are likely to have two stages, the political and the educational. In the case of the National Curriculum, they suggest that

> In the former, from the context of general influence, through opportunity and initiation, and text production, through to the context of immediate reception, the policies of the New Right dictated the course and reception of action. The Secretary of State had sustained and enhanced in some quarters, his political standing by his policies. Educationists and LEAs had been disempowered, teachers put in their place, progressive policies derided, more traditional ones saluted. An election had been won. By the time it arrived in schools its political purposes had been largely served, and the accompanying 'noise' made primarily by the media, had disappeared.   (p. 138)

It may well be argued, therefore, that the combination of a relative loosening in curriculum prescription coupled with a growing confidence to manage such requirements at school level has allowed at least some teachers to feel more positive and to exercise more professional discretion than the above account would suggest. This interpretation is reinforced by the findings of Archbald and Porter (1994) in the USA, who found that the perception of strong external control did not, in itself, lower teachers' job satisfaction. Rather, teachers' morale, and hence their level of professional commitment, depends on the characteristics of the job itself, on the degree of feedback, participation, collaboration, learning opportunities and resources that together enable them to fulfil their professional vision. Differential incentives, merit pay and career ladders were found to be much less important in increasing job satisfaction than increasing collaboration, feedback and participation. Similar findings for English primary teachers have been reported by Nias (1989) on the basis of a study carried out before the impact of the National Curriculum, and by Campbell and Neill (1992), both of whom found that the pressures experienced by primary teachers in terms of time and lack of recognition were most effectively mitigated by working in a supportive and collaborative professional environment. In confirming the importance of a supportive institutional context, these findings help to explain the range of responses to the National Curriculum and its associated requirements in terms of pedagogy that we have documented among the teachers who formed the PACE sample. They also suggest that some of the more recent government policy initiatives – notably the commitment to introducing merit payments and a differentiated reward structure which were heralded by the Green Paper *Excellence in Teaching* – may well not achieve their intended purpose.

Thus in broad terms the PACE study tells a story of both change and continuity with regard to primary teachers' perspectives and practices since the passing of the Education Reform Act in 1988. The many changes have centred on a progressive loss of professional freedom to determine what and how to teach which has resulted in a perceived loss of creativity and a more or less grudging compliance on the part of teachers. The climate of increased managerialism based on targets and performance indicators has served to reinforce this compliance and to encourage a sense of instrumentalism in the pursuit and judgement of learning outcomes. Where teachers have been conscious of such an increased instrumentality in their teaching, this has been experienced by some as a source of conflict. However, other teachers, either as individuals or as groups, have been able to integrate these new pressures into their existing professional values. They have developed more collegial ways of working and new understandings about how to achieve their underlying professional values. These have in turn become the basis for a new 'professionalism' which is a synthesis of past and present ideologies.

Thus, depending on the particular mixture of both individual teachers' and whole-school circumstances, the specific blend of change and continuity that has resulted can range from demoralization and disaffection at one extreme to empowerment at the other. Moreover, this range of responses may also be experienced by the same teacher at different times or in relation to different aspects of his or her work, as we demonstrated in our discussion of the notion of 'fragmented identities' in Chapter 4. One important lesson from our results is to reinforce the point that the impact of policy change is rarely homogeneous – that it needs to be understood as a reflexive process that is governed by a variety of individual and institutional factors that inform the subsequent perceptions and actions on the part of those involved.

Perhaps the most crucial question raised by these broad generalizations is that concerning the factors that govern the capacity creatively to mediate change; to ask which schools and teachers in what circumstances found it difficult to respond to the new requirements placed on them and why. For in seeking to answer this question, our study begins to illuminate some more fundamental issues about the impact of the prevailing educational discourse and its potential longer-term significance for English primary education. In particular, it addresses arguably the most significant of the dimensions identified above. This is the issue of 'commitment'. In seeking to understand teachers' different responses to recent policy initiatives and the significance of these differences, the issue of professional motivation – both in terms of the overall level of personal commitment and in terms of the nature of individual teachers' involvement in the task of teaching young children – is arguably crucial. For, as we suggest in the companion PACE book on pupils (Pollard *et al.*, 2000), whether motivation is intrinsic and associated with the satisfaction inherent in the task itself or extrinsic, based on the promise of subsequent rewards, has a profound effect on the quality of pupils' learning and, even more importantly, on their subsequent *disposition* to learn. Here we argue a very similar point concerning teachers. We hypothesize that there has been a pressure to move from a covenant-based professionalism in which a good deal of a teacher's day-to-day motivation is dependent on the *intrinsic* satisfaction of trying to achieve self-imposed goals to a contractual, performance-based motivation driven by the promise of external rewards. This is likely to lead in the longer term to an overall diminution in the quality of teachers' commitment. This in turn may result in a decline in the largely indefinable, but nevertheless fundamentally important facets of professionalism that are bound up in teachers' sense of moral, self-imposed accountability. We explore these issues in more detail in the next section.

11.3 FROM COMPETENCE TO PERFORMANCE

Whilst our first priority in this book has been to describe and analyse the impact of the 1988 Education Reform Act on primary teachers and primary schools, we are also concerned to analyse the changes that have taken place in English primary schooling as an illustration of wider social developments. In particular, we are concerned to understand the changing focus of education policy as a reflection of the emerging conditions of late modernity, or 'post-modern' society, with its new priorities and new forms of contestation, regulation and discourse.

In 1994 we described the PACE project as 'one of the many stepping stones in the quest to understand the nature of the educational enterprise and hence, how to provide for it most effectively' (Pollard *et al.*, 1994a, p. 4) in a changing context. Thus our research has been designed to help understand the origin and significance both of the policy initiatives imposed by government and of those that are the product of attempts by teachers and headteachers to reconcile these requirements with their professional values and understandings. What, ultimately, is likely to be the significance of these policy initiatives set in motion in the England of the late 1980s for the nature and quality of teachers' professional motivation and practice?

As we suggested in Chapter 1, the work of Basil Bernstein has proved particularly apposite as a foundation framework for these theoretical interpretations. The capacity of Bernstein's theory of educational codes to embrace curriculum, pedagogy and assessment, and its concern with power, knowledge and consciousness as key variables, made it possible to use it to integrate the diverse perspectives of the PACE project into three core themes, which we identified as *values, understanding* and *power*.

Central to the early analyses of the PACE project was the argument that schools, as well as teachers and pupils, are 'embedded in a dynamic network of personal identity, values and understandings that are constantly developing in the light of internal and external interaction, pressure and constraint' (Pollard *et al.*, 1994a, p. 156). Because of this, policy directives are translated into classroom practice through a series of 'mediations'. Such 'mediations', we have argued, should not be conceptualized in engineering terms as a series of articulated levers that relay a load through the structure. Rather they are the creative reinterpretation by the actors involved at each successive stage of the process of delivering education.

In these terms, too, Bernstein's analysis of the pedagogic code and its power to define, and hence control, which is embodied in the discourse of primary, secondary and subsequent reconceptualizations of the original message, provides a powerful theoretical model with which to examine the significance of the changes documented in the PACE data. Bernstein locates the 'pedagogic discourse' of primary education, which has been progressively eroded in recent years, within a number of broad social science traditions of the 1960s. These had a common emphasis on 'competencies' and were characterized by a 'universal democracy of acquisition'. He cites, for example, the psychology of Piaget, the linguistics of Chomsky and the sociology of Garfinkel as instances of social scientific conceptualizations which in turn came to underpin the creation of educational approaches based on 'competencies'. These identified the subject as active and creative in the construction of a valid world of meaning and practice, and favoured an educational approach that 'celebrated what we are rather than what we have become' and in which the role of formal instruction is replaced by accomplishments that are intrinsically creative and tacitly acquired.

Radical as these educational ideas may seem, Bernstein argued that they found 'official' expression in the report of the Plowden Committee, *Children and Their Primary Schools* (CACE, 1967), and the next twenty years of primary school practice, which the report's ideas profoundly shaped. He contrasts this 'competence'-based pedagogic model with one based on 'performance' which emphasizes a specific output from the acquirer, a particular text that the learner is required to construct and the acquisition of the specialized skills necessary to the creation of the required output. Through the operation of explicit assessment procedures, learners are made aware of the learning outcomes that will be valued. Their performance will in turn be a means of locating them in terms of a hierarchical judgement. These are ideas that we have explored in some detail in the companion volume to this, which is concerned with pupils (Pollard *et al.*, 2000).

However, it is apparent from the developments that we have described in this book that teachers too are now similarly subject to such a 'performance' model. As with pupils, the orientation towards performance is a comprehensive strategy that embraces the inputs and processes, as well as the outputs, of the education system. Thus recent years have witnessed increasing central specification of the range of competencies to be achieved in initial teacher training and, hence, of the 'inputs' to the education system. They have witnessed, too, the growing powers of OFSTED and the imposition of a comprehensive inspection system based on a framework that defines what constitutes 'quality' in educational 'processes'. Last but not least, teachers are subject to the control of externally imposed definitions of 'outputs' through the pervasive dissemination of published tables of pupil results. Moreover, as has already been suggested, the radical reforms to teachers' pay and career structure which were heralded in the 1998 Green Paper *Teachers: Meeting the Challenge of Change* are also based on the assumption that it is both possible and desirable to judge an individual teacher's performance in relation to explicit criteria. Thus teachers, like pupils, are increasingly being required to respond to a 'performance'-orientated system of education based on external measures of quality. Both teachers' working lives and pupils' learning experiences are increasingly the subject of formal, 'categorical' assessments.

Thus the characteristics of Bernstein's 'performance' pedagogic model are readily recognizable in the developments that have taken place in primary schools as documented by the PACE project. As Tables 11.1 and 11.2 illustrate, the increasingly tight classification of the curriculum into clearly delineated subjects, the growing strength of the framing of both teachers' and pupils' work so that they have less and less autonomy and choice, and the designation of times and spaces for particular purposes are all clear indicators in this respect. Perhaps most powerful of all, however, is the changing assessment discourse and the way in which the language of levels and achievement for pupils and institutional evaluation, standards and 'value-added' for schools reflect a profound change in both the definition of educational priorities and assumptions about the most effective way of achieving them.

Tables 11.1 and 11.2 below display some of these issues in contrasting ways for analytic purposes, though of course the situation is more complex than this device allows. This form of modelling derives from Bernstein (1996, p. 58), although he is in no way responsible for our adaptation and extension of his work.

The significance of these changes and findings may be examined in terms of two broad issues. First, they suggest a deep tension between the rhetoric of the much-

Table 11.1 Some contrasting aspects of competence and performance models in relation to schools and teachers

	A 'competence model': LIBERAL PROGRESSIVE EDUCATION	A 'performance model' PERFORMANCE EDUCATION
Management style	'Invisible management', with relative professional autonomy	'Visible management', with relative professional regulation
Organizational form	Professional, with flat management structure. Control through self-regulation, socialization and internalization of norms	Mechanistic, with hierarchical structure and bureaucracy. Standardization for control and coordination
Management style	Collegiate, with emphasis on proficiency, dialogue and consensus. Informality in relationships	Managerial, with emphasis on efficiency and target-setting for results. Greater formality in relationships
Teacher roles	Teachers as facilitators, with affective dimensions seen as intrinsic to the teaching role	Teachers as instructors and evaluators, with emphasis on cognitive and managerial skills
Teacher professionalism	Professional covenant based on trust, and commitment to education as a form of personal development. Confidence, sense of fulfilment and spontaneity in teaching	Professionalism as the fulfilment of a contract to deliver education, which is seen as a commodity for individuals and a national necessity for economic growth. Less confidence, fulfilment and spontaneity in teaching
Teacher accountability	Personal and 'moral' accountability	External and contractual accountability, backed by inspection
Whole-school coordination	Relative autonomy and informal teacher collaboration	Formal school planning, with 'managed' collegiality
Economic costs	Expensive, because of sophisticated teacher education and time-consuming school practices	Cheaper, because of more explicit teacher training and systematized school practices

vaunted 'learning society' and the empowerment for both teachers and pupils that it implies, and the reality of the 'performance' culture which is being promoted by current policy-making and by the accountability requirements that are being placed on schools. The educational ideology of the learning society is one in which learners are empowered to want and to be able to manage their own learning in an individualistic manner; where there will be more openness and opportunity, and

Table 11.2 Some contrasting aspects of competence and performance models in relation to classrooms and pupils

	Competence model	Performance model
	'Invisible pedagogies', with weak classification and frame	'Visible pedagogies', with strong classification and frame
Autonomy	Considerable	Limited
Space	Flexible boundaries and use	Explicit regulation
Time	Flexible emphasis on present experiences	Strong structuring, sequencing and pacing
Activity	Emphasis on the realization of inherent learner capabilities through subject-integrated and learner controlled activities, such as projects	Strong control over selection of knowledge and explicit promotion of specialized subjects and skills
Evaluation	Emphasis on immediate, present qualities using implicit and diffuse criteria	Emphasis on correct products or capabilities using explicit and specific performance criteria
Control	Relatively 'invisible', with control inhering in interpersonal communications and relationships	Explicit structuring and systems for classification, setting and differentiation through instruction
Pupil products	Pupil products are taken to indicate a stage of cognitive, affective or social development. Teachers 'read' and interpret learner products using specialized professional judgement and knowledge	Pupil products are simply taken to indicate performance, as objectified by grades. Teachers instruct and assess using nationally defined procedures and criteria.
Pupil learning	Highlighting intrinsic motivation and encouraging mastery orientation. Potential for 'deep learning', but tendency to produce routinization and evasion.	Highlighting performance orientation and explicit attainments. Tendency to produce instrumentalism and 'surface learning'. Risk of learned helplessness and withdrawal

fewer prescribed spaces and times for learning, or defined outcomes or prescribed bodies of knowledge. One manifestation of this is the set of proposals from the Labour government on lifelong learning, *The Learning Age: A Renaissance for a New Britain* (DfEE, 1998).

However, we believe that the call for resilient and flexible learners whose intrinsic motivation and mastery orientation will provide the foundation of future national economic and social development is in tension with the systemic, performance-oriented changes that are still being strengthened within the schools system. In the same way, the growing emphasis on performance management strategies for teachers which is clearly evidenced, for example, in the 1999 DfEE Consultation Document *Performance Management Framework for Teachers* is likely to inhibit the emergence of the kind of flexible professionals that such developments are likely to require. As Gray (1990, p. 10) has argued, the

> rhetoric about 'driving up standards' can be read as an attempt to realign education to the commodity values that increasingly define worthwhile or legitimate knowledge in post-industrial societies ... [i.e.] 'the task of education is not the dissemination of a general model of life, not to transform students' minds but to supply the system with the merchandise it needs in the form of information and skills.

This suggests that we have reached a stage in the development of 'performativity' as a policy device in which its role is not just to hold schools (and other institutions) accountable for educational standards, but rather the redefining of the educational standards themselves in terms of economic commodity values. Referring to the current policy preoccupation with school effectiveness – itself a manifestation of the prevailing preoccupation with 'performativity' – Elliott (1996, p. 16) argues that the new emphasis on performativity as a policy device is not simply, or even mainly, about raising standards, but rather plays a central role in

> changing the rules which shape educational thought and practice. They are part of a language game which serves the interests of power and legitimates those interests in terms of the performativity criterion ... The more successful such reviews are in manufacturing a consensus about the properties that characterised good schools, the more marginalised and silenced are the voices who would articulate, given the social space to do so, a different vision of quality in education, of the pedagogical conditions which make it possible and of the contribution of research to its realisation.

To the extent that such voices are silenced, however, the likelihood of developing the type of educational institution that is needed to foster 'lifelong learning for all' is correspondingly reduced. On the one hand, increasingly pervasive 'categoric assessments' mean that a substantial, and probably correspondingly increasing, number of learners are put off the business of learning at a relatively young age by the experience of failure. On the other, the institutions themselves are condemned to pursue and prioritize those learning goals which form the basis of the 'league tables' and other external quality assessments on which they will be judged.

In this book we have suggested that the process of accommodating to new, externally imposed obligations is characterized by a variety of mediations based on the values and understandings of the individuals involved concerning the goals of education and how they may best be achieved. The effect of this process of accommodation is gradually to change the discourse through which the ideology and practice of education at any particular level are expressed.

One of the most significant features of the contemporary preoccupation with 'performativity' is its apparent neutrality. Changes in the discourse of education eventually become 'normalized' such that the validity of its underpinning assumptions are increasingly taken for granted. However, any exercise that is concerned with the evaluation of quality involves more than the application of a neutral technology. Such evaluations are not 'valid irrespective of human expectation, ideas, attitudes and wishes' (Feyeraband, 1987, p. 5). Rather, they must be understood as a 'social technology' (Madaus, 1994) rooted in contemporary power relations. Assessment devices are necessarily instruments of power. 'They are not, and cannot be, measures or indicators of some purely objective, independently-existing state of affairs', writes Hanson (1993, p. 52); rather they 'act to transform, mould and even to create, what they supposedly measure'. The prevailing culture of 'performativity' moulds individual teachers' and pupils' views of themselves; it moulds and controls notions of success and failure and the reasons for it; and increasingly it forms the basis for the way in which institutions are both managed and judged. Above all, it shapes the vision of English primary education and its priorities in the late twentieth century. Increasingly, as its contribution to economic competitiveness has become the overriding goal of education, so society begins to lack any more fundamental basis for social solidarity (Broadfoot, 1996b). One important consequence of this has been the recourse to 'performativity' measures. This in turn has had the result of silencing alternative voices concerning the goals of education and how these goals may best be achieved. As Pollard (1997) has argued, the trends that we have identified suggest the likelihood of growing tensions in the social fabric.

11.4 TOWARDS A NEW PROFESSIONALISM? IS THERE A THIRD WAY?

The PACE study has focused on a particular sector of English society, primary education, which is located within the broader sweep of history and social, cultural, economic and political change. In this book we have documented in some detail the contemporary characteristics of English primary teaching and how these have changed in response to the major policy initiatives of recent years. In concluding, it is appropriate to speculate a little about what the future might hold in the light of the conflicting pressures we have identified between an increasingly explicit concern with performativity on the one hand and primary teachers' traditionally rather different values and understandings on the other.

It is appropriate too, to recognize that these tensions are not confined to one small country even if they find their more extreme expression in the hitherto unfettered freedoms of English primary schooling. As Sultana (1994) suggests in his analysis of teachers' work in a uniting Europe, the preoccupation with 'performativity' in the field of education has led to the predominance of what Habermas refers to as 'instrumental rationality' where the criteria for establishing the best course of action are decided not with reference to the best reasons, but with reference to the most efficient and effective course to achieve desired ends. Instrumental, technocratic rationality has become all-pervasive and hegemonic, he suggests, with the results that education is increasingly conceived in instrumental terms. As a parallel development, democracy becomes a system of political management rather than a distinctive form of social and moral life.

The logical extension of this form of rationality is the conceptualization of teachers' work as a skilled craft based on technical expertise despite the fact that education as a moral project and the teacher as a transformative intellectual are historically at the heart of the European educational tradition. Sultana (1994) calls for teachers to recapture this larger vision and to reject the role of 'deliverer, tester, and technician' (p. 178). Another European writer, Perrenoud (1996), sounds a similar call to arms. Sketching out the choice that confronts teachers in many developed societies between proletarianization or professionalization, he argues that teachers have a choice and can exert an influence but that they must have a clear vision and use it to negotiate a new role.

Clearly, policy-makers in England and elsewhere are faced with a choice. Evidence from the PACE study, which is reinforced by that of related studies of English primary schooling, confirms that the shift towards managerialism at all levels of the system – in the classroom, in the school and in the system as a whole – goes against the development of effective collegiality (Hargreaves, 1991; Webb and Vulliamy, 1996a). It confirms, as we suggested at the beginning of this chapter, that teachers' job satisfaction and, by implication, their commitment, are rooted in complexity and a sense of empowerment (Rowan, 1994). As we have argued in both this book and its companion volume about pupils (Pollard *et al.*, 2000), our study has led us to pose the most fundamental questions about the nature of teaching and learning. As we have documented, primary teachers struggled over recent years with the question. 'Is this the kind of teacher I want to be?' So we are now bound to ask, by implication, 'What kind of teacher do we want to form the future citizens of our society?'

The choice, as Ball (1999) suggests, is between the 'authentic' teacher whose practice is based upon the values of 'service' and a shared moral language that provides for reflection, dialogue and debate, and the 'reformed' teacher, whose practice is based upon the achievement of targets and the calculation of 'costs' in relation to outputs. Within all this schools will become whatever it seems necessary to become in order to flourish in the market. But there is a choice.

Appendix: Systematic Observation: Definition of Categories

TEACHER OBSERVATION

Teacher activity

Coded at each ten-second interval. The code relates to what is happening at the 'bleep', not to a summary of the previous ten seconds.

I   Instruction: Teacher is involved with child/children directly on a curriculum activity (excluding hearing reading, encouraging and assessment, as defined below). This includes explaining a task and watching/listening to children doing a task. It does not include managing the task.

C   Control: Control/discipline relating to children's behaviour, e.g. 'This room is getting noisy', 'Sit down, Marilyn', 'Andrew!' It does not include non-disciplinary directions, e.g. 'Stop what you are doing and listen to me.'

D   Direction: Management of curriculum task activity, e.g. 'Blue group go to the library', 'Put your things away now', 'When you've finished you can colour it in.'

A   Assessment: Explicit assessment, such as marking or correcting work, recording attainment or reviewing work with a pupil as an assessment activity.

E   Encouragement: Positive praise, support or encouragement, e.g. 'That's really good', 'You have all worked really well today.' It does not include routine feedback, e.g. 'Yes, that's right', which is coded I.

N   Negative: Negative feedback and comment on curriculum activity, e.g. 'That's no good at all', 'Why didn't you do it the way I told you?' It does not include routine feedback, e.g. 'There are two h's in "chrysanthemum".'

R   Hearing children read: This refers to 'reading to teacher' as a one-to-one activity.

O   Other: Including teacher talking to adult, teacher not involved with class and non-curriculum activities such as class administration. (NB. Class administration is not included in planned observation but may occur unexpectedly.)

Teacher interaction

Coded every ten seconds. The code relates to what is happening at the bleep. It is the teacher's interaction that is coded. Interaction includes verbal interaction (speaking and listening) and also other forms of interaction, such as touch, gesture and writing on the blackboard with the class watching.

O   Alone means not interacting. Children may be physically present.

TC   Teacher interaction with the whole class. It is coded whenever the teacher is working with all the children who are present in the room, even if some children from the class are missing. But if over half the children are out of the room, one of the group codes should be used. This code encompasses a range of settings, e.g. story time or discussions on carpeted areas, as well as more direct instruction.

A   Interaction with any other adult.

G   With individual girl: one-to-one interaction with a single female pupil.

B   With individual boy: one-to-one interaction with a single male pupil.

X   With group of boys: simultaneous interaction with more than one male pupil.

Y   With group of girls: simultaneous interaction with more than one female pupil.

M   With a mixed group: simultaneous interaction with a mixed group of pupils.

Note: A group is defined as two or more children but less than the whole class as defined above. For the teacher to be coded as interacting with a group, the children do not necessarily have to be working together.

Pedagogic context

'Pedagogic context' summarizes the teaching context of the teacher over the six minutes of observation. MAIN gives the overall summary of the teaching context and only one code should be used. PART is coded for any other teaching activity that took place and multiple codes may be used. Sometimes, if teaching is very varied or evenly balanced, there may be no main context.

CLASS INTERACTION is defined as for TC above.

INDIVIDUAL WORK is when pupils are working individually on tasks. These may be the same tasks as are being undertaken by other children.

COOPERATIVE GROUP WORK is when the teacher is working with a group of children who are also working cooperatively amongst themselves.

GROUP WORK WITH TEACHER is when the teacher is working with a group of children who are not otherwise working together (although they may be sitting together and doing similar tasks).

OTHER – if none of the above contexts applies; details are noted.

Curriculum context

'Curriculum context' summarizes the curriculum content with which the teacher has been engaged in the preceding six minutes. MAIN gives the principal curriculum area, largely in terms of National Curriculum categories, and is normally coded once. PART refers to any other aspect of the curriculum that has been present. Sometimes, if the content is highly integrated with no subject category dominating, there may be no main code. Sometimes, if there has been a shift in the content the teacher is engaged with, there may be more than one main code. Clarification may be sought from the teacher if required.

CHILD OBSERVATION

Teacher activity

Coded as for teacher activity above.

Child interaction

Coded every ten seconds. The code refers to interactions of the target child at the bleep. Interactions may be verbal (both speaking and listening) or by touch or gesture.

O   Alone: The child is not interacting.

TC   With teacher in whole class: the child is part of the teacher's class audience (teacher whole-class interaction as defined above).

TO   With teacher one-to-one: the child is the focus of the teacher's individual attention on a one-to-one basis (although other children may be listening).

TG   With teacher in group: the child is part of a group with which the teacher is interacting (group as defined above).

AO   With another adult one-to-one: any interaction with an adult other than the teacher.

G   With individual girl: one-to-one interaction with a female pupil.

B   With individual boy: one-to-one interaction with a male pupil.

X   With a group of boys: simultaneous interaction with more than one male pupil.

Y   With a group of girls: simultaneous interaction with more than one female pupil.

M   With a mixed group: simultaneous interaction with a mixed group of pupils.

Note: If a child is notionally part of a class or group with the teacher but is actually interacting with one or more other children, then the actual interaction should be coded.

Child activity

Coded every ten seconds. The code refers to the target child's activity at the bleep.

TE   Task engagement in curriculum task (excluding reading to teacher and being formally assessed). This includes listening to the teacher when the teacher could be coded as I.

TM   Task management activity associated with a curriculum task, e.g. moving around the classroom, fetching or arranging books or materials, moving desks and equipment, getting out or sharpening pencils, listening to the teacher when the content of the teacher's activity would be coded as D rather than I.

D   Distracted: includes behaviour that is not task-focused – messing around, talking to other children about something other than work, day-dreaming etc.

B   Both distracted and task management.

A   Assessment: Child being explicitly assessed by his or her own or another teacher. Assessment as defined for teacher activity.

W   Waiting for teacher: usually either as part of a queue or with hand up.

X   Waiting (other): as above for another adult.

O   Out of room/sight.

R   Reading to teacher: reading to the teacher as a one-to-one reading activity.

Pedagogic context

Summary of pedagogic situation of the target child for the six minutes of observation. MAIN is the overall summary of the child's teaching context and is coded once. PART refers to any other teaching context that occurred, and may have multiple codes. Sometimes, if the teaching context is very varied or evenly balanced, there may be no main context. Categories are defined as in the teacher observation schedule. It is the context, not the actual activity, that is coded. If the child is part of a class lesson but has actually been interacting with other children, CLASS TEACHING is still coded. If the child is part of a cooperative group but has not contributed, COOP GROUP is still coded.

Curriculum context

'Curriculum context' provides a summary of the curriculum content of the activities in which the target child was engaged. MAIN gives the principal curriculum context, mainly in terms of National Curriculum areas. PART refers to any other aspect of the curriculum that was present in the work being observed. Normally there will be only one code for MAIN and there may be several for PART. If the content is highly integrated, with no subject dominating, there may be no MAIN context. Occasionally, if the focus of a child's work has changed during the period of observation, there may be more than one MAIN code.

References

Abbott, D., Broadfoot, P., Croll, P., Osborn, M. and Pollard, A. (1994) 'Some sink, some float: National Curriculum assessment and accountability', *BERA Journal*, **20**(2), 155–74.

Acker, S. (1990) 'Teachers' culture in an English primary school: continuity and change', *British Journal of Sociology of Education*, **11**(3), 257–73.

Acker, S. (1995) 'Carry on caring: the work of women teachers', *British Journal of Sociology of Education*, **16**(1), 21–36.

Acker, S. (1999) *The Realities of Teachers' Work: Never a Dull Moment*. London: Cassell.

Agambar, C. (1996) 'HMI findings on use made of National Curriculum assessment', SCAA seminar, June.

Alexander, R. (1991) *Primary Education in Leeds*. 12th and final report from the Primary Needs Independent Evaluation Project, University of Leeds.

Alexander, R. (1995) *Versions of Primary Education*. London: Routledge.

Alexander, R. (1997) *Policy and Practice in Primary Education*. London: Routledge.

Alexander, R. J., Willcocks, J. and Kimber, K. M. (1989) *Changing Primary Practice*. Basingstoke: Falmer.

Alexander, R., Rose, J. and Woodhead, C. (1992) *Curriculum, Organisation and Classroom Practice in Primary Schools*. London: Department for Education and Science.

Apple, M. W. (1986) *Teachers and Texts: A Political Economy of Class and Gender Relations in Education*. London: Routledge.

Archibald, D. and Porter, A. (1994) 'Curriculum control and teachers' perceptions of autonomy and satisfaction', *Educational Evaluation and Policy Analysis*, **16**(1), 21–39.

Association of Teachers and Lecturers (ATL) (1996) *Doing Our Level Best: An Evaluation of Statutory Assessment in 1995*.

Association of Teachers and Lecturers (ATL) (1997) *The Validity of the 1996 Key*

Stage 2 Tests in English, Mathematics and Science.

Ball, S. (1999) *Educational Reform and the Struggle for the Soul of the Teacher!* Hong Kong: Chinese University of Hong Kong.

Ball, S. J. (1990) *Politics and Policy Making in Education: Explorations in Policy Sociology.* London: Routledge.

Bennett, S. N., Wragg, E. C., Carre, C. G. and Carter, D. S. G. (1992) 'A longitudinal study of primary teachers' perceived competence in, and concerns about, National Curriculum implementation', *Research Papers in Education*, 7(1), 53–78.

Bernstein, B. (1975) *Class, Codes and Control*, vol. 3: *Towards a Theory of Educational Transmission.* London: Routledge and Kegan Paul.

Bernstein, B. (1990) *Class, Codes and Control*, vol. 4: *The Structuring of Pedagogic Discourse*: London: Routledge and Kegan Paul.

Bernstein, B. (1996) *Pedagogy, Symbolic Control and Identity.* London: Taylor and Francis.

Black, E. (1996) 'Managing to change? The role of primary school head', in P. Croll (ed.) *Teachers, Puils and Primary Schooling.* London: Cassell.

Blase, J. and Anderson, G. (1995) *The Micropolitics of Educational Leadership: From Control to Empowerment.* London: Cassell.

Bourdieu, P. and Passeron, J. (1970) *La Reproduction: éléments pour une théorie du système d'enseignement.* Paris: Les Éditions de Minuit.

Bourdieu, P. and Passeron, J. (1977) *La Reproduction.* Paris: Sage.

Bowe, R., Ball, S. J. and Gold, A. (1992) *Reforming Education and Changing Schools.* London: Routledge.

Broadfoot, P. (1996a) 'Do we really need to write it all down? Managing the challenge of national assessment at Key Stage 1 and Key Stage 2', in P. Croll (ed.), *Teachers, Pupils and Primary Schooling: Continuity and Change.* London: Cassell.

Broadfoot, P. M. (1996b) *Education, Assessment and Society.* Buckingham: Open University Press.

Broadfoot, P., Osborn, M., Gilly, M. and Bûcher, A. (1993) *Perceptions of Teaching: Primary School Teachers in England and France.* London: Cassell.

Broadfoot, P., Osborn, M., Planel, C. and Pollard, A. (1994) 'Primary teachers and policy change: a comparative study. Final report to ESRC', University of Bristol/ University of the West of England, mimeo.

Broadfoot, P., Osborn, M., Planel, C. and Pollard, A. (1996) 'Teachers and change: a study of primary school teachers' reactions to policy changes in England and France', in T. Winther-Jensen (ed.), *Challenges to European Education: Cultural Values, National Identities and Global Responsibilities.* Berne: Peter Lang.

Broadfoot, P., Osborn, M., Planel, C. and Sharpe, K. (2000) *Promoting Quality in Learning: Does England Have the Answer?* London: Cassell.

Brown, B., McCallum, B., Taggart, B., Branson, J. and Gipps, C. (1995) 'Validity and the impact of national tests in the primary school: a teacher's view', Paper delivered at the European Conference on Educational Research, University of Bath.

Campbell, J. (1996) 'Professionalism in the primary school', Papers presented at ASPE Conference.

Campbell, R. J. and Neill, S. R. S. J. (1992) *Teacher Time and Curriculum Manageability at Key Stage 1*. London: AMMA.

Campbell, J. and Neill, S. R. (1994) *Primary Teachers at Work*. London: Routledge.

Campbell, R. J., Evans, L., Neill, S. R. S. J. and Packwood, A. (1991) *The Use and Management of Infant Teachers' Time: Some Policy Issues*. Coventry: University of Warwick Policy Analysis Unit.

Campbell, J., Emery, H. and Stone, C. (1993) 'The broad and balanced curriculum at Key Stage 2: some limitations on reform', Paper given at the BERA Annual Conference, University of Liverpool.

Central Advisory Council for Education (1967) *Teachers and Their Primary Schools*. London: HMSO.

Conduit, E., Brookes, R., Bramley, G. and Fletcher, C. L. (1996) 'The value of school locations', *British Educational Research Journal*, **22**(2), 199–206.

Conservative Party (1997) *You Can Only Be Sure with the Conservatives*, election manifesto.

Cortazzi, M. (1991) *Primary Teaching, How It Is: A Narrative Account*. London: David Fulton.

Cox, C. B. and Dyson, A. E. (eds) (1969) *Fight for Education: A Black Paper*. London: The Critical Quarterly Society.

Cox, T. and Sanders, S. (1994) *The Impact of the National Curriculum on the Teaching of Five Year Olds*. London: Falmer.

Croll, P. (ed.) (1996) *Teachers, Pupils and Primary Schooling: Continuity and Change*. London: Cassell.

Croll, P., Abbott, D., Broadfoot, P., Osborn, M. and Pollard, A. (1994) 'Teachers and educational policy: roles and models', *British Journal of Educational Studies*, **42**(2), 333–47.

Dale, R. (1981) 'Control, accountability and William Tyndale', in Dale, R., Esland, G., Fergusson, R. and MacDonald, M. (1981) *Politics, Patriarchy and Practice: Education and the State*, Vol. 2. Lewes: Falmer.

Darling-Hammond, L. (1990) 'Teachers and teaching: signs of a changing profession', in W. R. Houston, M. Haberman and J. Sikula (eds) *Handbook of Research on Teacher Education*. New York: Macmillan, pp. 267–90.

Darmanin, M. (1990) 'Maltese primary school teachers' experience of centralised policies', *British Journal of Sociology of Education*, **11**(3), 275–308.

Dearing, R. (1993) *The National Curriculum and Its Assessment: An Interim Report*. London: National Curriculum Council/School Examinations and Assessment Council.

Dearing, R. (1994) *The National Curriculum and Its Assessment: Final Report*. London: HMSO.

Densmore, K. (1987) 'Professionalism, proletarianisation and teachers' work', in T. Popkewitz (ed.), *Critical Studies in Teacher Education*. Lewes: Falmer.

Department for Education and Employment (1999) *Performance Management Framework for Teachers: Consultation Document*. London: DfEE.

Department for Education and Employment (1997) *Excellence in Schools*. London: DfEE.

Department for Education and Employment (1998a) *The Learning Age: A*

Renaissance for a New Britain. London: DfEE.

Department for Education and Employment (1998b) *Teachers Meeting the Challenge of Change.* London: HMSO.

Department for Education and Employment (1999) *A Fast Track for Teachers.* London, DfEE.

Department for Education and Employment (1999b) An update on the revised National Curriculum for Schools in England. News 402/99, 9 September.

Department for Education and Science (1985) *Better Schools.* Cmnd 9467. London: HMSO.

Elliott, J. (1996) 'Quality assurance, the educational standards debate, and the commodification of educational research', *Curriculum Journal*, **8**(6), 63–83.

Elliott, J., Bridges, D., Ebbutt, D., Gibson, R. and Nias, J. (1981) *School Accountability.* Oxford: Blackwell.

Evetts, J. (1990) *Women in Primary Education.* London: Methuen.

Evetts, J. (1994) *Becoming a Secondary Head Teacher.* London: Cassell.

Feyeraband, P. (1987) *Farewell to Reason.* London: Verso.

Filer, A. and Pollard, A. (2000) *The Social World of Pupil Assessment.* London: Continuum.

Fullan, M. (1982) *The Meaning of Educational Change.* New York: Teachers College Press.

Fullan, M. (1991) *The New Meaning of Educational Change.* London: Cassell.

Galton, M. (1995) *Crisis in the Primary Classroom.* London: David Fulton.

Galton, M. and Fogelman, K. (1998) *The Use of Discretionary Time in the Primary School.* Research Papers in Education.

Galton, M., Simon, B. and Croll, P. (1980) *Inside the Primary Classroom.* London: Routledge and Kegan Paul.

Galton, M., Hargreaves, L., Comber, C., Wall, D. and Pell, A. (1999) *Inside the Primary Classroom: 20 Years On.* London: Routledge.

Gewirtz, S. (1997) 'Post-welfarism and the reconstruction of teachers' work in the UK', *Journal of Education Policy*, **12**(4), 217–31.

Gipps, C. V. and Murphy, P. (1994) *A Fair Test? Assessment, Achievement and Equity.* Buckingham: Open University Press.

Gipps, C. V., Brown, M., McCallum, B. and McManus, S. (1995) *Intuition or Evidence? Teachers and National Assessment of Seven-Year-Olds.* Buckingham: Open University Press.

Grace, G. (1995) *School Leadership.* London: Falmer Press.

Gray, J. (1990) 'The quality of schooling: frameworks for judgement', *British Journal of Educational Studies*, **38**(3), 204–23.

Hall, V. (1996) *Dancing on the Ceiling: A Study of Women Managers in Education.* London: Chapman.

Halsey, A. J., Heath, A. F. and Ridge, J. M. (1980) *Origins and Destination: Family, Class and Education in Modern Britain.* Oxford: Clarendon Press.

Handy, C. (1994) *The Empty Raincoat: Making Sense of the Future.* London: Hutchinson.

Handy, C. and Aitken, R. (1986) *Understanding Schools as Organizations.* Harmondsworth: Penguin.

Hanson, A. (1993) *Testing Testing: Social Consequences of the Unexamined Life.* Berkeley, CA: University of California Press.

Hargreaves, A. (1994) *Changing Teachers, Changing Times: Teachers' Work and Culture in the Postmodern Age.* London: Cassell.

Harlen, W. and Qualter, A. (1991) 'Issues in SAT development and the practice of teacher assessment'. *Cambridge Journal of Education,* **21**(2), 141, 151.

Haviland, J. (1988) *Take Care, Mr Baker!* London: Fourth Estate.

Helsby, G. (1999) *Changing Teachers' Work.* Buckingham: Open University Press.

Helsby, G. and McCulloch, G. (eds) (1997) *Teachers and the National Curriculum.* London: Cassell.

Her Majesty's Inspectorate (1978) *Primary Education in England.* London: HMSO.

Hill, T. (1994) 'Primary headteachers: their job satisfaction and future career aspirations', *Educational Research,* **36**(3), Winter.

Hoyle, E. (1974) 'Professionality, professionalism and control in teaching', *Educational Review,* **3**(2), 15–17.

Hoyle, E. (1986) *The Politics of School Management.* Sevenoaks: Hodder and Stoughton.

Hoyle, E. and John, P. (1995) *Professional Knowledge and Professional Practice.* London: Cassell.

Huberman, M. (1993) *The Lives of Teachers.* London: Cassell.

Hughes, M., Wikely, F. and Nash, T. (1990) 'Parents and the National Curriculum: an interim report', University of Exeter, mimeo.

Husen, T. (ed.) (1967) *International Study of Achievement in Mathematics: A Comparison of Twelve Countries* (Vols 1, 2). Stockholm; Almqvist and Wiksell.

Jackson, P. W. (1968) *Life in Classrooms.* New York: Holt, Rinehart and Winston.

Jeffrey, B. and Woods, P. (1995) 'Panic on parade', *Times Educational Supplement, Primary Update,* 13 September, p. 13.

Jeffrey, B. and Woods, P. (1996) 'Feeling deprofessionalised: the social construction of emotions during an OFSTED inspection', *Cambridge Journal of Education,* **26**(3), 325–43.

Keys, W., Harris, S. and Fernandes, C. (1997) *Patterns of Mathematics and Science Teaching in Upper Primary Schools in England and Eight Other Countries.* The Third International Mathematics and Science Study 2nd National Report. Slough: NFER.

Krespi, A. (1995) 'Greek primary teachers and the National Curriculum'. Unpublished poster presentation, BERA Conference, University of Bath.

Labour Party (1997) *New Labour because Britain Deserves Better,* election manifesto.

Lawn, M. (1987) 'The spur and the bridle: changing the mode of curriculum control', *Journal of Curriculum Studies,* **19**(3), 227–36.

Lawn, M. (1995) 'Restructuring teaching in the USA and England: moving towards the differentiated flexible teacher'. *Journal of Education Policy,* **10**(4), 347–60.

Lawn, M. and Ozga, J. (1981) 'The educational worker: a reassessment of teachers', in M. Walker and L. Barton (eds), *School, Teachers and Learning.* London: Falmer.

Lawlor, S. (1993) *Inspecting the School Inspectors.* London: Centre for Policy Studies.

Lightfoot, S. L. (1983) 'The lives of teachers', in L. Shulman and G. Sykes (eds), *Handbook of Teaching and Policy*. New York: Longman.

Lipsky, M. (1980) *Street-level Bureaucracy: Dilemmas of the Individuals in Public Services*. New York: Russell Sage Foundation.

Little, J. W. (1990) 'The persistence of privacy: autonomy and initiative in teachers' professional relations', *Teachers College Record*, **91**(4), 509–36.

Lortie, D. C. (1975) *Schoolteacher*. London: Routledge and Kegan Paul.

Madaus, G. F. (1994) 'Testing's place in society: an essay review of *Testing, Testing: Social Consequences of the Examined Life* by F. A. Hanson', *American Journal of Education*, **102**, 222–34.

Menlo, A. and Poppleton, P. (eds) (1999) *The Meanings of Teaching: An International Study of Secondary Teachers' Work Lives*, London: Bergin and Garvey.

Menter, I., Muschamp, Y. and Pollard, A. (1995) 'The primary market place: a study of small service providers in an English city', Mimeo presented to the American Educational Research Association, San Francisco.

Menter, I., Muschamp, Y., Nicholls, P., Ozga, J. and Pollard, A. (1997) *Work and Identity in the Primary School: A Post-Fordist Analysis*. Buckingham: Open University Press.

Mortimore, P., Sammons, P., Stoll, L., Lewis, D. and Ecob, R. (1988) *School Matters: The Junior Years*. Wells and London: Open Books.

Moses, D. and Croll, P. (1990) 'Perspectives on the National Curriculum in primary and secondary schools', *Educational Studies*, **16**(1).

NCC (1993) *The National Curriculum at Key Stages 1 and 2*. York: National Curriculum Council.

Nias, J. (1989) *Primary Teachers Talking: A Study of Teaching as Work*. London: Routledge.

Nias, J. (1996) 'Thinking about feeling: the emotions in teaching', *Cambridge Journal of Education*, **26**(3), 293–306.

Nias, J. (1997) 'Would schools improve if teachers cared less?', *Education*, **3**(13).

Nias, J. (1999a) 'Teachers' moral purposes: stress, vulnerability and strength', in R. Vandenberghe and M. Huberman (eds), *Understanding and Preventing Teacher Burnout: A Sourcebook of International Research and Practice*. Cambridge: Cambridge University Press.

Nias, J. (1999b) 'Primary teaching as a culture of care', in J. Prosser (ed.), *School Culture*. London: Paul Chapman, pp. 66–81.

Nias, J., Southworth, G. and Yeomans, R. (1989) *Staff Relationships in the Primary School: A Study of Organisational Cultures*. London: Cassell.

Nias, J., Southworth, G. and Campbell, P. (1992) *Whole School Curriculum Development in the Primary School*. Lewes: Falmer.

Nixon, J., Martin, J., McKeown, P. and Ranson, S. (1997) 'Towards a learning profession: changing codes of occupational practice within the new management of education', *British Journal of Sociology of Education*, **18**(1): 5–29.

OFSTED (1993) *Curriculum Organisation and Classroom Practice in Primary Schools*. London: DFE.

OFSTED (1995) *Guidance on the Inspection of Nursery and Primary Schools*.

London: Office for Standards in Education.

OFSTED (1996) *Setting Targets to Raise Standards: A Survey of Good Practice*. London: Office for Standards in Education.

OFSTED (1997) *Using Subject Specialists to Promote High Standards at KS2*. London: Office for Standards in Education.

Osborn, M. and Black, E. (1994) *Developing the National Curriculum at Key Stage 2: The Changing Nature of Teachers' Work*. Birmingham: University of Bristol/ NASUWT.

Osborn, M. (1996a) 'Identity, career and change: a tale of two teachers', in P. Croll (ed.), *Teachers, Pupils and Primary Schooling*. London: Cassell.

Osborn, M. (1996b) 'Teachers as adult learners: the influence of the national context and policy change', Paper given at the International Conference on Education and Training, Warwick, March.

Osborn, M. (1996c) 'Teachers mediating change: Key Stage 1 revisited', in P. Croll (ed.), *Teachers, Pupils and Primary Schooling*. London: Cassell.

Osborn, M., Broadfoot, P., Abbott, D., Croll, P. and Pollard, A. (1992) 'The impact of current changes in English primary schools on teacher professionalism', *Teachers College Record*, **94**(1), 138–51.

Osborn, M., Broadfoot, P., Planel, C. and Pollard, A. (1997a) 'Social class, educational opportunity, and equal entitlement: dilemmas of schooling in England and France', *Comparative Education*, **33**(3), 375–93.

Osborn, M., Croll, P., Broadfoot, P., Pollard, A., McNess, E. and Triggs, P. (1997b) 'Policy into practice and practice into policy: creative mediation in the primary classroom', in G. Helsby and G. McCulloch (eds), *Teachers and the National Curriculum*. London: Cassell.

Perrenoud, P. (1996) 'The teaching profession between proletarianization and professionalization: two models of change', *Prospects*, **26**(3 September): 509–29.

Peters, T. (1989) *Thriving on Chaos*. London: Pan.

Plowden Report (1967) *Children and their Primary Schools: Report of the Central Advisory Council for Education in England*. London: HMSO.

Pollard, A. (1985) *The Social World of the Primary School*. London: Cassell.

Pollard, A. (1997) 'Learning and a new curriculum for primary schooling', Paper presented to the SCAA conference Developing the Primary School Curriculum: The Next Steps, School Curriculum and Assessment Authority, London, June.

Pollard, A. and Filer, A. (1996) *The Social World of Pupil Learning*. London: Cassell.

Pollard, A. and Filer, A. (1999) *The Social World of Pupil Career*. London: Cassell.

Pollard, A. and Triggs, P., with Broadfoot, P., McNess, E. and Osborn, M. (2000) *Policy Practice and Pupil Experience: Changing English Primary Education*. London: Cassell.

Pollard, A., Broadfoot, P., Croll, P., Osborn, M. and Abbott, D. (1994a) *Changing English Primary Schools? The Impact of the Education Reform Act at Key Stage One*. London: Cassell.

Pollard, A., Broadfoot, P., Croll, P., Osborn, M. and Abbott, D. (1994b) 'Changing the classroom curriculum: the acid test of policy intervention', PACE Working Paper 17, presented at American Educational Research Association Conference,

New Orleans, April.

Pollard, A., Broadfoot, P., Osborn, M., McNess, E., Triggs, P. and Noble, J. (1997) 'Primary assessment, curriculum and experience', Symposium papers, British Educational Research Association, York.

Poppleton, P. (1999) 'The teacher's roles and responsibilities', in A. Menlo and P. Poppleton (eds), *The Meanings of Teaching: An International Study of Secondary Teachers' Work Lives.* London: Bergin and Garvey.

Poulson, L. (1996) 'Accountability: a key-word in the discourse of educational reform', *Journal of Education Policy*, **11**(5), 579–92.

Radnor, H. (1996) *Evaluation of Key Stage 3 Assessment in 1995 and 1996.* London: School Curriculum and Assessment Authority.

Radnor, H. A., Poulson, L. and Turner-Bisset, R. (1995) 'Assessment and teacher professionalism', *The Curriculum Journal*, **6**(3), 325–42.

Richards, C. (1998) 'Curriculum and pedagogy in Key Stage 2: a survey of policy and practice in small rural primary schools', *The Curriculum Journal*, **9**(3): 319–32.

Robertson, S. L. (1998) 'Restructuring and re-regulating teachers' labour in New Zealand'. Paper presented to the Annual Meeting of the American Educational Research Association, San Diego, CA, 13–17 April.

Rowan, B. (1994) 'Comparing teachers' work with work in other occupations: notes on the professional status of teaching', *Educational Researcher*, **23**(6): 4–17, 21.

SCAA (1995a) *Report on the 1995 Key Stage 2 Tests and Tasks in English, Mathematics and Science.* London, HMSO.

SCAA (1995b) *Key Stage 2 Assessment Arrangements 1996.* London: HMSO.

Shipman, M. (1990) *In Search of Learning: A New Approach to School Management.* Oxford: Blackwell Education.

Smith, M. L. (1991) 'Meanings of test preparation', *American Educational Research Journal*, **28**(3), 521–42.

Stone, C. (1993) 'Topic work in the context of the National Curriculum', *Journal of Teacher Development*, **2**(1), 27–38.

Sultana, R. (1994) 'Conceptualising teachers' work in a uniting Europe', *Compare*, **24**(2): 171–82.

TGAT (1988) National Curriculum Task Group on Assessment – A Report. London: DES/WO.

Troman, G. (1995) 'The rise of the new professionals? The restructuring of primary teachers' work and professionalism', Paper presented at the British Educational Research Association Annual Conference, University of Bath.

Troman, G. (1996) 'The rise of the new professionals? The restructuring of primary teachers' work and professionalism', *British Journal of Sociology of Education*, **17**(4): 473–87.

Vulliamy, G. and Webb, R. (1993) 'Progressive education and the National Curriculum: findings from a global education research project', *Educational Review*, **45**(1), 21–41.

Wallace, M. (1991) 'Coping with multiple innovations in schools', *School Organisation*, **11**(2), 187–209.

Waller, W. (1932) *The Sociology of Teaching.* New York: Russell and Russell.

Webb, R. (1993) *Eating the Elephant Bit by Bit: The National Curriculum at Key*

Stage 2. London: ALT.

Webb, R. and Vulliamy, G. (1996a) 'A deluge of directives: conflict between collegiality and managerialism in the post-ERA primary school', *British Educational Research Journal*, **22**(4): 441–58.

Webb, R. and Vulliamy, G. (1996b) *Roles and Responsibilities in the Primary School: Changing Demands, Changing Practices.* Buckingham: Open University Press.

Webb, R. and Villiamy, G. with Hakkinen, K., Hamalainen, S., Kimonen, E., Nevalainen, R. and Nikki, M. (1997) *A Comparative Analysis of Curriculum Change in Primary Schools in England and Finland.* York: University of York Department of Education.

West, A., Hailes, J. and Sammons, P. (1997) 'Children's attitudes to the National Curriculum at Key Stage 1', *British Educational Research Journal*, **23**(5), 597–613.

Woods, P. (1977) 'Teaching for survival', in P. Woods and M. Hammersley (eds), *School Experience.* London: Croom Helm.

Woods, P. (1990) 'Cold eyes and warm hearts: changing perspectives on teachers' work and careers' (review essay), *British Journal of Sociology of Education*, **11**(1), 101–17.

Woods, P. (1995) *Creative Teachers in Primary Schools.* Buckingham: Open University Press.

Woods, P. and Jeffrey, B. (1996) *Teachable Moments.* Buckingham: Open University Press.

Woods, P. and Jeffrey, B. (1997) 'Creative teaching in the primary National Curriculum', in G. Helsby and G. McCulloch (eds), *Teachers and the National Curriculum.* London: Cassell.

Woods, P. and Wenham, P. (1995) 'Politics and pedagogy: a case study in appropriation', *Journal of Education Policy*, **10**(2), 119–41.

Woods, P., Jeffrey, B., Troman, G. and Boyle, M. (1997) *Restructuring Schools, Reconstructing Teachers: Responding to Change in the Primary School.* Buckingham: Open University Press.

Wragg, E. C., Bennett, S. N. and Carre, C. G. (1989) 'Primary teachers and the National Curriculum', *Research Papers in Education*, **4**(3), 17–37.

Young, D. (1991) 'Managing for change: the strategic route to making organisational change sustainable' *Multinational Business No. 2.*

Name Index

Subject Index